Management of Digital Library

Omesh Aadhavan

Oxford Book Company
Jaipur New Delhi

Published By

Oxford Book Company

Regd. Off. "Bony Residency", Gate No. 2
Opp. Tilak Public School, Vishweswariya Nagar,
Gopalpura Road, Jaipur - 302018, India
Ph: 0141 - 2761280, Telefax: 2761381
email - oxfordbookjpr@gmail.com
website - oxfordbookcompany.com

Delhi Office: 102, 1st Floor, Satyam House,
4327/3, Ansari Road, Darya Ganj,
New Delhi - 110002, India
Ph: 011-45652440

Distributed by
KEYA INTERNATIONAL PRESS LLP
E-mail: keyainternationalpressllp@gmail.com

Published in India, 2026

ISBN : 9789380179834

Typeset by Shivangi Computers, Jaipur

Printed and bound in India by Replika Press Pvt. Ltd.

Preface

Advances in internet technologies have made it seemingly possible and easy to create digital collections, repositories, archives and libraries. However, supporting diverse information uses that facilitate interaction beyond searching and browsing is in the early stages. Interactive digital libraries and digital archives are still evolving. The digital preservation techniques have brought revolutionary changes in the organisation and management of libraries and archives. To peep into it, library and information science professionals, need to be get ready to face challenges emerging due to the adoption of digital technologies.

The book has been written with a view to raise awareness level of library and information professionals about the wonderful body of knowledge and opportunities and challenges posed by information technology and build confidence among them to playa proactive role in the end-users in this insecure and unstable era. With the development of digital information and a knowledge society, libraries are changing their role from document provider to information provider.

Multidimensional knowledge management theories and practices backed up by emerging technologies and techniques is the first few sets of papers. Followed by these are the theoretical and practical illustrations of digital library technologies, architectures and standards centering around open source digital library software and open digital library standards.

Omesh Aadhavan

Contents

	Preface	v
1.	Digital Library	1
2.	Managing Creation of the Digital Library	42
3.	Establishing a Digital Library Centre	73
4.	Digital Library Architecture	93
5.	Cornell Digital Library Research Group	112
6.	Data Stream Management into Digital Library	136
7.	Library Support for e-Learners	140
8.	Information Management in Digital Libraries	159
9.	Management of Digital Library Education	175
10.	Digital Library from "Project" to "Production"	201
11.	Digital Information Preservation	234
12.	Digital Curation and the Management of Digital Library	254
13.	Impact of Digital Library on Higher Education and Research	262
	Index	273

Chapter 1

Digital Library

A digital library is a collection of documents in organized electronic form, available on the Internet or on CD-ROM (compact-disk read-only memory) disks. Depending on the specific library, a user may be able to access magazine articles, books, papers, images, sound files, and videos.

On the Internet, the use of a digital library is enhanced by a broadband connection such as cable modem or DSL. Dial-up connections can be used to access plain-text documents and some documents containing images, but for complex files and those with animated video content, a downstream data speed of at least several hundred kilobits per second (Kbps) can make the user's experience less tedious, as well as more informative. Internet-based digital libraries can be updated on a daily basis. This is one of the greatest assets of this emerging technology.

On CD-ROM, the amount of data is limited to several hundred megabytes (MB) per disk, but access is generally much faster than on an Internet connection. Several CD-ROMs can be combined in a set, and because the disks are small, a large library can be accommodated in a reasonable physical space.

The main limitation of CD-ROM is the fact that updating cannot be done as frequently as on the Internet. In addition, producing and distributing CD-ROMs involves overhead costs that are largely nonexistent in Internet-based libraries.

Some institutions have begun the task of converting classic books to electronic format for distribution on the Internet. Some files can be viewed directly in HTML format; others can be downloaded in PDF format and printed. Some publishers keep electronic files of books and produce them one unit at a time in printed and bound form on demand.

Electronic distribution of intellectual and artistic property has authors, agents, and publishers concerned about the possibility of copyright infringement. It is much easier to copy a CD-ROM, or to download an electronic book and make unauthorized copies of it, than it is to reproduce bound volumes and distribute them illegitimately.

Fundamental changes in copyright law and/or changes in the way in which the laws are enforced are likely to occur as digital libraries expand and their use becomes more widespread.

HISTORY AND DEFINITION OF DIGITAL LIBRARIES

In this unit we ask two questions:

- What is a digital library?
- What are its characteristics?

In answering these questions we will learn about digital coherence, discuss the origins of digital libraries, and discover synonyms and metaphors for digital libraries. We will also touch on assumptions about a digital library, technologies of library collections, and the act of information seeking.

Digital Coherence

The term digital library has been applied to a wide variety of offerings from collections of electronic journals to software agents that support inquiry-based education to collections of email to electronic versions of a public library, to personal information collections, and even to the entire Internet. The one property these various entities have in common is their digitization or digital coherence (Daniel Atkins).

Digital coherence means all the objects in a digital library, whether sounds, images, texts, or some other media, can be treated in essentially the same way.

Prior to digital coherence, libraries needed to treat various media, for example, books, journals, videos, and musical recordings, differently.

One could say that digital coherence is the mechanism which permits a form of equality among various information resources. This equality has importance for delivery and integration of information.

Envisioning a World Brain and The Memex

The concept of a digital library is not new. In fact, the concept of digital libraries pre-dates the development of the first computer. H. G. Wells was one of the first authors to write about idea of a world brain that could supplement, add functionality to, and even replace traditional libraries.

It is generally agreed that Vannevar Bush's 1945 article in the Atlantic Monthly, in which Bush conceives of a memex machine, inspired much of the early application of computers to information retrieval. The memex is a mechanical device based on microfilm technology.

The concept of the memex included [a community of scholars indexing and creating] links between pieces of information in a [microfilm-based] research library combined with [microfilmed] personal notes (and classification system) and notes of colleagues, anticipating the ideas of both hypertext and personal information retrieval systems.

Lesk assures us that by 2015 (70 years after Vannevar Bush published his memex dream) "we will have the equivalent of a major research library on each desk. And it will have searching capabilities beyond those Bush imagined".

Synonyms for the Term Digital Library

In the early 1950s computers entered library services in the form of punched card applications in technical services operations and through the development of the MARC (MAchine-Readable Cataloging) standard for digitizing and communicating library catalog information.

The vision of a fully computer-based library began to emerge in terminology in the mid-60s with J. C. R. Licklider's the library of the future.

Over the years, other terms have been coined to refer to the concept of a digitized library, including electronic library, virtual library, library without walls, and bionic library. Library science professor Winfred Lancaster extended this concept beyond the functions of the library, using the term paperless society.

The use of the term digital library can be traced to the Digital Libraries Initiative, established through funding in 1994, by the National Science Foundation, the Advanced Research Projects Agency, and the National Aeronautics and Space Admini-stration in the United States. Under this funding, six U.S. universities were granted a total of $24.4 million for digital library research.

Two events motivated this funding: the sudden explosive growth of the Internet and the development of graphical Web browsers.

These two developments significantly increased the viability of extending library resources and services beyond their current walls and communities, facilitating the sharing of scarce resources and the reaching of under-served populations.

Metaphors for Digital Libraries

There is little discussion or agreement in the literature about what constitutes a digital library. Harter juxtaposes two extreme views: the most inclusive view, which takes a digital library to be essentially what the Internet is today, and the metaphor of the traditional library.

The essential differences between these two metaphors deal with their [presumed] properties of location, content, selection criteria, organization, authority control*, authorship, stability, access, and user groups, services and fees. The Internet has no physical or logical location; no quality control and no entry barriers; no organization scheme, authority control, or surrogates; no concept of author; and is fluid and transient.

Everyone has access to the Internet, but access may require payment and purchase of equipment by the individual user. The traditional library is perceived to have their properties and no entry fee for the individual.

*Names of authors, variants of works (editions), and subject headings or descriptors are all controlled and common variants are cross-listed to the designated official form.

CHARACTERISTICS OF A DIGITAL LIBRARY

Assumptions about a Digital Library

There are certain assumptions in discussions of a digital library. Levy and Marshall summarize these as: digital libraries are collections containing fixed, permanent documents which are based on digital technologies and are used by individuals working alone.

Fixity of Content

The concept of a fixed and permanent document is based on the printed book: While a title may be reissued in a revised version, once a specific volume is printed and bound, it remains unchanged. Fixity creates a comfortable environment in which to perform certain library functions.

Cataloguing practices have evolved around the largely fixed and permanent document. Fluid or transient documents, such as pamphlets and news clippings have been largely uncatalogued and stored in unclassified areas, such as the vertical file [cabinet].

The perception of lack-of-fixity in fluid digital documents, especially internet-based documents, leads to the assumption that digital items are ill-equipped for cataloguing and other library functions.

This concept of the fixity and permanence of a volume is, itself, flawed. For example, marginalia entered by the reader gives a book some degree of fluidity. Marginalia can contribute error-correction, critique, and even new content to the volume.

Marginalia is viewed as an important addition to certain texts. In addition to marginalia, vandalism— such as removal of pictures or pages from a book—makes it difficult to predict that two books, identical at binding, still contain the same contents on any library shelf.

In classifying books as fixed and permanent, the ways of altering a book after issue have been dismissed. What has, in fact, been catalogued is the pristine just-off-the-press edition. Certainly, many digital-based texts could be archived as a pristine edition, with many fluid copies existing at other sites, and perhaps even linked to and from the archived edition.

While the range of variation from a digital pristine copy would certainly have the potential to facilitate and exceed the variation from a print pristine copy, the practice of cataloging and archiving documents at certain points of development can extend to digital media.

Fluid copies on the internet could be considered manuscripts in progress (just as some authors circulate paper-based working drafts of manuscripts to colleagues for reading, comment and use) and at some point a revised version could be catalogued and archived, not unlike revised editions of print-based texts.

This is a simplistic discussion of fixity in print and digital media, however, it does illustrate the point that fixity is a relative concept and does not necessarily belong exclusively to the print medium.

Technologies of Library Collections

The develop of the concept of a library based on digital technologies has revolved around the concept of a library based on the book. As Levy and Marshall point out, the book is not the only material contained in library collections.

In addition to holdings of books, photographs, unbound and handwritten manuscripts and correspondents, and other ephemera which are adaptable to digital representation, libraries also contain three-dimensional artifacts, such as models, dioramas, toys and games, and realia—for example, a chameleon (for a borrow-a-pet service) or a wooden crate marked with 'Papers of [author].

Do not open until [date]. [Name of custodian or executor].' Realia and certain other three-dimensional items in a library's collection do not easily convert to digital format. Therefore, even if all currently convertible library materials were digitized, not all materials in the library would be in digital form.

The current concept of a digital library, then, is a subset of the larger concept of library, just as a video or a film library is a subset of the concept of library and not a substitute for it.

While it is possible that certain libraries will collect only digital materials, it is more likely that libraries in general will make use of digital material where it best serves their patrons' needs and their libraries' budgets, much like libraries have used microforms and paperback editions.

While some materials will not be suitable for digitalization, representations of these materials, such as the products of indexing and abstracting, will be. At some point in the future when applications such as virtual reality develop sufficiently, we may be able to satisfactorily convert much of the informational content of librariesU 3-D holdings to digital format.

At least for now, a comprehensive library will of necessity be a multiple format collection.

The Act of Information Seeking

The perception seems to be that the work in which the user engages in seeking information and the work in which the practitioner engages in supporting his or her patrons is a solitary act.

Contrary to this impression, research finds that the library is a meeting place where collaborative work takes place among patrons, among practitioners, and between practitioners and patrons.

For digital libraries to pattern the work capabilities of the traditional library, and to pattern the work habits of the library's patrons and practitioners, collaborative functionality must be included in digital library design. An exceptional example of progress toward this goal, the work of Robertson, Jitan and Reese of the US WEST Research & Information Group, is discussed later.

THE SCOPE OF THE DIGITAL LIBRARY

INTRODUCTION AND BACKGROUND

The term "Digital Library" has a variety of potential meanings, ranging from a digitized collection of material that one might find in a traditional library through to the collection of all digital information along with the services that make that information useful to all possible users. As the WG discussed possible scenarios and challenge problems to drive our discussion of metrics, we found the need to come to at least a loose agreement on the scope of the digital library. This document is intended to serve that purpose.

Much of the question about the scope of the term is how broad a view should be taken of the digital library. Does it encompass all of information management or is a more tightly constrained view appropriate?

In this document, and for the purposes of the deliberations of the WG, we choose to take a very broad view. This is driven by the recognition that to do otherwise would require setting boundaries that are fairly artificial.

The structure of this document is as follows. In the first section, a brief definition of the term "digital library" is given, as a set of characteristics. The remainder of the document elaborates each of those characteristics.

At the kickoff meeting of the WG (held January 7-8, 1998 at Stanford University), the following definition was proposed:

The Digital Library is:

- The collection of services
- And the collection of information objects
- That support users in dealing with information objects
- And the organization and presentation of those objects
- Available directly or indirectly
- Via electronic/digital means.

The Collection of Services

A digital library is much more than just the collection of

material in its repositories. It provides a variety of services to all of its users (both humans and machines, and producers, managers, and consumers of information). Thus we start our definition with the notion of the collection of services that the digital library represents.

There are a large and varied set of such services, including services to support management of collections, services to provide replicated and reliable storage, services to aid in query formulation and execution, services to assist in name resolution and location, etc.

The Collection of Information Objects

The basis for a digital library, however, must be the information objects that provide the content. A basic characteristic of the digital library is that the information objects are found in collections with associated management and support functions.

The types of information objects vary from traditional "documents" through to live objects (e.g. sensor readings) or dynamic query results.

Supporting Users Deal with Information Objects

The goal of the digital library is to assist users by satisfying their needs and requirements for management, access, storage, and manipulation of the variety of information stored in the collection of material that represents the "holdings" of the library. Users may be humans or they may be automated processes acting on behalf of or in support of human needs.

Users also vary and include those who are "end" users (those not involved in the management and operation of the library but rather are the customers), library operators, and information "producers" who want their material available through the library.

The Organization and Presentation of those Objects

The key to effective collections management is to implement simple structural organizations and be able to present those organizations in a way that library users find useful and can understand easily.

In traditional libraries, books are primarily stored by subject, title, author, and date, and accessed by following signs to the appropriate floor, room, bookcase, shelf, and spine-labeled book. The size and relative celebration of each portion of the collection gives patrons information about the collection and can reveal the library's collection management objectives as well.

A library is created to serve a community of users. Users who participate in the digital library should be aware of its design and be able collectively to refine that design to better serve their own information needs.

Therefore, the ongoing human usability of a digital library depends on the clear and unobtrusive exposure of the library's design, its near-term goals, and its overall objectives.

Furthermore, digital libraries should continue the ongoing tradition of coupling utility with aesthetics in the organization and presentation of materials.

Available Directly or Indirectly

These information objects may be digital objects or they may be in other media (e.g. paper) but represented in the library via digital means (e.g. metadata).

They may be available directly over the network (e.g., using a query service of the library to find and then retrieve electronically the information object) or indirectly (e.g., the result of the query may give instructions on how to obtain the object, but that is done outside the scope of the library itself.)

Electronic/digital Availability

Although the objects may not even be electronic, and although the objects themselves may not be available directly over the network, the objects must be represented electronically in some manner through, e.g., metadata or catalogs. Otherwise, we would not consider the objects to be part of the *digital* library.

The term *digital library* – denotes a collection of literature and its attendant metadata (data about data) stored electronically.

According to Herbert Samuel, a library is "thought in cold storage", and unfortunately digital libraries can be cold, isolated, impersonal places that are inaccessible to both machines and people.

Many scientists now organize their knowledge of the literature using some kind of computerized reference management system (BibTeX, EndNote, Reference Manager, RefWorks, etc.), and store their own digital libraries of full publications as PDF files.

However, getting hold of both the data (the actual publication) and the metadata for any given publication can be problematic because they are often frozen in the isolated and icy deposits of scientific publishing.

Because each library and publisher has different ways of identifying and describing their metadata, using digital libraries (either manually or automatically) is much more complicated than it needs to be, and with papers in the life sciences alone (at Medline) being published at the rate of approximately two per minute, only computerized analyses can hope to be reasonably comprehensive. What then, are these digital libraries, and what services do they provide?

As far as computational Biologists are concerned, and for the purposes of this Review, we shall define a digital library more broadly as a database of scientific and technical articles, conference publications, and books that can be searched and browsed using a Web browser.

As of early 2008, there is a wide range of these digital libraries, but no single source covering all information (in part because of the cost, given that there are some 25,000 peer-reviewed journals publishing some 2.5 million articles per year). Each library is isolated, balkanized, and has only partial coverage of the entire literature.

This contrasts with the historically pre-eminent library of Alexandria whose great strength was that it brought together all the useful literature then available to a single location. Like

Alexandria, most digital libraries are currently *read-only*, allowing users to search and browse information, but not to *write* new information nor add personal knowledge. Other digital libraries are in danger of becoming *write-only* "data-tombs", where data are deposited but will probably never be accessed again.

Indeed, the literature itself is now so vast that most scientists 1choose to access only a fraction of it, at potentially considerable intellectual loss.

Digital libraries provide electronic access to documents, sometimes just to their abstracts and sometimes to the full text of the publication. Presently, the number of abstracts considerably exceeds the number of full-text papers, but with the emergence of Open Access initiatives (e.g., –), Institutional Repositories (e.g., –), and the like, this is set to change considerably.

This is very important, as much additional information exists in full papers that is not seen in abstracts, and, in addition, full papers that are available electronically are likely to be much more widely read and cited –. The format of the full text of such documents can vary significantly among publishers.

Such formats can be described using a Document Type Definition (DTD), e.g., that provided by the (U.S.) National Library of Medicine and, since not all publishers (especially those of non-biomedical material) conform to the NLM DTD, this can considerably affect the types of analysis that can be done on such documents.

In a similar vein, there is not yet a recognized (universal) standard for describing the metadata, although some such as the Dublin Core are becoming widely used.

Since all of these libraries are available on the Web, increasing numbers of tools for managing digital libraries are also Web-based.

They rely on Uniform Resource Identifiers (URIs or "links") to identify, name, and locate resources such as publications and their authors. By using simple URIs, standard Web browser technology, and the emerging methods of the next generation Web or "Web 2.0", it has become possible for digital libraries to become not just *read-only* or *write-only*, but both *read–write*.

These applications allow users to add personal metadata, notes, and keywords (simple labels or "tags",) to help manage, navigate, and share their personal collections. This small but significant change is helping to improve digital libraries in three main ways: personalization, socialization, and integration.

The focus of this Review is largely about searching and organizing literature data together with their metadata. For reasons of space, we do not consider in any detail issues surrounding Open Access, nor structured digital abstracts, (note the recent initiative in FEBS Letters – and the RSC's Project Prospect for whole papers).

Neither do we discuss the many sophisticated tools for text mining and natural language processing, for joining disparate concepts for literature-based discovery, and for studies of bibliometrics literature dynamics, knowledge domains, detecting republication, and so on, all of which become considerably easier to implement only when all the necessary data are digitized and linked together with their relevant metadata.

This Review is structured as follows: the section Digital Libraries, DOIs, and URIs starts by looking at the range of information in digital libraries, and how resources are identified using URIs on the Web.

In the section Problems with Digital Libraries, we consider a fairly standard workflow that serves to highlight some problems with using these libraries.

The following section, Some Tools for Defrosting Libraries, examines what Web-based tools are currently available to defrost the digital library and how they are making libraries more personal, sociable, and integrated places. Finally, the section A Future with Warmer Libraries looks at the obstacles to future progress, recommends some best practices for digital publishing, and draws conclusions.

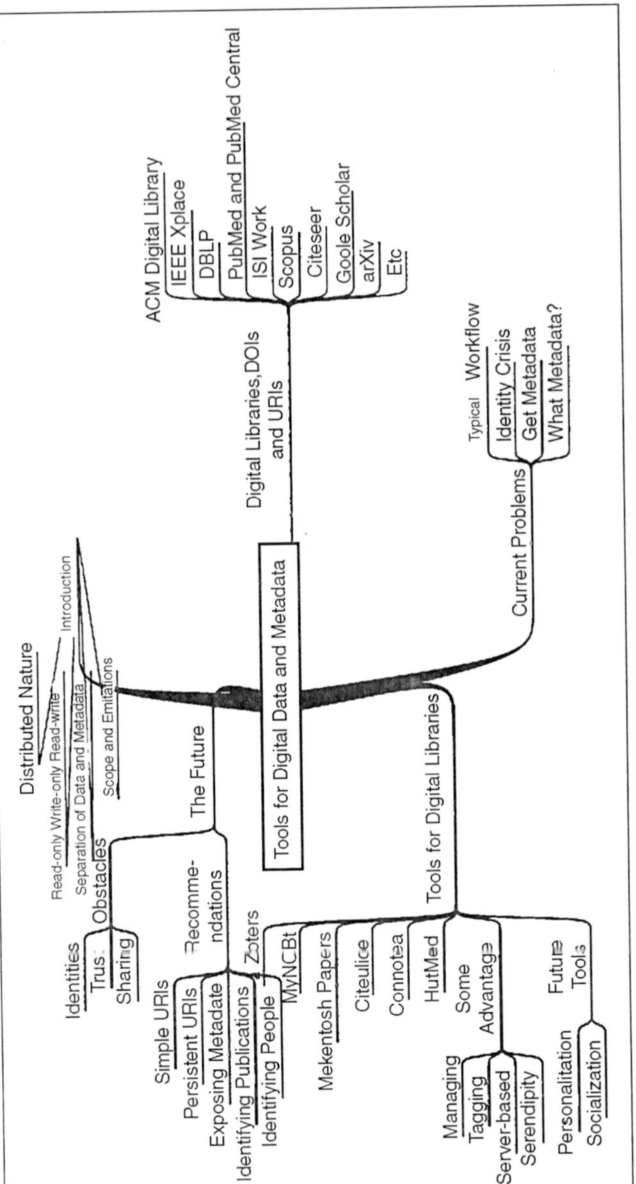

Fig. A Mind Map Summarizing the Contents of this Article in a Convenient Manner.

Digital Libraries, DOIs, and URIs

Because computational biology is an interdisciplinary science, it draws on many different sources of data, information, and knowledge. Consequently, there exists a range of digital libraries on the Web identified by URIs and/or DOIs, that a typical user requires, each with its own speciality, classification, and culture, from computer science through to biomedical science.

DOIs are a specific type of URI and similar to the International Standard Book Numbers (ISBN), allowing persistent and unique identification of a publication (or indeed part of a publication), independently of its location. The range of libraries currently available on the Web is described below, starting with those that focus on specific disciplines (such as ACM, IEEE, and PubMed) through to libraries covering a broader range of scientific disciplines, such as ISI WOK and Google Scholar.

For each library, we describe the size, coverage, and style of metadata used. Where available, DOIs can be used to retrieve metadata for a given publication using a DOI resolver such as CrossRef, a linking system developed by a consortium of publishers. We illustrate with specific examples how URIs and DOIs are used by each library to identify, name, and locate resources, particularly individual publications and their author(s).

We often take URIs for granted, but these humble strings are fundamental to the way the Web works and how libraries can exploit it, so they are a crucial part of the cyberinfra-structure required for e-science on the Web. It is easy to underestimate the value of simple URIs, which can be cited in publications, bookmarked, cut-and-pasted, e-mailed, posted in blogs, added to Web pages and 1wikis –, and indexed by search engines.

Simple URIs are a key part of the current Web (version 1.0) and one of the reasons for the Web's phenomenal success since appearing in 1990. As we shall demonstrate with examples, each digital library has its own style of URI for being linked to (inbound links) and alternative styles of URI for linking out (outbound links) to publisher sites. Some of these links are simple, others more complex, and this has important consequences for both human and programmatic access to the resources these URIs identify.

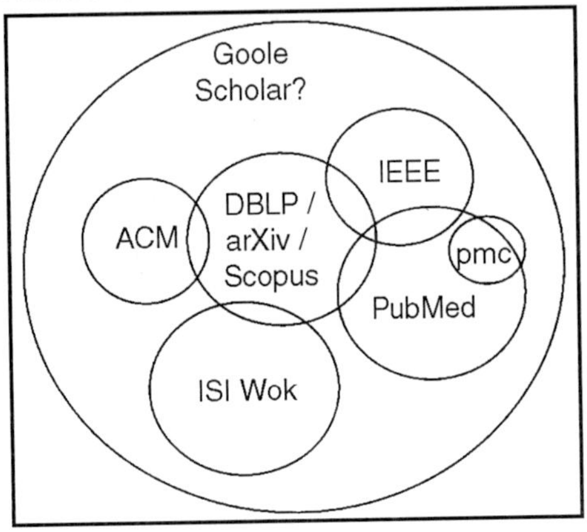

Fig. The Approximate Relative Coverage and Size of Selected Digital Libraries Described in the section Digital Libraries, DOIs, and URIs.

Of all the libraries described, Google Scholar probably has the widest coverage. However, it is currently not clear exactly how much information Google indexes, what the criteria are for inclusion in the index, and whether it subsumes other digital libraries in the way shown in the figure. Note: the size of sets (circles) in this diagram is NOT proportional to their size, and DBLP, Scopus, and arXiv are shown as a single set for clarity rather than correctness.

The ACM Digital Library

The Association for Computing Machinery (ACM), probably best known for the Turing award, makes their digital library available on the Web. The library currently contains more than 54,000 articles from 30 journals and 900 conference proceedings dating back to 1947, focusing primarily on computer science. Like many other large publishers, the ACM uses Digital Object Identifiers (DOI) to identify publications.

So, for example, a publication on scientific workflows from the 16th International World Wide Web Conference (WWW2007) is identified by the Digital Object Identifier DOI:10.1145/1242572.1242705. The last part of the DOI can be used in ACM-style URIs as follows: http://portal.acm.org/ citation.cfmdoid12 42572.1242705. Metadata for publications in the ACM digital library are available from URIs in the style above as EndNote and BibTeX formats; the latter is used in the LaTeX document preparation system.

IEEE Xplore

The Institute of Electrical and Electronics Engineers (IEEE) provides access to its technical literature in electrical engineering, computer science, and electronics, through a service called Xplore. The exact size of the Xplore archive is not currently described anywhere on the IEEE Web site.

Xplore identifies publications using Digital Object Identifiers that are supplemented with a proprietary IEEE scheme for identifying publications.

So, for example, a publication on text-mining in *IEEE/ ACM Transactions on Computational Biology and Bioinformatics* is identified by both the Digital Object Identifier DOI:10.1109/ TBME.2007.906494 and an internal IEEE identifier 1416852. These identifiers can be used in URIs as follows: http:// dx.doi.org/10.1109/TBME.2007.9064 94 and http:// ieeexplore.ieee.org/search/wrappe r.jsparnumber 1416852.

Metadata for publications in IEEE Xplore are available from URIs in the style above in EndNote, Procite, and Refman. Alternatively, publication metadata are available by using a DOI resolver such as CrossRef. Currently, the IEEE offers limited facilities for its registered members to build a personal library and to share this with other users.

DBLP

The Digital Bibliography and Library Project (DBLP) created by Michael Ley, provides an index of peer-reviewed publications in computer science. Recently, DBLP has started to index many popular journals with significant computational biology content such as *Bioinformatics* and *Nucleic Acids Research*, and currently indexes about 900,000 articles, with links out to full text, labeled EE for electronic edition.

Thus an article by Russ Altman on building biological databases is identified by the URI http://dblp.uni-trier.de/rec/bibtex/jour nals/bib/Altman04. Metadata for publications in DBLP are available in BibTeX format only. Unlike some libraries that we describe later, DBLP is built largely by hand, rather than by bots and crawlers indexing Web pages without human intervention.

One of the consequences of this is that authors are disambiguated more accurately, e.g., where an author's middle initial(s) is not used or alternative first names appear in metadata. This kind of author disambiguation is particularly relevant to the naming conventions in some countries.

PubMed gov and PubMed Central

PubMed is a service provided by the National Centre for Biotechnology Information (NCBI). The PubMed database includes more than 17 million citations from more than 19,600 life science journals. The primary mechanism for identifying publications in PubMed is the PubMed identifier (PMID); so, for example, an article describing NCBI resources is identified by the URI http://pubmed.gov/18045790.

Publication metadata for articles in PubMed are available in a wide variety of formats including MEDLINE flat-file format and XML, conforming to the NCBI Document Type Definition, a template for creating XML documents. PubMed can be personalized using the MyNCBI application, described later in the section Some Tools for Defrosting Libraries.

PubMed Central, a subset of PubMed, provides free full-text of articles, but has lower coverage as shown in Figure. Related sites are also emerging in other countries, such as that in the UK. A URI identifying the NCBI resources article in the US PubMed Central is: http://www.pubmedce-ntral.nih.gov/article render.fcgiartid1781113. Metadata are available from URIs in PubMed Central as either XML, Dublin Core, and/or RDF by using the Open Archives Initiative (OAI) Protocol for Metadata

Harvesting (PMH), a standard protocol for harvesting metadata.

For example, embedded in the page identified by the URI above, there are Dublin Core terms such as DC.Contributor, DC.Date, and DC.title, which are standard predefined terms for describing publication metadata. In addition to such standard metadata, PubMed papers are tagged or indexed according to their MeSH (Medical Subject Heading) terms, curated manually.

ISI Web of Knowledge (WoK)

ISI WoK is The Institute for Scientific Information's Web of Knowledge, a service provided by The Thomson Reuters Corporation, covering a broad range of scientific disciplines (not just computer science or biomedical science). The size of the library is somewhere in the region of 15,000,000 "objects" according to the footer displayed in pages of search results.

Unfortunately, ISI WoK does not currently provide short, simple links to its content; so, for example, the URI for an NCBI publication in ISI WoK is hidden behind a script interface called cgi; this is usually displayed in the address bar of a Web browser, regardless of which publication is being viewed, as in this example: http://isiknowledge.com It is possible to extract individual URIs for publications, but regrettably they are usually too long and complicated and contain "session identifiers," which make them expire after a set period of time (usually 24 hours).

Temporary and long URIs of this kind cannot be easily used by humans, and prevent inbound links to the content. ISI WoK also provides various citation tracking and analytical features such as Journal Citation Reports, which measures the impact factor, of individual journals. Metadata for publications in ISI WoK are provided in BibTeX, Procite, Refman, and EndNote. WoK provides citation tracking features, particularly calculating the H-index for a given author, as well as "citation alerts" that can automatically send e-mail when a given paper is newly cited.

Scopus.com

Scopus is a service provided by Reed Elsevier and seems to be the Digital Library with individually the most comprehensive coverage, claiming (June 2008) >33,000,000 records (leaving aside Web pages). As far as linking is concerned, Scopus allows links <1?show=[to]?>to its content using OpenURL, which provides a standard syntax for creating URIs.

For example, the URI http://www.scopus.com/scopus/openurl/doc ument.urlissn03029743volume3298spage350 identifes a publication from the Semantic Web conference, with the ISSN, volume, and page as part of the URI. The Scopus OpenURL link shown above is the simplest kind that can exist; many get much more complicated as more information is included in the URI, doubling the length of the one shown.

The longer and more complicated URIs become, the less likely they are to be useful for humans. Scopus also links out to content using OpenURL and provides citation tracking. Metadata can be exported in RefWorks, RIS format (EndNote, ProCite, RefMan), and plain text, etc.

Citeseer

Citeseer is a service currently funded by Microsoft Research, NASA, and the National Science Foundation (NSF), covering a broad range of scientific disciplines and more than 760,000 documents, according to Citeseer. The URI http://citeseer.ist.psu.edu/apweiler04un iprot.html identifies a paper about UniProt.

Publication metadata are available from Citeseer in BibTeX format, and citation tracking is performed annually in the Most Cited Authors feature.

Google Scholar

Google Scholar is a service provided by Google which indexes traditional scientific literature, as well as preprints and "grey" self-archived publications from selected institutional Web sites. A typical page from Google Scholar is shown in Figure. The size and coverage of Google Scholar does not seem to have been published, and the exact method for finding and ranking citations has not yet been made completely public.

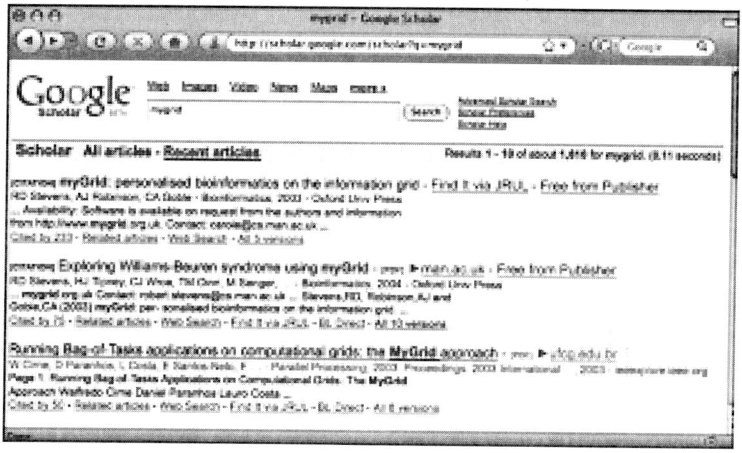

Fig. Google Scholar Search Results, Identified by http://Scholar.google.com/scholar?q = mygrid.

Google Scholar links out to external content using a number of methods including OpenURL, shown here by the "Find it via JRUL" (JRUL is a local library) links. Unlike, e.g., WoK, it is relatively easy to create inbound links to individual authors and publications in Google Scholar.

In contrast to some other digital libraries, Google Scholar provides simple URIs that link to different resources.

For example, http://scholar.google.com/scholarcites 9856542662207029505 identifies citations of a publication by Tom Oinn.

At the time of writing, Google Scholar does not currently offer any specific facilities for creating a personal collection of documents or sharing these collections with other users, other than using simple links such as the one above. Publication metadata can be obtained from Google Scholar where OpenURL links are found in its search results; otherwise, metadata can be obtained by clicking through the links to their original sources.

ArXiv.org

ArXiv provides open access to more than 44,000 e-prints in physics, mathematics, computer science, quantitative biology, and statistics, and was created by Paul Ginsparg. It is a leading example of what *can* be done, although it is presently little used by biologists.

The arXiv has a different publishing model from that of the other digital libraries described in this paper, because publications are peer-reviewed *after* publication in the arXiv, rather than before publication. (A related but non-identical strategy is pursued with PLoS ONE, where papers are peer reviewed before being made accessible, but if they do not pass peer review they do not appear.)

The arXiv is owned, operated, and funded by Cornell University and is also partially funded by the National Science Foundation. arXiv uses simple URIs to identify publications that incorporate the arXiv identifier. Because arXiv acts as a preprint server, some of its content eventually becomes available elsewhere in more traditional peer-reviewed journals.

For example, an article on social networks published in *Science* is also available from http://arxiv.org/abs/cond-mat/0205383. Metadata for publications in arXiv are available in BibTeX format, with various citation-tracking features provided by the experimental citebase project.

This alternative approach to manual citation counts works by calculating the number of times an individual paper has been downloaded, as with the Highly-accessed feature on BioMedCentral journals.

In a short review such as this one, it is not possible to describe every single library a computational biologist might use, because there are so many. Also, it is surprisingly hard to define exactly what a specific digital library is because the distinction between publishers, libraries, and professional societies is not always a clean one.

Thus, we have not described the digital libraries provided by Highwire, WorldCat, JSTOR, the British Library, the Association for the Advancement of Artificial Intelligence (AAAI), the Physical Review Online Archive (PROLA), and the American Chemical Society (ACS) (e.g., SciFinder).

Neither do we discuss commercial publisher-only sites such as SpringerLink, Oxford University Press, ScienceDirect, Wiley-Blackwell, Academic Press, and so on here, since *most* of this content is accessible, typically via abstracts, via the other libraries and databases described in the section on digital libraries with links out to the publishers' sites.

Summary of Libraries

Although they differ in size and coverage, all of these digital libraries provide similar basic facilities for searching and browsing publications. These features are well-documented elsewhere, so we will not describe them in detail here.

With the exception of arXiv and PubMed Central, which provide full free access to entire articles, all other libraries described here provide free access to metadata (author, year, title, journal, abstract, etc.) and link to data (the full-text of a given article), which the user may or may not be licensed to view. The approximate relationship between the different libraries, as far as coverage is concerned, is shown in Figure.

Where these libraries differ is in the subscription, personalization, and citation-tracking features. So, for example, ISI WoK is a subscription-only service, not freely accessible, but which offers more extensive citation tracking features (such as ranking papers by citation counts, the impact factor and h-index) than other libraries.

Other services, such as the NCBI, are available freely, and provide additional features using custom tools to freely registered users. Other services such as Google Scholar and Citeseer are free, but currently offer no personalized view. Both ISI and Google Scholar provide services for counting and tracking citations of a given paper, which are not provided by most other libraries.

These libraries also differ considerably in the nature and power of their indexing by which users can search them on specific topics of metadata. Most permit Boolean searches on the basis of authors, keywords, words in a title or abstract, and so on, though none does this in real-time, and comparatively few allow sophisticated combinations.

All of this reflects the fact that these libraries and the means of searching them evolved independently and largely in isolation.

Consequently, it is generally difficult for a user to build their own personalized view of *all* the digital libraries combined into one place, although tools described in the section Some Tools for Defrosting Libraries are now beginning to make this more feasible.

Before we describe these further, we shall look at some of the current issues with using these digital libraries, as it is exactly these kinds of problems that have motivated the development of new tools.

These tools, and the digital libraries they are built on, have to manage two inescapable facts:

- *Redundancy*: any given publication or author can be identified by many different URIs;
- *Representing metadata*: there are many different ways of identifying and describing

Problems Using Digital Libraries

The digital libraries outlined in the previous section all differ in their coverage, access, and features, but the abstract process of using them is more standard.

Figure shows an abstract workflow for using any given digital library.

We do not propose this as a universal model, which every user will follow, but provide it to illustrate some of the problems with managing data and metadata in the libraries described in the previous section on digital libraries.

Tasks represented by white nodes are normally performed exclusively by humans, while tasks shown in blue nodes can be performed wholly or partly by machines of some kind.

The main problematic tasks that make digital libraries difficult to use for both machines and humans are "GET" (publication) and "GET METADATA". These are shown in bold and discussed further in the Identity Crisis section of this paper.

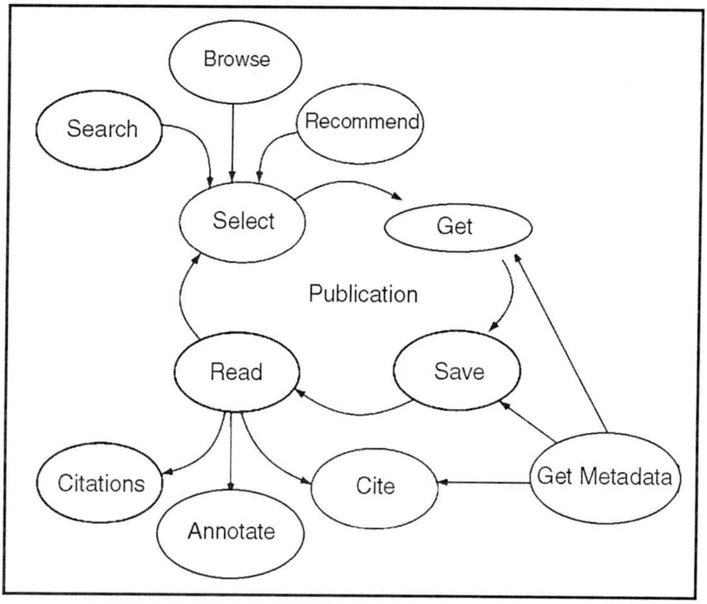

Fig. A Typical Workflow for Using a Digital Library Representing a Subset of the Literature.

To begin with, a user selects a paper, which will have come proximately from one of four sources:

- Searching some digital library, "SEARCH" in Figure;
- Browsing some digital library ("BROWSE");
- A personal recommendation, word-of-mouth from colleague, etc., ("RECOMMEND");
- Referred to by reading another paper, and thus cited in its reference list ("READ").

Once a paper of interest is selected, the user:

- Retrieves the abstract and then the paper (i.e., the actual paper itself as a file), "GET" in Figure)
- They save the paper, for example by bookmarking it, storing on a hard-drive, printing off, etc., ("SAVE"). Saving often involves getting the

metadata, too, ("GET METADATA"). By metadata, we again mean the basic metadata about a publication, such as the author, date, journal, volume, page number, publisher, etc. In practice, this means any information typically found in an EndNote or BibTeX entry;

- They read the paper, "READ" in Figure;
- They may annotate the paper, ("ANNOTATE");
- Finally, they may cite the paper ("CITE"). Citing requires retrieving the metadata, if these have not been retrieved already.

This abstract workflow is idealized, but highlights some problems with using current digital libraries, for both humans and machines.

- *Identity Crisis*: There is no universal method to retrieve a given paper, because there is no single way of identifying publications across all digital libraries on the Web. Although various identification schemes such as the PubMed identifier (PMID), Digital Object Identifier (DOI), ISBN, and many others, exist, there is not yet one identity system to "rule them all."
- *Get Metadata*: Publication metadata often gets "divorced" from the data it is about, and this forces users to manage each independently, a cumbersome and error-prone process. Most PDF files, for example, do not contain embedded metadata that can be easily extracted. Likewise, for publications on the Web there is no universal method to retrieve metadata. For any given publication, it is not possible for a machine or human to retrieve metadata using a standard method. Instead there are many inadequate options to choose from, which add unnecessary complexity to obtaining accurate metadata.
- *Which metadata*? There is no single way of representing metadata, and without adherence to common standards (which largely already exist, but in a plurality) there never will be. EndNote (RIS) and BibTeX are common, but again, neither format

is used universally across all libraries.

We describe each of these issues more fully in the following sections.

Identity Crisis

We are suffering from an acute identity crisis in the life sciences. Just as sequence databases have trouble managing the multiple identities of sequences, digital libraries also suffer from being unable to identify individual publications and their authors.

These are essential pieces of information that make libraries easy to use, and also help to track citations, but in the present implementation they create considerable barriers to users and machines. Any single publication or author is identified by numerous different URIs.

An important task for managing these disparate collections involves reconciling and normalizing these different identity schemes, that is, calculating if two different URIs identify the same resource or not.

For example, a human can fairly easily determine that each of these URIs identify the same publication, but writing a generic programme to automate this for arbitrary URIs is more challenging: http://nar.oxfordjournals.org/cgi/conten t/full/36/suppl_1/D13; http://www.ncbi.nlm.nih.gov/pubmed/18045 790; http://www.pubmedcentral.nih.gov/article render.fcgiartid1781113; and http://dx.doi.org/10.1093/nar/gkm1000.

Where DOIs exist, they are supposed to be the definitive URI. This kind of automated disambiguation, of publications and authors, is a common requirement for building better digital libraries. Unlike the traditional paper library, machines play a much more important role in managing information.

They come in many forms, typically search-engine bots and spiders such as Googlebot, but also screen-scrapers, feed-readers workflows programs, Web services,, and ad hoc scripts, as well as semantic Web agents and reasoners.

They are obviously of great importance for text-mining,

–, where computer algorithms plus immense computing power can outperform human intelligence on at least some tasks. Publication metadata are essential for machines and humans in many tasks, not just the disambiguation described above. Despite their importance, metadata can be frustratingly difficult to obtain.

Metadata: You can't Always GET What you Want.

As well as the problem of extracting metadata from PDFs, getting metadata for any given URI which identifies a publication is also problematic. Although the semantic Web has been proposed as a general solution to this –, it is currently a largely unrealised vision of the future.

The Open Archives Initiative mentioned previously provides a solution to this problem, though it is not adopted by all publishers. So, given an arbitrary URI, there are only two guaranteed options for getting any metadata associated with it. Using http, it is possible to for a human (or machine) to do the following.

- *Http GET the URI*: Getting any URIs described in the previous section Digital Libraries, URIs, and DOIs will usually return the entire HTML representation of the resource. This then has to be scraped or parsed for metadata, which could appear anywhere in the file and in any format. This technique works, but is not particularly robust or scalable because every time the style of a particular Web site changes, the screen-scraper will probably break as well. Some Web sites such as PubMed Central make this easier, by clearly identifying metadata in files, so they can easily be parsed by tools and machines.
- *Http HEAD the URI:* This returns metadata only, not the whole resource. These metadata will not include the author, journal, title, date, etc., of the publication but basic information such as the MIME type which indicates what the resource is (text, image, video, etc.), Last-Modified date, and so on.

The lack of an adequate method for retrieving metadata has led to proposals such as the Life Sciences Identifier (LSID), and BioGUID (Biological Globally Unique IDentifier).

These may be useful in the future if they become more widely adopted, but do not change the current state of the digital library.

As it stands, it is not possible to perform mundane and seemingly simple tasks such as, "get me all publications that fulfill some criteria and for which I have licensed access as PDF" to save locally, or "get me a specific publication and all those it immediately references".

Metadata for Publications

Even if there were a standard way to retrieve metadata for publications, there is still the problem of how to represent and describe them. In addition to EndNote (RIS) and BibTeX, there are also various XML schemas such as the U.S. Library of Congress Metadata Object Description Schema (MODS) format and RDF vocabularies, such as the Dublin Core mentioned earlier.

Having all these different metadata standards would not be a problem if they could easily be converted to and from each other, a process known as "round-tripping". However, some conversions gain or lose information along the way. Lossy and irreversible conversions create dead-ends for metadata, and many of these mappings are non-trivial, e.g., XML to RDF and back again.

In addition to basic metadata found in EndNote and BibTeX, there are also more complex metadata such as the inbound and outbound citations, related articles, and "supplementary" information.

The identity crisis, inability to get metadata easily, and proliferation of metadata standards are three of the main reasons that libraries are particularly difficult to use and search as automatically as one would wish. These are challenging problems to overcome, and the tools we describe in the next section tackle these problems in different ways.

Some Tools for Defrosting Libraries

Although libraries can be cold, the tools described in this section could potentially make them much warmer. They do this in two main ways. Personalization allows users to say this is my library, the sources I am interested in, my collection of references, as well as literature I have authored or co-authored.

Socialization allows users to share their personal collections and see who else is reading the same publications, including added information such as related papers with the same keyword (or "tag") and what notes other people have written about a given publication.

The ability to share data and metadata in this way is becoming increasingly important as more and more science is done by larger and more distributed teams rather than by individuals.

Such social bookmarking is already available on the Web site of publications such as the Proceedings of the National Academy of Sciences (http://www.pnas.org) and the journals published by Oxford University Press.

The result of personalization and socialization is integration of a kind that cannot be achieved by machines alone. First, we look at personalization-only style tools, then we examine tools that also allow socialization of the library through sharing.

Zotero.org and Mendeley

Zotero is an extension for the Firefox browser that enables users to manage references directly from the Web browser. As with most Web-based tools, Zotero can recognise and extract data and metadata from a range of different digital libraries. Users can bookmark publications, and then add their own personal tags and notes.

Currently, Zotero does not allow users to share their tags in the same way that more "sociable" tools such as CiteULike and Connotea do, although enhancements to the current 1.0 version of Zotero may include this feature. Zotero bookmarks cannot be identified using URIs, so it is not possible to link in from external sources to these personal collections.

Mendeley is a similar application that helps to manage and share research papers, although as well as having a Web-based browser version it is possible to store bibliographies using a more powerful desktop-based client that automatically extracts metadata from PDF files, but it can only do this where metadata is available in an amenable format.

MyNCBI

MyNCBI allows users to save PubMed searches and to customise search results. It also features an option to update and e-mail search results automatically from saved searches. MyNCBI includes extra features for highlighting search terms, filtering search results, and setting LinkOut, document delivery, and external tool preferences.

Like Zotero, MyNCBI currently allows personalization only, with no socialization features. It is also limited to publications in PubMed. As we have previously seen, computational biologists frequently require access to many publications outside PubMed, so they cannot capture their entire library in MyNCBI alone. Like Zotero, it is currently not possible to link to personal collections created in MyNCBI.

Mekentosj Papers

Papers, is an application for managing electronic publications, originally designed by Alexander Griekspoor and Tom Groothuis. Although it is not a typical browser-based Web application, it can be closely integrated with several services on the Web-like Google Scholar, PubMed, ISI Web of Knowledge, and Scopus mentioned in the Digital Libraries section of this paper.

The Papers application demonstrates how large collections of PDF files can be managed more easily. Papers provides a simple and intuitive interface shown in Figure to a collection of PDF files stored on a personal hard drive.

It looks and behaves much like Apple's iTunes, an application for managing music files, because the user does not have to know where the data (PDF file) is stored on their hard drive. Unfortunately, Papers is only available for Apple Macintosh users, and there is no version for Windows, which limits its uptake by scientists.

It looks and feels much like the popular iTunes application, allowing users to manage their digital libraries by categories shown at the top. It is presently available only under Mac OS/X.

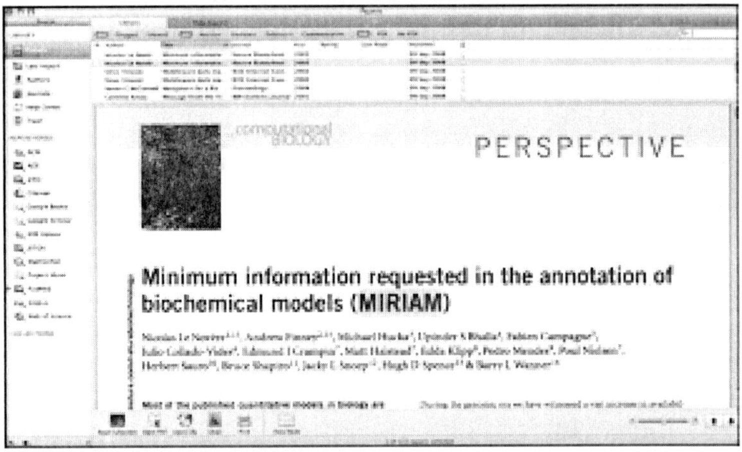

Fig. Mekentosj Papers can Organize Large Collections of Locally Stored PDF files, with their Metadata.

The personalization of libraries is nothing especially new or groundbreaking, and scientists have been creating personal libraries for years, for example by having their own EndNote library or BibTeX file. Tools such as Zotero, MyNCBI, and Papers just make the process of personalization simpler.

However, socialization of digital libraries *is* relatively new, in particular the ability of *multiple* users to associate arbitrary tags with URIs that represent scientific publications. This is what CiteULike, Connotea, and HubMed all allow, thereby capturing some of the supposed "wisdom of crowds" in classifying information.

CiteULike.org

CiteULike is a free online service to organize academic publications, now run by Oversity. It has been on the Web since

October 2004 when its originator was attached to the University of Manchester, and was the first Web-based social bookmarking tool designed specifically for the needs of scientists and scholars.

In the style of other popular social bookmarking sites such as delicious.com it allows users to bookmark or "tag" URIs with personal metadata using a Web browser; these bookmarks can then be shared using simple links such as those shown below.

The number of articles bookmarked in CiteULike is approaching 2 million, indicated by the roughly incremental numbering used. While the CiteULike software is not open source, part of the dataset it collects is currently in the public domain. Publication URIs are simple: http://www.citeulike.org/article/1708098.

CiteULike normalizes bookmarks before adding them to its database, which means it calculates whether each URI bookmarked identifies an identical publication added by another user, with an equivalent URI. This is important for social tagging applications, because part of their value is the ability to see how many people (and who) have bookmarked a given publication.

CiteULike also captures another important bibliometric, viz how many users have potentially *read* a publication, not just cited it. It seems likely that the number of readers considerably exceeds the number of citers and this can be valuable information. Time lags matter, too.

This is particularly the case with Open Access, where the "most-accessed" *Journal of Biology* paper of 2007 had in June 2008 been accessed in excess of 12,000 times, but has been cited just nine times (note that early access statistics can provide good predictors for later citations).

CiteULike provides metadata for all publications in RIS (EndNote) and BibTeX, providing a solution to the "Get Metadata" problem described in the previous section Metadata: You Can't Always GET What You Want, because every CiteULike URI for a publication has metadata associated with it in exactly the same way.

Connotea.org

Connotea is run by Nature Publishing Group and provides a similar set of features to CiteULike with some differences. It has been available on the Web since November 2004. Connotea uses MD5 hashes to store URIs that users bookmark, and normalizes them after adding them to its database, rather than before.

This post-normalization means Connotea does not always currently recognize when different URIs (such as the examples in the section Identity Crisis) identify the same publication, a bug known as "buggotea", which also affects CiteULike to a lesser extent. Like CiteULike, URIs in Connotea are simple.

A publication about Connotea, for example, is identified by the URI http://www.connotea.org/uri/685b90ae66cf bc3fc8ebeed0a5def571. Metadata are available from Connotea in a wider variety of formats than from CiteULike, including RIS, BibTeX, MODS, Word 2007 bibliography, and RDF, but these have to be downloaded in bulk only, rather than individually per publication URI.

The source code for Connotea is available, and there is an API that allows software engineers to build extra functionality around Connnotea, for example the Entity Describer.

HubMed.org

HubMed is a "rewired" version of PubMed, and provides an alternative interface with extra features, such as standard metadata and Web feeds which can be subscribed to using a feed reader. This allows users to subscribe to a particular journal and receive updates when new content (e.g., a new issue) becomes available.

An example URI for a publication on HubMed is http:// www.hubmed.org/display.cgiuids168 45111. Like CiteULike, HubMed also solves the "Get Metadata" problem because metadata are available from each HubMed URI in a wide variety of formats not offered by NCBI.

This is one of HubMed's most useful features. At the time of writing, HubMed provides metadata in RIS (for EndNote),

BibTeX, RDF, and MODS style XML. Users can also log in to HubMed to use various personalized features such as tagging.

Advantages of using CiteULike and Connotea

Both CiteULike and Connotea require users to invest time and effort learning how to use them, and importing or entering bibliographic information. Why should they bother? Managing bibliographic metadata using these tools has several advantages over the common scenario of storing un-indexed PDF files locally on a personal computer.

Both CiteULike and Connotea provide a single place (a Web server) where data (PDFs) and metadata can both be shared and more tightly coupled; this has the following benefits.

Searching

Easier and more sophisticated searching is possible. Conversely, given a collection of PDFs on a hard drive, it is typically difficult (or impossible) to make simple queries such as "retrieve all papers by [a given author]".

Managing

When authoring manuscripts, managing references in a Web-based repository can save some of the pain of re-typing metadata (e.g., author names) for a given publication. Provided the publication has a URI that is recognized by these tools, metadata are automatically harvested on behalf of the user, saving them time.

Tagging

Tags are just keywords, but these allow both personalisation and socialisation of bibliographic data, see for papers cited in this Review as an example.

Tagging of papers by other users allows non-expert users to explore related papers in ways that may not be possible through traditional reference lists, since exploring a subject of research in which you are not expert is made easier by following links added by other potentially more expert users.

Server-based

Hosting a bibliography on a Web server means that, if and when the user moves computer, the library is still accessible. However, keeping local and remote versions requires appropriate synchronisation, which can be problematic.

Serendipity

Many serendipitous discoveries or intellectual linkages that may be determined via co-occurrences (e.g., –) exist in science, and these can be assisted by browsing links provided via social tagging.

Future Tools

The tools described here are the first wave of Web 2.0, Library 2.0, or even Science 2.0 style tools that are helping to defrost the digital library. There will certainly be plenty more in the future; for example, the Research Information Centre from the British Library is investgating innovative new tools in this area, backed by Microsoft.

Some are calling it "Web 3.0", but, whatever the name, it seems likely that we will see many digital library applications that will exploit the novel social features of platforms such as Facebook, and OpenSocial. Here they can exploit the identity mechanisms already built into those systems.

Personalization and socialization of information will increasingly blur the distinction between databases and journals, and this is especially true in computational biology where contributions are particularly of a digital nature. Scientific contributions to digital knowledge on the Web often do not fit into traditional scientific publishing models.

This is usually because they are either too "small" or too "big" to fit into journals. Web logs or "blogs" are beginning to fill the "too small" gap and can be used for communicating preliminary results, discussion, opinion, supplementary material, and short technical reports – in the style of a traditional laboratory notebook. Biological databases, such as those listed in the annual NAR database review, have long filled the "too big" gap in scientific publishing.

They are clearly more significant than their publications alone. As we move in biology from a focus on hypothesis-driven to data-driven science, it is increasingly recognized that databases, software models, and instrumentation are the scientific output, rather than the conventional and more discursive descriptions of experiments and their results.

In the digital library, these size differences are becoming increasingly meaningless as data, information, and knowledge become more integrated, socialized, personalized, and accessible. Take Postgenomic, for example, which aggregates scientific blog posts from a wide variety of sources.

These posts can contain commentary on peer-reviewed literature and links into primary database sources. Ultimately, this means that the boundaries between the different types of information and knowledge are continually blurring, and future tools seem likely to continue this trend.

A Future with Warmer Libraries

The software described in the section Some Tools for Defrosting Libraries are a promising start to improving the digital library. They make data and metadata more integrated, personal, and sometimes more sociable. While they are a promising start, they face considerable obstacles to further success.

Obstacles to Warmer Libraries

We suggest that the main obstacles to warmer libraries are primarily social rather than technical in nature. Identity, trust, and privacy are all potential stumbling blocks to better libraries in the future.

One Identity to Rule them all?

The basic ability to identify publications and their authors uniquely is currently a huge barrier to making digital libraries more personal, sociable, and integrated. The identity of people is a twofold problem because applications need to identify people as *users* in a system and as *authors* of publications.

The lack of identity currently prevents answering very simple questions such as, 'show me all person *x* publications', unless the authors concerned are lucky enough to have unique names. Both the NCBI and CrossRef have initiatives to identify authors uniquely in digital libraries, but these have yet to be implemented successfully.

The use of Single Sign-On (SSO) schemes such as Shibboleth and OpenID (the latter is used in projects such as myExperiment.org and Connotea) could have a huge impact, enabling identity and personalization, without the need for hundreds of different usernames and password combinations. It remains to be seen what their impact on scientific literature will be.

Technically, there are also tough challenges for creating unique author names such as synonymy, name changes, and variable use of initials and first names, which are ongoing legacy issues.

Passing valuable data and metadata

Passing valuable data and metadata onto a third party requires that users trust the organization providing the service. For large publishers such as Nature Publishing Group, responsible for Connotea, this is not necessarily a problem.

That said, many users are liable to distrust commercial publishers when their business models may unilaterally change their data model, making the tools for accessing their data backwards incompatible, a common occurrence in bioinformatics.

Smaller startup companies, who are often responsible for innovative new tools, may struggle to gain the trust of larger institutions and libraries. Most of the software described in the section Tools for Defrosting Libraries require a considerable initial investment from users to import their libraries into the system. Users have to trust service providers that this investment has a good chance of paying off in the longer term.

Scientists also have to decide how much to trust and rely

on commercial for-profit companies to build and maintain the cyberinfrastructure they require for managing digital libraries. Not all commercial companies provide the best value-for-money services, and this is often true in scientific publishing.

Paul Ginsparg, for example, has estimated that arXiv operates with a cost that is 100 to 1,000 times lower than a conventional peer-reviewed publishing system. If the market will not provide scientists with the services they require, at a price they are willing to pay, they need to build and fund them themselves.

The danger is that too much electronic infrastructure will be owned and run by private companies, and science will then be no better served than it was with paper-based publishing.

data Scientists want to Share

Although the practice of sharing raw data immediately, as with Open Notebook Science, is gaining ground, many users are understandably cautious about sharing information online before peer-reviewed publication.

Scientists can be highly secretive and reticent at times, selfishly not wanting to share their data and metadata freely with everyone and anyone, for fear of being "scooped" or copied without proper credit and attribution. Some tools provide security features, e.g., both CiteULike and Connotea allow users to hide references. However, this requires users to trust external providers to respect and protect their privacy, since the information is on a public server, and out of users' control.

Recommendations

Warmer digital libraries cannot be achieved by software tools alone. The digital libraries themselves can take simple steps to make data and metadata more amenable to human and automated use, making their content more useful and useable. Only with proper and better access to linked data and metadata can the tools that computational biologists require be built. We make the following recommendations to achieve this goal.

Simple URIs

URIs for human use should be as simple as possible, to allow easy linking to individual publications and their authors. Short URIs are much more likely to be used and cited than longer, more complicated URIs.

Persistent URIs

It has been noted many times before but it is worth repeatedly restating: persistent URIs make digital libraries a much more useful and usable place. Although URIs will inevitably decay many (but not all) will be preserved by the Internet Archive and every effort should be made to keep them persistent where possible.

Exposing Metadata

Publication metadata, in whatever style (EndNote, BibTeX, XML, RDF, etc.), should be transparently exposed and readily available, programmatically and manually, from URIs, HTML, and PDF files of publications.

Identifying Publications

URNs (such as Digital Object Identifiers) should be used to identify publications wherever possible. Most large publishers already do this, although there are still many confounding exceptions.

Identifying People

This problem is twofold. people need to be identified as users of a system and as authors of publications. To tackle the first issue, tools and libraries should use Single Sign On (SSO) schemes, such as OpenID to provide access to personalized features where possible, as this prevents the endless and frustrating proliferation of username/passwords to identify users in Web applications. The second requires unique author identification, an ongoing and as yet unsolved issue for digital libraries.

By following these recommendations, publishers, scientists, and libraries of all kinds can add significant value to the information they manage for the digital library.

Conclusions

The future of digital libraries and the scientific publications they contain is uncertain. Rumours of the death of printed books and the death of the journal have (so far) been greatly exaggerated. In scientific publishing, we are beginning to see books and electronic journals becoming more integrated with databases, blogs, and other digital media on the Web.

These and other changes could lead to a resurgence in the role of nonprofit professional societies and institutional libraries in the scientific enterprise as the cost of publishing falls. But the outcome is still far from certain.

What is certain is the fact that we can look forward to a digital library that is more integrated, sociable, personalized, and accessible, although it may never be completely "frost-free".

Ultimately, better libraries will be a massive benefit to science. The current breed of Web-based tools we have described are facilitating this change, and future tools look set to continue this trend. Ultimately, data and metadata will become less isolated and rigid, moving more fluidly between applications on the Web. There are still issues with trust, privacy, and identity that may hinder the next generation of Web-based digital libraries, and these social problems will need addressing.

It has frequently been observed that scientists lag behind other communities in their use of the Web to communicate research, and that this is ironic given that the Web was invented in a scientific laboratory for use primarily by scientists.

Most scientists are painfully familiar with the shortcomings of the databases and software described in this Review, because these tools are at the very heart of science. Digital libraries are, and always will be, fundamental components of e-science, and of the "cyber-infrastructure", –, necessary for both computational and experimental biology in the 21st century.

Chapter 2

Managing Creation of the Digital Library

It is an important starting point to define the Digital Library in all its complexity. The section dedicated to it examines the various possible definitions which librarian circles all over the world have been pondering for over five years, as well as the practical and operational consequences that a correct definition implies. In the light of the examined debate the roles of the Digital Library are identified, and the way these are variously reported in the literature is examined.

This process has produced what has been recognised, not by us but by the IFLA at an international level, as the most ample and circumstantiated possible definition of the Digital Library.

Two aspects of this definition should here be underlined:

- The fact that the Digital Library is necessarily positioned within the context of other

Digital Library

- The fact that it is, no more and no less than other libraries, a centre providing services.

Models: Defining the Digital Library has also led to identification of models. Above all in the Anglo-American context, these models have been developed theoretically with the nonetheless very practical aim of deducing from them concrete indications for action and for the development of new solutions or modification of existing ones. Of the various models examined two have been particularly mentioned:

- Model of Bawden and Rowlands. Models which reveals the technical but also social complexity of the Digital Library and which recalls the need for a constant, detailed study, such as had never before occurred in the traditional library world.
- Model of EFQM, Pt.

Models which stresses the need for the Digital Library to develop the profession in a managerial and productive sense, linked to the fact that the reference area is expanding, the agents with whom contact is to be made are part of a productive and commercial world with which we must interact on a new basis and in new capacities.

Being a body which certifies quality, EFQM places emphasis on the managerial part of the Digital Library, in terms of Leadership, Human Resource management and Entrepreneurial Capacity.

The practical consequence, which emerges in the continuation of the study and above all in the proposals part, is the need for a strong commitment in the direction of retraining the professional forces already working, above all in terms of management, of identification of the new professional skills necessary for handling the new complexities, and finally, the need for preparing the ground for a different degree of flexibility towards the world of digital information and its relations with the existing situation.

Actually the prevalent model is that of a library which is not purely digital (since this is unrealistic), but rather hybrid, in the sense that known and new ways of using, optimising and producing the information product are followed in conjunction with each other.

Aims of the Digital Library

The main aim, considering our hugely rich heritage, is and remains an eminently cultural one. The cultural aim is and remains in any case the main one also in all the other countries in the world, both where the Digital Library is used to create a support to academic studies and where the intention of documentation of historical memory prevails.

Actually, as is clearly seen from the international account which is widely summarised below, the two aims are complementary and the problem shifts to the choice to be made at the start, so that the Digital Library can be developed in a coherent and uniform way in both directions.

In the case of Italy, the attention to local memory and the support for research might be the two ideal boundaries within which Digital Library initiatives should be directed and maintained.

It should also be pointed out that this cultural aim is seen as the cog-wheel for the creation of new work, professional growth and recognition of national culture at an international level.

The Technical/librarianship Framework

Both from the definition and from indications deriving from the models analysed, the Digital Library undoubtedly presents itself as an extraordinarily complex structure. This complexity is analysed from various points of view, both the purely technical and the specifically librarianship ones.

Given the implications that the latter more than any other has in our view on the success of any project, we will focus on these themes in the summary and omit others for which we will simply refer to the main study.

Organisational Aspects

On the basis of the proposed analysis, the Digital Library is seen to be a "complex Library" and as a new information system in terms of:

- Objects to be handled
- Format of data
- Means of description (metadata)
- Organisation of research (search engines)
- Interfaces (informatics and/or human)
- Production activities (Workflow, Budgeting)
- Integration of different types of applications and systems
- Complex and distributed system

The Digital Library which organises production activities needs to define the methodologies for the treatment of the various materials in the context of a project (Workflow) and consequently the investment policies (Budgeting) both for the moment of production and for the subsequent conservational maintenance. A functional profile of the Digital Library is outlined with indication of the following functions:

Net infrastructures	Pac/web opac
Database bibliographic/metadata	Ocument management system
Digital repository	Maging
Storage	Raphics
Interface	Tatistics
Safety	

For each of these the functional requirements to be fulfilled in the Digital Library are specified. In particular it is stressed that in a Digital Library the objects to be handled are very different in nature:

- They can integrate metadata for description and management
- They can be local and remote
- They can concern other information data (online courses, Web pages)
- They can be multi-format (text, audio, video, images,....)
- They can be original digital objects: electronic publications

Evolution of Services and the Profession

The evolution of the potentialities of the services generated by the Digital Library and the parallel evolution of the profession are among the most significant and complex aspects of the Digital Library.

With the greater availability of information, the Digital Library still presents itself as a service structure. Some of the many statements and definitions indicated and analysed strongly stress the function of service-provider in relation to other similar institutions. For example:

- The appeal for cooperation ("the Digital Library is not a separate entity")
- The appeal to the particular use of technologies ("the Digital Library needs technologies for connecting the resources of different libraries with information services")
- The appeal relative to access ("the aim of the Digital Library is universal access to its collections and services").

The characteristics of the service also change because of the changed attitude of the user and the different interaction between user and intermediary. This leads to a careful consideration of the qualitative evolution of the reference services, in which this mediation will be a strategic element in the development of the Digital Library.

Undoubtedly the problem of professionalism is one of the most significant of those related to the Digital Library, both because of how this professionalism is defined and how it is changing with the new services and the new skills which are required.

It is agreed that we are in the face of a true revolution, mostly brought about by facts which are outside the librarianship field in the strictest sense, but have evident repercussions on the functions and the very nature of the library, hence of the librarian. The librarian's work is the fruit of different, complementary kinds of know-how which mean that he/she operates as a:

- Professional handigital libraryer of digital information
- Producer of digital information
- Communicator of digital knowledge to provide this type of service the librarian of the digital library
- To know the users with whom he/she is in contact better in order to adapt adequate tools and products to specific demands
- To adapt the procedures for presenting data-

interface and not to propose them according to a single standard procedure

- To give access also to non-bibliographical information available on the Web From the analysis it emerges that there will be an affirmation of professional figures who are able to unite the more classic principles of librarianship with the prospects offered to the profession by digital technologies and telematic connections. The most substantial changes will be seen in the most classic areas of the librarian's profession, i.e.:
- *In the description of resources*: With the advent of metadata and the implications dictated by the reflections deriving from the debate on Functional Requirements for Bibliographic Records;
- *In the services*: With particular regard to the sector of Reference and Document Delivery;
- *In conservation*: Where simple conservation is united with production and extended access to resources which were once inaccessible.

These changes are inevitably translated into practice by the emergence of new qualifications and new professional figures. At the basis we can identify a strong demand for entrepreneurship on the part of the managerial class, as has already been noted in the illustration of the model proposed by EFQM.

In this regard it appears that the prevailing librarian will be a professional with the ability to combine different solutions, different public and private operators within and outside the structure: a sort of professional who moves between the classic principles of the profession and the new technological possibilities and suggestions, a professional who is able to unite opportunities and risks in a productive way.

The Italian scene does not favour great optimism in this sense. In many libraries we perceive a widespread situation of unawareness of the change in progress and a growing gap between those who know and those who do not, with the growing risk of a sort of "returning illiteracy".

This phenomenon seems particularly present in the large Italian libraries which are mainly government-run, and which are seriously behind as regards basic training, continuous updating and the retraining of the managerial class. Attending to basic and continuous training, also taking advantage of the possibilities offered nowadays by distance learning technologies, is becoming more and more a priority goal.

Thorough study of digital themes reveals that, though technology is important, it is more than ever an instrumental fact and hence secondary to that of giving staff the means for dominating the change.

Technologies and Standards

Undoubtedly the technological component is the factor through which a Digital Library is set up. The same can be said of the attention necessary for the application of descriptive standards (metadata) for access to the resources and their sharing, as well as for their fruition.

However, although the study reserves a significant part for these themes, it seems to us correct to emphasise here that technology presents itself above all as an instrumental and not a priority fact, due to its continual evolution.

In fact within a precise cultural and organisational reference framework, and with the availability of adequate skills, we should be careful to adopt market standards and move towards solutions which are technologically open to continual evolution. The study deals with the following themes under a series of sections:

- Digital supports (Text, Audio, Images, onwards: a comprehensive survey of the "objects" of the Digital Library.
- Telematic infrastructures and Internet onwards: an analysis of web demands and of the current range of offers in our country. The services offered by Infostrada, Albacom, I-net, Telecom, Garr and Rupa are examined.
- Automated management systems: a survey of to what extent and how the present library automation

systems are being adapted to the advent of the digital. With a brief examination also of the Italian scene and of the features of SBN (servizio bibliotecario nazionale), which at the present time does not seem to be prepared for any kind of digital function.

Among the most innovative services is the ASP: "A further evolution, which may significantly influence the market in the years to come, is the starting-up of the so-called ASP (Application Service Provider). In practice, ASP is a service for library management which is completely entrusted to the outside.

The only thing which the library has to manage locally is the connection to Internet. All the functions, from research to data input to the management of all the other functions are the concern of the system provider." It seems to us useful to recall this particular solution since it is proposed as one of the services that could be offered by the Digital Library., although with a different significance.

- Data Storage on the function of storage. It should be pointed out that in the face of a continually changing situation from both the technological viewpoint and that of competitiveness of the offer, a continual updating on each of these themes is crucial.

Digitisation

One of the most important technical aspects is that of acquiring a mastery of the materials and modes of treatment for digitisation. "The project of setting up a digital library needs thoroughly to evaluate the different types of document which are involved in the scanning process, whether it be a question of books, archive documents or more specifically museum documents, since also the latter are involved in the process of technological transformation of conservation and of fruition through informatics and telematic instruments".

The theme of hybridism is dealt with. "(...) a theme which is closely related to the conservation of the library document at the moment when we are planning the setting-up of digital library. The demands of a conservation system are, in fact, better fulfilled by a combination of technologies".

"The practice of hybridism thus consists of combining the two technologies: converting into digital and producing microfilms from the digital or viceversa producing microfilms and converting them into digital". For each type of material, technical and methodological indications are provided in the second part. Indications are given in particular for the following materials:

- Supports of vegetable origin (papyri)
- Cloth supports
- Wooden supports
- Paper supports (with particular regard to manuscripts [illuminated, illuminated with close binding, loose binding or loose-leaf, monochromatic], printed books, postcards and prints in general, tissue paper)
- Supports of animal origin (parchments)
- Supports of mineral origin
- Supports of chemical origin (microfilms, slides) Indications are given regarding the general criteria to apply for photographic and digital resolution.

The Organisation of a Project

Granted that each project has a separate story, a general reference scheme for the typical operations of a digitisation project is however proposed on the basis of what is offered by the professional literature.

Description of the Resources

In the Digital Library the problems of description take on more and more importance and a large part of the study is dedicated to these. What determines special attention to the problem is the need to understand all the different features of the digital object.

The various categories of Metadata necessary for identifying the object for its conservation and transmissability in time are analysed.

A survey of the standards of description and their evolution, directly influenced by the nature of the objects to which they will be applied, is proposed. Mention is made of ISBD (ER), of bibliographical formats such as MARC and Unimarc, of the problem of resource identifiers URN, DOI, URL, PURL, and finally a part is dedicated to the most significant standard so far developed for the purpose, i.e. Dublin Core.

The debate on description also regards environments other than the library, in particular archives and museums; the EAD and CRM developed standards take this debate into account. Some international projects dedicated to this theme are of great importance. Some of these also include Italian participants.

The problems of the standards and Metadata return in the second part within a series of operational proposals and recommendations.

"The importance is underlined that some specific applications of projects for a digital library should start up the experimentation of the model IFLA FRBR because of its potential for analysing and documenting in a precise way the work, the expression, the manifestation, the copy, connections among them and respectively to the intellectual responsibility and the concepts treated.

This model is suitable for the treatment of electronic resources in their multiple versions, allowing documentation of critical editions, versions, new editions, translations, transpositions and revisions on similar or different supports.

This could be adequately applied in the treatment of prestigious collections which boast a rich literary history, thus furnishing a precious, rich access to which the function of digital conservation can be associated". And " metadata are necessary for the management of transactions which require the precise identification of the users of the objects treated, of the use that is to be made of them".

The initiatives of the digital library cannot ignore this function; they must define the parties involved and their role, the object of the transactions, the action to be carried out on the requested objects (e.g. read, listen, see, save, transfer), the parameters which limit it (in terms of place, time, amount, repeatability, hence the number of times in which the action may be repeated), and also the action of whoever uses the service in exchange for acquired rights".

For conservation: "Regardless of the technique used to guarantee conservation and the future use of the digital resources, it is necessary to document clearly how to put these functions into practice and hence to define the features of the format of the software and of the instruments in order to use a certain resource over time".

"Besides the previously-expressed recommendations relative to the features of the metadata for the functions of identification and access, management of rights and conservation of the digital resources, some proposals are put forwards which cover on the one hand the activity of support to the description and management of the digital resources, on the other the actions of coordination which are necessary at an institutional and interinstitutional level, on both a national and an international scale".

Legal Problems (Copyright) in Italy

In this as in other cases, uncertainty prevails as to the behaviour to be adopted in the face of laws which are still mainly orientated towards traditional documentation. "The reference norms for copyright in a digital environment derive from the interpretation of the existing norms, from analogical application and from the appeal to the general principles of the law. In general there is even a lack of a consolidated jurisprudential doctrine and practice.

In view of the particular nature of the new technologies and the many different possibilities that they offer in comparison with traditional supports (paper, videocassettes, photographs etc.), the recourse to analogy and to interpretation of the existing norms is sometimes difficult.

Thus for a more complete protection, contractual solutions are often used to clarify the conditions of use of digital material, either through contracts (or licenses) or through regulations of access (or general conditions)."

Regarding services:

"In offering services to the users of a databank we must necessarily follow the legislation established for that type of support or negotiate with copyright-holders. If we wish to offer certain paid services on material which is still protected by copyright, we must necessarily negotiate the procedure to be adopted with the author, since he/she has all rights over the work".

Concerning the protection of the rights of a database: "In this case we can establish services, conditions of access to the database, limitations of liability, guarantees, applicable legislation and so on.

The contractual solution has undoubted advantages since the creator of the database defines his own liabilities and the conditions of access within a legislative picture which is not always clear and complete".

Even in the case of copyright we are faced with a situation which is continuously changing. "the legislation on this matter is still evolving, and there is very little jurisprudential doctrine and practice; despite this some guidelines can be already identified in current legislation or in analogical application. There are numerous problems regarding the possibility of offering paid services, in that obligations deriving from legislation on copyright, as well as some regulations about electronic trading, would emerge.

While the offering of "traditional" non-profit-making services on material not protected by copyright (public property) in any case seems to be easier, even if a clear legal framework is lacking ". In this as in other cases, the need for constant observation of the evolution of the law remains open.

There is a similarly strong need to acquire the necessary skills in the case of negotiation for the acquisition of original digital resources. This is possible both by means of an internal process (special training as required), and thanks to the activation of external references (outsourcing) which are specifically dedicated to negotiation.

Examination of the Existing Situation

One of the fundamental elements in the setting-up of Digital Library in the world (but also in Italy for few but significant examples) is cooperation in terms of sharing of experience, knowledge and programmes. This assumption can clearly be drawn from the observation of what has actually happened and is in progress, above all outside our country.

A significant part of the study is that dedicated to an inventory of what has been created in Italy and abroad from all the previously-mentioned points of view. It is from this survey that the most significant part of the proposals arise; they are outlined concretely in the second section of the study.

General Summary

The Digital Library took off abroad much earlier than in Italy and this allows us to learn from a series of experiences, analyses, mistakes which have been identified and corrected, and thus to start from this point, exploiting the experiences metabolised by the library system thanks to forms of extended cooperation.

Features Chosen for the Study

The study has chosen from all the experiences analysed and has focused on the organisational aspects and the results which, thanks to these experiences, are being obtained in various, differentiated situations.

Situation Abroad

The study examines more or less in detail both the American and the European experiences.

To sum up, the elements that we feel it opportune to recall in this report are:

- The financial investment
- The political investment (understood as the politics of information)

- The training and professional investment
- The technological investment
- The constant investment of study and analysis

Let us examine the various points briefly:

- *The financial aspect is fundamental*: Not only in the sense that to set up any Digital Library project large funds have been invested, but also in the sense that in all countries the allocation of funds has been effected with extreme care and submitted to constant verification. Setting up a digital project not only costs a lot at the moment of its setting-up, but it costs as much again for its maintenance, digital resources not being static objects like traditional documents, but extremely dynamic ones.
- They are in fact subject to continual technological updating and, because of their possibilities of diffusion, produce expectations of service with consequences which must be continually foreseen, examined and dealt with opportunely.
- *The political investment*: This investment is clearly meant at an international level as the need to determine beforehand the "rules of the game", i.e. guidelines of development of the digital within which to direct and coordinate the various initiatives, to avoid dispersion of resources of all kinds. In almost all the countries examined a sort of "Charter of Constitution of the digital" has been made out: this is wide and flexible but able to provide an indispensable reference point for any future initiative.

These declarations of intent, destined to constitute the "mission" of the various Digital Librarys, also have generic elements and in any case have the characteristic of being comprehensive of all the facets that local cultures inevitably carry with them. They are such as to fulfil all the requirements that the various countries regard as priority. As an example we cite (there are in fact others) the principles emanated by the National Library of Australia *"Digitisation Policy"* for the years 2000-2004.

The Training and Professional Investment

The advent of the Digital Library has overturned or, let us say, has better clarified, the idea of what the lines of investment for retraining and basic training should be.

In other countries where those working in libraries have a background of basic studies in librarianship, the greatest investment is being made in several directions: staff retraining in the sense of planning skill, management according to quality requirements, providing of new services and technological ability.

Particular attention is placed on what is nowadays offered by the possibilities of continuous distance training.

There are numerous initiatives at various basic and higher levels, to guarantee a homogenous level of knowledge.

- *The technological investment*: The Digital Library obvio-usly has a strong technological component. Not only in the sense of the greater possibilities of application given by greater and more powerful means of production, storage and communication, but above all in the sense of using the technologies in the direction of all the categories of possible users.

From this derive the diffusion of studies and applications in the field of interfaces, in the qualification of services so as to cover all possible user groups from the scientific to the purely entertainment ones.

Another sector in which there is a large investment is that relative to the conservation of digital products, thanks to means of reconverting existing materials at the highest current technological level and according to the new market standards. Finally, the infrastructural aspect, which in many of the countries examined does not constitute a problem but which however is rightly pointed out as a precondition for the correct use of digital products. Some examples (continuously growing in number) are indicated both in the Bibliography and in the Bookmarks.

- The constant investment in study and analysis. The Digital Library is not static and this involves the presence in many countries of *ad hoc* structures for continuous study and extended sharing of studies and researches. International cooperation is no longer seen only as the sharing of information resources (also that), but above all as a sharing of experiences of research and technological results.

Many of the examples examined have within them structures suitable for scientific research in the digital field. T

Situation in Italy

A large section is dedicated to the Italian situation, whose main characteristics are the extremely fragmentary nature of the initiatives and poor coordination.

Features and Limitations

In our country a considerable number of initiatives have been undertaken or are in progress in the digital field. Most of these are aimed at the exploitation of single parts of collections (music, geographical maps, Galileo estate, etc.), rather than subscribing to wider projects with precise goals directed towards study or the systematic re-evaluation of areas of national culture.

In some universities and in the CNR (Consiglio Nazionale delle Ricerche), advanced projects are also created (three-dimensional digitisation, advanced workstations), but always in a way which is absolutely independent from other universities and, it sometimes seems, even in competition with them.

The same can be said of libraries, both government-run ones and those belonging to local government, in the absence of an overall plan. Almost all the initiatives also seem to obey the rule of incompleteness, in the sense that maintenance costs and the relative services are not planned ahead; the importance of elements like the implementation of metadata and conservation are not considered beforehand.

That cooperation in the Italian libraries (apart from SBN (servizio bibliotecario nazionale)) is a sort of "optional", is clear also to those bodies which observe them in relation to international initiatives. This is, and it should be emphatically underlined, an element of great weakness in the case of the digital, where the complementary interaction of individual efforts acts to the advantage of better use of the financial resources, and not only of these.

A case apart, to which we will return in the proposals part, is SBN (servizio bibliotecario nazionale), whose main legacy is the very fact of having introduced a cooperative mentality into the Italian library environment. Organisations which differ in size and geographical location have learnt, thanks to the SBN (Servizio Bibliotecario Nazionale) principles, to discuss, take joint decisions and work for common objectives of resource sharing.

Despite the confusion which still prevails in the Italian digital situation, there are however initiatives which should be observed very carefully, these by no coincidence being those which show a joint effort on the part of different organisations towards a single goal (e.g.: the CeBIT – Biblioteca Italiana Telematica, cited and described in the section on the Italian situation).

Introduction to Proposals

The proposal to which a large part of this summary as well as the study itself is dedicated, is fundamentally to:

- Fix precise criteria within which to carry out the activity of digitisation in our country.
- Opt for a strong series of initiatives of retraining and basic training.
- Set up a constant study.
- For the application of standards specific to the digital.
- For the definition of methodologies.
- For the definition of productive models directed at quality.

All this is to be done starting from the group of 46 libraries belonging to the government which, besides having the advantage of being under a single administration also have that (by no means secondary) of being part of one of the largest and most prestigious cultural heritages in the world.

Proposals

The proposals which are developed in the second part of the study are the fruit of a reflection on all the needs which have emerged in the light of the problems of all kinds highlighted in the inventory. The first part of the study ends with a mention of some aspects which are judged important and with a sort of summary of the problems.

"Two necessary levels of coordination are identified: local and central. By local coordination is meant everything pertaining to the single library structure. (...) It is thus a question of analysing the nature and extension of the new services and of the new professional figures required to handle these. The library also becomes a production centre, in that part of its collections will be destined to digital transposition; in this case we need

- A choice of the materials according to the ends which are proposed (conservation or service)
- Identification of the most appropriate methodologies for their treatment
- Creation of special operational task-forces or at least
- Coordination of outside forces in total or partial support of the digitization

From the central point of view, this coordination activity must have the function of supporting the initiatives of the single institutes, and they must be conceived as follows:

- According to general principles of coherence with the programmes of other institutions
- In compliance with consolidated standards which are updated each time
- Contributing to the financial support of the initiatives on the basis of the analysis of actual needs
- Providing where necessary the technical/logistic support for the setting-up and carrying out of digitisation initiatives
- Setting up the necessary training programmes for the acquisition of specific skills in the digital sector
- Creating the conditions for uncomplicated norms and regulations which fit the new tasks awaiting the single libraries".

The needs to be fulfilled should also be fixed, with particular regard to the features of the libraries belonging to the Ministry. The mixed features of these libraries requires a thorough knowledge of the users of the services provided.

"It does not appear that the government administration underst-ands these needs at a qualitative level but, from what emerges from the use made of statistical data, only at a quantitative one, even though data are collected which could help to define the characteristics of the users and their demands, on the basis of services provided. In the same way it does not seem that procedures of investigation specific to the users and their satisfaction (customer satisfaction) are ever undertaken.

This is an essential step in our opinion, one that should precede any project for the setting-up of Digital Librarys, as well as being coherent with the initiatives already underway relative to the quality of services. It is also coherent with debates at professional level on the so-called "Service Cards" in the library.

This would lead us to identify within the administration deficits related to regulations, organisation and the professional training of the staff, which may constitute a restriction to be overcome in order to achieve the effective working of a Digital Library project.

The analysis suggests the need for particular identification of:

- Which professional figures are today contemplated by the administration
- Which of these figures are coherent with the new professions which have become available with the advent of the digital
- How regulations and job descriptions fulfil the needs of the digital And from the point of view of regulations
- What the obstacles are which prevent the setting-up of value-added services (pricing of services etc.)
- What restrictions dictated by the budget items prevent the acquisition and activating of electronic

sources (databases, electronic magazines as an alternative to printed ones, etc.)

"The proposal is moreover developed from a series of considerations which are the object of the "Analysis and Diagnosis" which we report herewith. ".

- In Italy, as in the rest of the world, digital projects are being developed but we have the sensation that "despite the technological and cultural validity of many of these projects each of them has taken off on a separate impulse, without any thought of inserting the initiative into a wider picture of coordinated and shared planning".
- "The majority of projects has a single structure as its promotor and main participant, thus generating the legitimate doubt that no attention has been paid to similar initiatives in a national field nor even to those at the international level."
- "It is very difficult to know the measure [and] the duration of investments".
- The destined use of the projects underway does not seem clear and hence also their practical application seems to lack consideration, above all regarding certain librarianship aspects (e.g. use of metadata etc.)
- The large majority of library structures does not seem to be ready from the point of view of professional skills either for the starting up and running of the projects or for the offering of new services or of traditional services through new methods.
- More generally we note a lack of linkage among the *structures belonging to the various administrations, but also among offices belonging to the same administration".*

Operational Proposals

These are a series of options which are compared regarding feasibility and times. We might call this series "transitory" and actually it is proposed as the necessary initial application of the more complex proposal, to be considered as the point of arrival of a wide process of reorganisation as a function of the setting-up of the Italian Digital Library.

Proposed Model

From the analysis it emerges that the proposed model can be seen as a centre which must interact with the existing systems. These existing systems are understood as hybrid bodies, hence libraries which extend their activities and services to the digital environment.

The solution which emerges is thus not a purely technical one which quite simply stores in a single large "warehouse" the digital which is produced in Italy, but is instead orientated towards the coordination, support and management of the digital; in the Italian situation it will be above all new initiatives which will take on such service functions.

In this way the single initiatives which will have to be constructed according to standard and quality criteria, will be able to flow together into that single entity which we can call the Italian Digital Library (IDL).

The Strategic Value of Cooperation and the Tradition of SBN (Servizio Bibliotecario Nazionale)

As already said several times during both the study and the present summary, cooperation, understood not in a formal but in a substantial way as sharing of intellectual, organisational and economic efforts orientated towards the digital, is the winning factor all over the world. It is in any case the factor which blocks impractical initiatives or those without any great prospects, as well as those which simply waste public resources.

As already mentioned before, SBN (Servizio Bibliotecario Nazionale) is a positive "anomaly" on the Italian scene which has been nurturing the element of cooperation in the Italian library mentality and working habits for almost thirty years. It seems to us important to emphasise the following results:

- SBN (Servizio Bibliotecario Nazionale) is a distributed system.

- It is already in itself a "federation" of libraries.
- It has a wide, consolidated national extension.
- It has developed programmes and initiatives in a context of inter-institutional negotiation.
- It has developed a way of working and a transverse decisional model at both geographical and institutional levels (Government/Regions; relations among different Ministries)
- It has contributed to establishing operational relations among different sectors within the Ministry of Culture and Heritage itself.
- It has worked extensively with the private world.

These are elements which must in our opinion all be included without exception in the future Italian Digital Library, since they have furnished important political, technical and librarianship experiences.

Setting up of the Italian Digital Library

Despite the fragmentary nature of Digital Library experiences in Italy, we cannot ignore the presence of episodes which are valid from every point of view. These experiences have generated within the structures where they have been carried out a series of specific skills which must constitute the starting-point for any future development in the field.

We have also said that the group of libraries pertaining to the Ministry, to which can be added those active in the web thanks to SBN (Servizio Bibliotecario Nazionale), make up a potential Italian *"Digital Library Federation"*. It goes without saying that in the case of our proposal for setting up the Italian Digital Library we must consider the role and experiences of at least three of these libraries:

The Biblioteca Nazionale Centrale of Florence, the Biblioteca Nazionale Marciana of Venice, the Biblioteca Nazionale Braidense of Milan. Next to these must also be put the ICCU with all the weight of its skills in the field of applications of bibliographical standards, and the Discoteca di Stato (National Sound Archive), for its specific skills in the field of sound resources.

The areas of responsibility of these structures are thus: ICCU bibliographical standards and metadata Government Record Library sound resources BNCF Conservation of digital resources; methodologies of digitisation BNMV- special materials (music, geographical maps) BNBM Periodicals The definitions of the themes to be treated with continuity must be fixed from the start by representatives from these institutes, who will gradually be joined by other institutes and other skills.

Coordination Structure (CS)

It is however felt that a series of duties must be entrusted to a coordination structure. "The need to have an organised structure which deals with coordinating and monitoring the various initiatives in the digital field arises from the complexity inherent in the Digital Library from the technical, organisational and economic points of view.

The survey conducted both in Italy (few but significant examples) and above all abroad gives us a series of strong indications about the characteristics that the Digital Library must have in our country to give those guarantees of success and good return of investments.

The creation and running of a Digital Library is only partly comparable to the creation and running of a library automation system. In general, in our opinion, only in those parts regarding the technological choices (hw/sw solutions) and the activation of maintenance for the system

All the rest is instead part of a production process which lies outside normal library functions. The complexity of these initiatives is obviously proportionate to the dimensions of the "production object". Hence the need at a national level of a CS which has the task of observing, directing and monitoring the various projects".

"This CS would have strong powers of directing and monitoring compliance of the fixed standard requirements. The tasks and limitations of the CS will also be defined in relation to other ministerial bodies, particularly all those directly dealing with matters in the library, archive and museum environment. It must in fact be remembered that the

Digital Library goes beyond the mere library sphere and indeed, as has been amply demonstrated by numerous examples, has its maximum significance in the interaction among different institutions such as libraries, archives and museums".

The tasks which must be undertaken at a central level are such because they cannot be delegated to peripheral structures, whose roles must concentrate more on operations and applications.

The "Mission" of the Italian Digital Library: its Definition and Creation

For the creation of the Italian Digital Library it is indispensable, as has already happened and is happening in other countries, to define the guidelines of the new Italian Digital Library.

We are talking about a sort of "Charter of Principles" of the digital, in which the fundamental principles and the cultural and scientific reference frameworks within which the existing initiatives will be placed and new initiatives will be set up, must be fixed.

We must define " a series of reference points which can be modified in time and adapted to the changing conditions and developments of the world of information.

The CS will have as its prime task that of monitoring compliance with the principles which have been fixed, in the sense of encouraging and sustaining all the initiatives which are coherent with these principles and discouraging those which diverge from them.

Study and Research

The setting-up of the Digital Library involves a huge interaction of knowledge and experience from both the technological and the librarianship points of view. The primary task of the CS of the Italian Digital Library will thus be to act as a real "clearing-house" for the various problems that are encountered in the projects, in their creation and in their running in time.

For the various subjects of interest it may divide up into permanent working groups with specialists in the sector and "temporary guests" who are able to contribute with their concrete experience to the acquisition of information. We see four main paths along which to develop this type of organisation:

- Methodologies (planning, quality processes etc.)
- Technologies (hw/sw solutions, compression systems, new digital formats, etc.)
- Legal aspects (copyright, internal regulations, professional figures, deregulation directed to the service, etc.)
- The services (interfaces, pricing, joint ventures directed to resource sharing, etc.)

A National Directory of the Italian Digital Library

The starting point for any planning or goal definition is awareness of the existing situation. Also in Italy there are already numerous initiatives on the digital and some (very few) also of a certain significance; many are interesting as regards goals and less so as regards results.

In any case a Directory of the Digital must be set up, which is coordinated with other similar initiatives (for example the new one of the ICCU, more directed towards the use of metadata.

It can contain data both on the projects carried out (providing the necessary access via URL) and on those still in the planning stage, identified through inventories, papers, conventions, mention in professional and non-professional periodicals. It will cover both technical, organisational and content aspects. There will be a parallel compilation of a kind of "Who's Who?" of the digital in Italy. It will need a stable inventory and editing structure.

Planning Support

The CS of the Italian Digital Library must become the reference point for providing consultancy services to the regions or to the large library structures for the correct formulation of the projects.

To this end it will from the start have to identify all the standards towards which the various projects must be directed, guaranteeing a tendency to homogeneity in the results.

It must succeed in imposing a workflow standard for production and provide support for the drawing-up of plans according to quality requirements (Pert, GANNT). It will identify, also on the basis of indications by experts, programmes for optimising the national culture, themes (anniversaries, historical subjects) and types of material (periodicals, posters, statutes, etc.) which should all move towards the setting up of a complete Italian Digital Library (on the lines for example of the American Memory promoted by the Library of Congress), focusing on the integration of single projects which are developed on a local basis.

It will favour the growth of these local initiatives (always within the standard reference grid) incentivating them with ad hoc grants and funding, on the basis of tenders as happens in other countries.

It must in any case encourage projects which are the fruit of joint efforts (several bodies, complementary projects etc.). It must favour projects integrating national and international projects which have already been started and particularly which regard themes of interest for Italian culture. The task force responsible for this important task of project definition must necessarily include: librarians, pure technicians, project management experts, marketing experts.

Training

The identification of training needs for adapting basic and advanced skills is another vital task. "The setting up of the Digital Library involves a revolution of skills, duties and roles which is not comparable to what was involved in the advent of automation of the library system. The librarian, seen both as manager and as employee responsible for certain duties, must necessarily be submitted to updating and often to a new technological literacy process.

This is not so much in order to transform librarians into pure technicians but to offer him/her all the tools for the understanding of the various technological components introduced by the Digital Library. The profession of librarian is transforming itself more and more into a sort of "aggregator" of solutions, aimed at obtaining a certain "object" (in our case: digital products) or at the activation of a certain service (in the case in question: new services of access to information).

The CS of the Italian Digital Library will play an important role in:

- Identifying training needs
- Defining the level of training/updating
- Developing new training methods and contents or having them developed
- Activating monitoring tools for verification of results

A task force for training will set up training paths and can also have the most suitable contents developed by outside companies which specialise in training. Particular use must be made of distance learning.

It can also set up agreements with community and extra-community countries for periods of study and updating exclusively aimed at the acquisition of skills in the Digital Library sector.

A particularly important point will be that related to the relations with schools and universities. Primary schools can be stimulated to become vehicles of Internet literacy and some of the first and most extensive users of Digital Library initiatives. Secondary schools and universities can instead be the main users of services offered by the Digital Library in terms of creativity, planning, distance learning.

Communication, Promotion and Outside Relations

One of the weak points of the present structures of the libraries is the low ability to communicate. The Cs and Italian Digital Library must break this negative tradition, setting up a continuous communication with the potential users of the proposed services. Not only through publicity campaigns but also above all thanks to detailed, constant strictly digital information on the current or finished initiatives, on projects and the various related initiatives.

The CS portal of the Italian Digital Library will be the natural vehicle of this information flow. The promotion of initiatives in progress or those already available must pass through the portal.

The CS of the Italian Digital Library must have a stable active editorial board (even located remotely and not necessarily centralised) which is coordinated by experts in communication able to constantly update the Web with information pertaining to the Digital Library. An electronic newsletter can be published in the currently fashionable method of brief review with links to the news or resource.

The aim of proposing Italian partnership in the great international initiatives will be particularly important for this PR Office. Expanding public relations also means activating channels of constant relations with interlocutors such as the publishing world, firms interested in the digital, as well as of course all those traditional partners like the Regions, the Provinces and the Boroughs.

With the latter in particular permanent negotiations must be set up to launch and/or monitor initiatives directed towards the Digital Library. The prototype developed shows how such a structure could communicate and provide specific services on the digital.

A National Conference on a Regular Basis

An extremely important task due to its communication value is that of organising a "National conference on the Digital" on a regular basis (for example every two years).

This will be the national and international showcase of the results obtained, with sessions of presentation of the most significant projects in progress or completed, technical workshops in cooperation with similar international structures, exhibition of specific technological solutions for the digital.

Times, Costs and Quality Requirements

Not all these objectives can be achieved at the same time and the last part of the study compares times, methods and costs of the proposals. Emphasis is on the requirement of quality as an element to be focused on and in this sense a synoptic classification of the characteristics which a quality Digital Library should have is proposed.

These requirements are examined both in regard to the local Digital Library (which is transformed into a centre of production of digital products and of supply of value-added services) and in regard to the true object of the study and of our proposal, i.e. the Digital Library and its various services orientated towards the various local structures belonging to the system as a whole.

One section is dedicated to the "planned interventions on non-informative components" which are in particular training and organisation. "The setting up of the Digital Library faces the traditional library with some questions finding the answer to which is a necessary prelude to the setting up of any initiative.

In particular the answer to what the essential conditions are for the feasibility of a project from the point of view of the processes which will be activated and their organisational impact on the functioning of the library and its staff".

This involves the redefinition of services, job definitions and training schemes. The final part of the study shows a list in table form of the main steps in this process of construction and an estimate of the costs to be faced at least during a first two-year period.

Breakdown of the Project

The overall plan of the project for the setting-up of the Italian Digital Library is developed using the formalism of the Work Breakdown Structure, which provides a proposal for the segmentation of the project, defining the varies activities (Work packages) of which it is composed. "*The main stages of the project which have been identified are:*

- *Pre-set-up Stage:* One of the stages for the setting up of the Italian Digital Library where the founding principles of the Italian Digital Library are outlined
- *Set-up Stage:* Where concreteness is lent to the action

through a planning stage. It is in this stage that the tender specifications and/or outsourcing contracts for the creation of the technical/editorial infrastructures will be defined.

- *Creation Of Infrastructures:* Stage of development and transfer online of the Italian Digital Library services
- *Implementation Of Advanced Services:* this stage refers to the conception of the evolutionary nature of services offered by the Italian Digital Library." Through GANTT and Pert the project is described in its time course and in terms of the milestones of verification and/or checking of the activities.

Risks

"By risks we must above all understand non-exploitation of the resource potential in the processes and activities. But we can better judge this "non-exploitation" on the basis of the distinction of risks formulated as: -wastage (of human resources, materials, potential of internal functioning; organisational processes and activities) -losses of quality (dissatisfaction about the relations with the local Digital Library; with the final user; creation of a product not wholly complying with expectations and needs).

Costs

The costs expressed in the table refer to two orders of greatness:

- External costs refer to the adoption of resources outside the ministry such as: consultancies, telematic infrastructures, projects, outsourcing etc., to be found through contracts or tenders.
- Internal costs refer to the use of resources inside the organisational structure of the UCBL; in this case man-days were used as the unit of measurement to quantify the estimated expense.

A scheme is also provided for the calculation of the variable costs of a digitisation project, remembering that no universal scheme of budgeting so far exists for digitisation projects and that the orientation is rather that of working out a model on the basis of a prototype which is then extended to the whole project.

Benefits

In some final tables a methodology of evaluation is proposed without going into the attribution of the values expressed by the coefficients which will depend on the analysis of the various project situations. This illustration in table form is developed both for local Digital Librarys and for the Italian Digital Library. In the first case (Digital Library) it involves while in the second (Italian Digital Library) it instead involves

Conclusions

As explained in the introduction we have tried with this summary to provide a simpler and more direct key to the main concepts expressed in the study as a whole. We recommend however that this summary be used as an "entry key" to the complete study.

There are many subjects dealt with in it that are difficult to summarise without losing much of their value from the point of view of information or reflection on the complexity of the Digital Library.

Chapter 3

Establishing a Digital Library Centre

This article discusses some of the issues that arise when an academic department, unit or institution moves from possessing a few digital library projects and services, to possessing an integrated digital library centre.

The article is based on:

- The experiences of the author, who has worked in four digital library centres (according to the definition in the next section) in UK higher education.
- Replies from various people who have been employed by digital/electronic library projects and services over the past decade, to emailed questions about various aspects of digital library centre culture
- Examples of incidents or case studies of things that have occurred within UK digital library centres

It does not prescribe a 'one model fits all' plan for all budding digital library centres. There are many factors and variables, some constantly changing, that influence a successful or unsuccessful centre; this article touches on a selection.

Having said that, large consideration is given to the issues of staffing and funding, which (along with the struggle for accommodation) appear to be the main issues that preoccupy people involved in running digital library centres.

DEFINING THE DIGITAL LIBRARY CENTRE

Before proceeding, it is necessary to define what a UK higher education-based digital library research centre is. As one reply to this question put it:

"It's one of those things that is obvious when you see it you can quickly say whether something is a digital library research centre or not. Trying to define an authorative catch-all definition that every centre and non-centre is happy with, is another thing altogether."

By its very title, such a centre is a place where research into 'the digital library' is carried out. However, both 'research' and 'the digital library' are themselves vague, all-encapsulating terms; the phrase 'digital library' alone signifies remarkably different things to different people.

In addition, it could be argued that many university, and some FE college, departments carry out some kind of digital library research. For example, identifying the right database system to store information relevant to the subject domain of a department could constitute 'digital library research', as could designing a web site in order to provide access to content produced by the department, or providing department-wide access to a range of third-party electronic information services.

Because of the fuzziness of terminology, and the pervasiveness of digital library technologies in most aspects of education and information systems, acceptable synonyms of 'digital library centre' could include 'electronic library centre', 'information management centre', 'virtual library unit', 'learning technology unit' and many others.

However, there are a number of groupings and departments in UK academia that explicitly promote themselves as digital (or electronic, networking, learning technology or IT) research, development or service-oriented centres. These include centres such as the CDLR, CERLIM, CIRT, ILRT, LITC and UKOLN.

There are also distinct groupings of projects within UK higher education departments of information science (more commonly known as 'library schools') such as the Information Management Research Institute, which promote themselves as some variation of a 'digital library (research)' centre.

We looked at a number of these centres and groupings in order to identify the activities they conducted. The ten most common were:

- *Digital library services*: Creation, maintenance, enhancement.
- Evaluation of digital library projects, services and programmes.
- Consultancy in digital library matters.
- Developing digital library demonstrators usually, but not always, as part of a funded project.
- Research in a variety of aspects of digital/electronic library matters.
- Training in some aspect of ICT, or digital library usage.
- Fund raising for the centre.
- Digital library project and service coordination either as the sole partner, or as the lead partner of a consortium.
- Digital library centre, service and project-oriented publicity and promotion.
- Organising and promoting digital library events.

As an added complication, it could be argued that there are a number of centres carrying out most of these activities that do not market themselves as digital library (research) centres. For example, EDINA provides a wide range of electronic data-oriented services, in addition to events, service coordination, promotion and so forth.

In addition, the JISC-funded Resource Discovery Network coordinates a number of 'hubs' i.e. centres that provide a range of internet resource discovery and related electronic services in specific subject domains; these are either based around a long-established service, such as EEVL, OMNI and SOSIG, or are based around newly established resource discovery systems.

These hubs, though service-oriented as opposed to research-oriented, are typically involved in seven or more of the aforementioned ten activities. In addition, as one subject gateway research officer put it:

".even though we maintain a service, we still need to carry out research on a continuous basis. Better interfaces, methods of integrating our service with the RDN and others, faster information download, techniques to increase recall and precision, monitoring usage."

For the purpose of this article, we will drop the word 'research', so as to include those centres that provide mainly digital library services, therefore leaving us with the 'Digital Library Centre', or DLC for short. We will define the DLC somewhat unscientifically as being:

'A centre containing two or more digital library-oriented services or projects, where the services and projects interact in technical, personnel, promotional or other ways, and where the majority of activities in the aforementioned list of ten are carried out.'

The Benefits and the Drawbacks

What are the benefits of running a DLC?

- The skills and experience of staff can be used across a range of projects, and the non-project components of the centre, as opposed to being used on one discrete project. This benefits both the development of the staff, and the development of projects and services.
- The centre will have a higher profile than a disconnected collection of projects, therefore (theoretically) attracting potential funders and skilled staff.
- The more staff there is, the greater the pool of contacts and collaborators (through those staff), and the more people who may become aware of the more obscure sources of funding.
- Proposals can be submitted for work based on previous or current work in the centre, therefore increasing the chances of those proposals being funded.
- The centre should have more 'clout' within the host institution, and is therefore able to fight for better/ adequate accommodation and other institutional resources.
- With good (and independent) financial manage-

ment, there is more flexibility in moving monies between projects, services, initiatives and other budgets within the centre.

- Some activities can be carried out more efficiently; for example, a number of closely-related projects or services could carry out joint dissemination activities.

Obviously, there are drawbacks to establishing a DLC; otherwise, most HE institutions would possess one, and all DLCs would succeed and prosper.

Significant problems encountered by such centres include:

- Funding non-project staff, such as centre administrators and directors; many conventional funding sources will only fund staff directly employed on a project or service, and will expect the bidding centre or institution to provide appropriate administration, directorial and other non-project based staff out of its own funds.
- In the same vein, funding non-project activities, such as centre-oriented PR (web site, leaflets, presentational expenses).
- Finding increasing amounts of funding in order to retain staff who are increasing in experience and skills.
- *Accommodation*: This really should not be a problem; a successful DLC can bring in substantial funds to the host institution, raise the institutional profile, provide a range of services and information to other units within the institution, and assist in raising the RAE rating of several departments. You would therefore assume that Higher Education institutions would happily provide sufficient accommodation. This is not the case; most UK HE DLCs have fought a permanent struggle to gain satisfactory accommodation of anywhere near the standard of similarly sized units in the same institution.
- You will need to speculate before you can accumulate. Before hiring staff who will secure funding, the aformentioned accommodation has to

be located for them, in addition to desks, PCs, stationary and the like; this will easily run into several thousand pounds of spending before any member of staff of the new DLC actually starts to write the first funding application or proposal.

The 'Vision' of the Centre

Before establishing a DLC, you essentially need some kind of vision, agenda, remit or plan. This is useful when dealing with sponsors, funders, incoming staff, PR-related issues and so forth; it is not enough to mumble "we do digital library stuff" and leave it at that.

The vision of a DLC is usually oriented around one or more of the following:

- *Some subject domain or spectrum*: For example, a centre could offer a range of services including electronic journals, resource discovery access and internet training in a specific subject.
- *Some type of digital library service*: For example, a centre could specialise in providing services, research and consultancy in various aspects of electronic journal creation, maintenance, access and charging.
- *A geographic area*: A centre could aim to become the main higher education institution based centre of digital library research activity within its particular region of the country.
- A particular funding source or 'seam'.
- *Some particular user domain*: For example, a centre could research digital library issues applicable to teachers, lecturers, librarians, schoolchildren or some other type(s) of user.

The vision will be partially determined by the existing projects (and proposals for future projects currently submitted) which will form the new centre. In addition, the skill set and experience of staff who will work in the centre can be a significant factor in the scoping of the vision, as well as those digital library-related resources and services (usually within the host institution) on which the centre can rely. The vision (which needs to be updated as projects and services come and go) can be used to provide the basis of the centre mission statement and several other PR elements.

Funding the Centre

Unless your centre has several projects that involve large amounts of digitisation work, or invests in some hugely expensive specialist piece of hardware, then the large majority of expenditure will be on staff wages.

Focusing on the 'Vision' or the 'Money'

The two extremes of funding a digital library centre seem to be:

- Carefully evaluating the resource, skill and funding requirements necessary to fulfil a well-defined digital library centre vision, followed by locating and pursuing the appropriate funding sources.
- Throwing together a speculative proposal for every call or tender that contains a phrase similar to 'digital libraries'.

Most centres fall somewhere between these two extremes; if you work in a senior position in a DLC, it is an interesting exercise to (honestly) see what proportion of proposals submitted in the last year more closely match either of the two extremes.

In an ideal world, a DLC would firmly adhere to the first extreme. However, the culture in which typical DLCs are embedded is based upon short-term contracts, where there is a constant quest to find funding to keep individual staff members 'on' for as long as possible. Therefore, unless your DLC has managed to develop a successful financial mechanism for retaining significant reserves, it may need to step outside of the 'vision' and acquire funding via whatever means in order to retain key staff. As one ex-director of a DLC replied:

"I felt like a hamster on a wheel; as soon as funding was secured to extend the contract of one member of staff, it was time to secure funding for another. And before long, I was back to the first member of staff. So, we would 'squeak' to various funders on a regular basis, and every now and then one of them would throw us a bit of cheese to give us the energy to carry on running a while longer. That's quite a cynical way of looking at it, isn't it? Four whole years of my life and it reads like the lyrics of a Radiohead song."

In addition to acquiring funding to retain key staff, there is also the burden of perpetually funding a continuous service. Whereas a research project usually has some finite end, digital library services carry on until they are either sold, bought out or taken over, or are integrated into some other service, or become financially unviable. In addition, services can become obsolete in terms of either the content or the supporting technology, though this should not happen in a DLC which sufficiently maintains and upgrades its services.

Even if a service is discontinued in some manner, there is often a need to make available some publicly-accessible archive of the content, which in itself raises issues of continuous maintenance and cost. This is not always considered by people who submit proposals to create digital library services.

The Diversification of Funding Sources

One of the more interesting aspects of studying digital library developments in UK HE is that of seeing where the funding comes from. This is relatively easy, as most funders demand branding or mentions of themselves in the publicly-accessible deliverables of the project or service.

Looking at the completed projects and services of DLCs from the last decade, we see that the large majority were funded from three sources:

- The JISC (Joint Information Systems Committee) funded a large number of research-oriented projects, as well as a smaller number of more service-oriented developments. Many of these projects were funded under large programmes such as eLib and JTAP, through which much of the funding was awarded to groups working in HE institutions.
- Public organisations and bodies concerned with library and library-content development, such as the British Library.

- European funding programmes.

However, a cursory examination of recent and current projects and services in the more successful DLCs in the UK (in terms of personnel growth) indicates that funding now comes from a more diverse array of sources, many of which were not targeted explicitly at higher education institutions.

For example, recently funded projects in DLCs include 'providing ICT services aimed at benefiting disadvantaged communities', 'providing training for staff in public libraries', and 'providing work packages for secondary school ages'. Non of these needed to be provided by HE institutions in particular and were not advertised as such, being open calls to any appropriate public or private organisation. So, why are DLCs now locating funding from a wider range of sources?

Some of the more sensible answers put to this question were:

- The change in focus of traditional sources of funding. A key example is the JISC; though the JISC still fund a number of exploratory and research-based projects, the focus of many calls has moved to developing and sustaining integrated services, through initiatives such as the Distributed National Electronic Resource.
- The increase in collaborative ICT and digital library funding for, and work with, Further Education. This is a drive encouraged by a number of organisations including the JISC.

  The FE sector brings with it a range of characteristics starkly different to those of HE; for example, the number of institutions involved, the subject domains and qualifications, the network configuration, and the skill-set of staff. These and other factors often present interesting challenges when HE and FE organis-ations work together on digital library and ICT initiatives.
- *More commercial project sponsorship*: Companies are realising that providing funding for projects involving computers, training, networks, digital information and education reflects positively on themselves. For example, the BT-sponsored 'Lifelong

Learning Awards' aims to "support lifelong learning projects which use ICT to promote access, innovation and teamwork".

- Same cake, more slices. There are an increasing number of organisations not all of them DLCs applying for the same grants and pots of money: ".maybe it's just me getting older, but there seems to be many more people bidding for the same funding nowadays". Several funders now process proposals and responses to tender in a multi-stage manner; this is partially so all of the unsuccessful bidders do not have to submit a final, full (and time consuming) proposal, but also so that the funding organisation does not have to judge a large number of these full proposals in one go.

A holistic Approach to Funding

So, what are these diverse sources of funding that the more successful DLCs seem to be tapping into? The rest of this section lists eleven types of income; the more established DLCs use most, if not all of these in some form or other.

Source 1: conventional Digital Library Project and Service Funders

There are a surprisingly large number of funding organisations who either issue calls or tenders with a fixed deadline, or who take a 'submit whenever you want for consideration' approach. Though the competition for funding from many of these sources is quite steep, they are worth considering, especially if you can argue your case around relevant experience (through completed works or through staff). However, beware of creating your own tight deadlines on calls and tenders:

Example: Leaving it to the last meeting A DLC became aware of a call with a closing date seven weeks distant. As this was more than a month away, the call was not deemed to be 'urgent' and did not make the AOB section of several strategy-related meetings.

With three weeks to go, a meeting was called the following week for people interested in submitting a proposal to the call. At this meeting, all of the attendees stated that short term commitments ruled them out of writing part or all of the proposal. Eventually, the DLC director cancelled three external meetings, wrote a proposal overnight without the help of the more knowledgeable staff, and the proposal did not succeed.

Source 2: European Funding

European funding proposals can result in substantial amounts of money, and lead to working relationships and trips abroad to interesting cities and countries. However, such proposals often require an preposterous amount of paperwork; it is common for a member of staff to spend the best part of a month, and often more, working solely on such a proposal.

Source 3: Own Institution

There may be sources of funding within your own institution, especially if the project or service either raises the profile of the institution, or has a real chance of attracting future income.

The summative evaluation of phase three of the eLib programme (findings, point 16), states "Some of the eLib phase 3 projects have become self sustaining with funding provided by the host institutions themselves".

Source 4: E-commerce: Sell things on the Net

While lagging behind the more commercial sectors, there is an increasing awareness, and use of, e-commerce systems in higher education.

This leads to two opportunities for DLCs; either to use e-commerce to sell whatever they can, or to build, advise on, research and maintain the digital library components of such commercial systems within their own institution.

Source 5: Training

ICT and digital library-related training has been carried out within and by academic departments and projects for many years. Currently, public libraries and schools by the thousand are currently being connected to the Internet, resulting in a need for training. In addition, the recent emphasis on life-long learning, and the large increase in public PC ownership, should result in a substantial demand for good quality training in these areas for some time to come.

Source 6: Consulting

If your DLC contains staff that specialise in a particular subject, technology, user type or sector, then there are possibilities for offering their services on a consultancy basis. Academic consulting has the advantage of often being short-term, and therefore a contract-filler (and staff retainer) between longer periods of project or service funding.

Source 7: Commercial Funding

Most universities actively forge links with commercial organisations, especially those based nearby. The resident 'business opportunities' unit should indicate which commercial organisations that the university are chummy with would be interested in funding digital library research or services.

Source 8: Advertising and Affiliate Funding

This relatively controversial approach to fundraising is usually referred to in the context of placing advertisements and banners on web-based services and resources. A steadily growing number of UK higher education based services raise revenue in this manner.

However, a recent JISC-commissioned report on advertising on JANET highlights concerns at institutional and other levels regarding the implications of this approach, as well as the realistic amounts of revenue that could be generated.

Source 9: Sponsorship

Sponsorship is a more acceptable form of visible commercial involvement, whereby an organisation does not necessarily plaster your web site with adverts in return for monies. Sponsorship can take many forms, such as sponsoring a piece of equipment, a session at an event, part of the salary of one member of staff, or print-based PR materials.

Source 10: Hosting Events

Workshops, seminars and conferences can generate profit, though generally not substantial amounts especially when the final amount of staff resource used by an event is calculated.

Unsurprisingly, the key factor in many profitable DLC organised events seems to be whether the host institution has appropriate facilities that can be hired at attractive rates. However, events hosted by a DLC can be a great showcase for the projects, services and products produced by that centre.

Source 11: The RAE (Research Assessment Exercise)

The RAE occurs every four years. Very generally speaking, departments submit details of research they have undertaken, from which a panel in the subject area decide on a research rating (from 1 to 5 and 5*).

This rating determines the amount of core research funding that is awarded to the department. One of the main determining factors in the last few RAE exercises has been the amount of output published by researcher in peer-reviewed journals.

Therefore, various DLCs that are part of, or affiliated to, information science departments have often entered those staff who have published several such papers into the RAE, so as to maintain or increase their RAE rating and secure more core research funding.

STAFFING THE CENTRE

The Required Staff

As indicated throughout this article, a wide range of staff roles need to be filled in order to maintain a fully-functioning digital library centre. The core staff of a DLC may include:

- A director, with optional 'vision', who acts as a figurehead and 'public face' of the centre.

- Project management and coordination staff.
- Technical staff, for individual system and service maintenance, and PC and networking maintenance.
- Administration staff.
- Financial administration staff.
- Centre promotional staff i.e. people to create the centre web site, leaflets and so forth.
- Staff familiar with copyright and IPR issues.
- Staff experienced in fund raising and proposal writing.

...and, of course, staff to work on the individual projects and services.

It is important not to 'scrimp' on administration staff:

Example: "The director is busy emptying the bins" A DLC centre submitted a number of proposals for funding. Non of these included an element for administration staff; in addition, the centre had no dedicated staff due to budget cutbacks passed down from higher authority in the host institution. Most of the projects were funded, but immediately fell behind as the research staff, mostly unskilled in administration, had to carry out these tasks.

The (highly paid) director of the centre spent an increasing amount of time dealing with tasks such as emptying bins and rectifying the lack of paper in the toilets, when ideally he should have been negotiating with potential funders of the centre. The situation was exacerbated by several research staff leaving, partially as they viewed doing administration tasks as a demotion

Analysis of staff roles and numbers in UK DLCs indicate that, for every non-admin staff member, between 3.5 and 5.5 admin staff are required to fulfil core, project and financial administration roles in order for the centre to function at these levels.

Hiring Staff

Most digital library projects and a large number of services within the UK HE sector directly employ a very small (4 or less) number of people. Therefore, just one member of staff can have a large positive or negative effect on the progress of a project/service.

Hiring staff is therefore a risky business. These issues are not new; various projects in programmes such as eLib suffered delays due to difficulty in obtaining, and retaining, staff with sufficient technical abilities. These and related issues will be analysed by 'The Human Element', a study which aims '.to learn about the issues surrounding the recruitment, development and retention of project staff in UK HE libraries and archives, with special reference to RSLP and JISC projects.'

One ex-DLC co-director referred to staff hiring as: "...Russian roulette with five bullets, and the funders insisting you pull the trigger because the clock is ticking on the project and you cannot afford a further delay in order to re-advertise if all of the candidates are disappointing. What else can you do?"

The Digital Library Officer Skill Set

In August 2001, I asked a number of people who have been involved in selecting staff for DLCs to identify the most important criteria for a *good member of staff working within and across a Digital Library Centre.*

The criteria mentioned by several different people were:

- A 'team player', at both.
  - The level of the centre and
  - The level of the projects that they work on.
- Does their job with the minimum of supervision, and with no disruption to their (project and centre) work colleagues.
- A networker.
- Uses their skills to help other projects in the centre
  - Even ones with which they have no connection
  - Even if it does not benefit their own project.
- Promotes the centre as part of his/her project.
- Does not object to travel and overnight stays.
- Good communicator.
- Can produce good written and verbal English.
- Produces what they are supposed to produce, and on time.

- Iidentifies and 'grabs' opportunities for the centre as they arise.
- Is genuinely productive or as one reply stated, "...spends more time working than talking about working...".
- Is correctly motivated i.e. is politically oriented to support their project and the centre, as opposed to solely advancing their own career and reputation.

It is interesting to note that most of the criteria are concerned with communication, both within the centre and beyond.

Burrowing deeper: identifying the correct staff

Several people suggested techniques that can be used to identify the correct staff with a greater degree of accuracy. These include:

- Taking more time over the interview stage. This is a somewhat controversial measure, as several people strongly objected to spending "time I do not have" on long interview procedures.
  The counter argument to this is "hire in haste, carry someone at leisure" more time spent selecting the correct candidate can avoid the aggravation caused by hiring an unsuitable person.
- Interviewing as a group (in additional to individual panel interviews), over half or most of a day. As the aforementioned skill list has shown, communication is valued highly within DLCs. There are many scenarios where DLC staff have to deal directly with strangers, often with little or no warning; for example, meeting a potential funder at a conference. In addition, staff within a DLC typically have to negotiate and work with other staff in the centre, on the same project and different projects, and a range of people within the host institution of the centre. Therefore, interviewing in a larger group, and involving group activities such as role-playing or

a meal, can provide a better indication of relevant communication skills.

- Asking direct non-abstract questions, as opposed to traditional questions such as "Where do you see yourself in five years time". For example, if someone has worked for a period of time on a research project, then ask what they contributed to the project in terms of resource or effort.
- Giving the candidate some opportunity to demonstrate knowledge of relevance to the post that they are applying for; it is surprising how infrequently this occurs. For example, if a candidate is being interviewed for a post in a metadata registry service, then ask questions about metadata, contemporary metadata standards, where metadata research appears to be heading, and so forth.
- Asking other people who know the candidate, or their work. The digital library community in UK higher education is highly people-network oriented, and it is common to encounter current or previous work-colleagues of a specific person at an event such as a conference or workshop. If the timing is right, ask their opinions though be careful not to break the confidentiality of the job application procedure, for obvious legal and moral reasons.

Do not feel under pressure to take the 'best available' if none are suitable. This can be difficult, when dealing with a short-term project for a funder with whom you wish to forge a reputation for reliability. Have a back-up plan and schedule for quick re-advertisment of the post.

Keeping Good Staff

Good staff usually want to increase their experience and skill set, take on more senior roles in coordination and management, and see a subsequent increase in salary levels. Keeping good staff is vital, not only in terms of progressing the services and projects that they work on, but in terms of bringing in new funding most conventional digital library funding calls demand the CVs of relevant staff. Techniques for keeping good staff include:

- *Visibly rewarding good staff*: If someone is producing a good piece of work, encourage them to produce a paper concerning the work and submit to a digital library conference. An all-expenses paid trip to e.g. San Francisco in 6 months time can help to encourage staff to stay:-). In addition, such publications can count towards the RAE (thus increasing chances of funding through this route), and postcards from staff in exotic locations can often make other staff think "How can I get some of this conference action?"
- *Ensuring that staff roles in proposals have some element of flexibility*: A real example is that of a proposal for a resource discovery service, where the deliverables and schedule were based on staff doing nothing but cataloguing (at speed) 8 hours a day. Subsequently, the service had a relatively high turnover of staff, partially as the cataloguing staff had no opportunity to develop new skills through undertaking other tasks or roles.
- *Supporting and encouraging staff to write proposals*: Ideally, details of calls which may be of interest to staff should be circulated on internal mailing lists. Staff (especially those nearing the end of their contracts) should be supported via administration, training, and/or extra time to write proposals in subjects which interest them.

  This has the advantages of sustaining staff, bringing more funding into the centre, and staff moving onto projects and services in which they are directly interested.
- *Having a flexible work culture*: Two DLC director, on my first day of work, informed me that (paraphrased) "I don't care what hours people keep, so long as they get the job done". This is healthy, as to many people one of the attractive elements of

academic research is the informality; most of the time you do not need to wear a suit, do not need to be sitting at your desk at 9am sharp, and do not need to schedule coffee or meal breaks (or, compared to some call centres, need to put your hand up when you want to use the toilet). Accentuate this culture.

THE RELATIONSHIP WITH THE HOST INSTITUTION

While most, or all, of the funding for projects and services in a DLC will come from outside the host institution, the relationship with that institution is often the most important one for the DLC to cultivate.

Unless the DLC manages to acquire large amounts of excess revenue (this is unlikely), it will rely on the host institution for a diverse range of services and facilities, such as accommodation, financial system support, networking support, electricity, sanitation, interlibrary loans, and so forth.

Or, as one ex-DLC director put it, ".all the things that you don't notice while you are working in a digital library centre, until they break, leak, explode, go missing or become unavailable without notice."

Good relationships between the DLC and various units within the host institution are therefore essential. It is recommended that key DLC staff forge good working relationships with key staff in the following support units:

- Estates for everything to do with building, infrastructure and accommodation.
- Finance for receiving timely and detailed information about the financial state of projects and services, and answering financial queries.
- External relations for publicising the DLC in university publications.
- Print and reprographics for producing PR materials.
- Computing services for networking issues that impact on your digital library services.
- Catering so people at meetings, workshops and seminars are fed and watered.

- Room booking for space and facilities at meetings, workshops and seminars.
- Core institutional management senior principles, heads of departments and faculties so that people who make the key strategic decisions are aware of your centre, and it doesn't miss out on any internal digital library related work.
- Security especially useful when you start to possess expensive servers and other hardware.
- Personnel for contract renewal issues, and hiring new staff.
- The library for journal and book needs, as well as being a source of new staff who want to move into all things digital.
- Business opportunities for locating commercial partners and opportunities.
- Research support for project and service proposal approval.

Publicising the DLC throughout the institution on a regular basis is a wise option, as:

- Digital library work in various departments may come your way, if these departments are aware of you.
- Other departments are dissuaded from setting up such a centre if the university already hosts one.

Chapter 4

Digital Library Architecture

The Alexandria Project is a consortium of researchers, engineers, and educators, spanning the academic, public, and private sectors, working to develop distributed digital libraries for heterogeneous georeferenced information. *Distributed* means that a library's components may be spread across the Internet, as well as coexisting on a single desktop.

Heterogeneous means that a library may contain multiple types of digital information, including non-traditional items such as remotelysensed imagery, executable models, and multimedia instructional materials. *Georeferenced* means that, whenever possible, each item in a library is associated with one or more regions on the Earth's surface. (We refer to these regions as the item's *footprint*.)

The original motivation of the Alexandria Project was to create a digital library that could both reproduce and extend the content and functionality of a traditional research map library, specifically the Map and Imagery Laboratory (MIL) at the University of California, Santa Barbara (UCSB)

Davidson Library. In pursuit of this objective the project developed three successive versions of the Alexandria Digital Library (ADL) architecture: a "rapid prototype" system comprising a relational database of map and imagery metadata, accessed through a desktop geographic information system (GIS); a "web prototype" system which replaced the stand-alone GIS with an HTTP server, generating an HTML forms-based user interface accessible via the World Wide Web; and the "ADL-3" system which extended the HTTP server into full-fledged middleware, supporting HTTP interfaces to multiple clients, and connections to multiple catalog databases.

As our experience with digital libraries grew, the focus of the Alexandria Project broadened from a geospatial library to an integrated environment for managing, querying, and presenting geospatial information, especially for instructional applications. We refer to these new goals by the umbrella term Alexandria Digital Earth ProtoType (ADEPT). Digital Earth ProtoType (ADEPT). This paper presents the ADEPT digital library architecture. We introduce the architecture's fundamental concepts, and describe the

ADEPT bucket framework, the organizing principle for ADEPT queries and metadata. We then detail the architecture's standard interfaces and describe its current implementation. We conclude with a description of the new collection discovery service.

ARCHITECTURE OVERVIEW

In this section we describe the ADEPT architecture in terms of its component objects and the information flows between them.

Objects

The ADEPT architecture is composed of three kinds of objects: items, collections, and libraries. *Items* are the fundamental objects in ADEPT, and correspond directly to the "holdings" (e.g. books) in a traditional library. (We avoid the term "holding", with its connotations of physical custody, when referring to digital objects.) Items in ADEPT have identity, but no other innate properties all information or services available for an item must be accessed through higherlevel objects.

By not requiring items to do anything other than exist, ADEPT allows for the broadest possible definition of a digital library (e.g., a digital catalog of non-digital information).

Collections are sets of items. Information about individual items, as well as about the collection as a whole, is maintained at the collection level. It is thus possible for different information about the same item to appear in different collections. Collections may be heterogeneous (i.e., may "contain" different kinds of items); however, there are advantages, especially with respect to collection-level summarization, to having collections be homogeneous.

Libraries are sets of collections:

In most cases, "using" ADEPT means accessing the client-level services provided by a library. Libraries expose a single standard set of interfaces to all their collections, making it possible to issue a single query against multiple collections. (By contrast, the interfaces to collections are not standardized; instead, a library has standard mechanisms for adapting itself to whatever interfaces the collection exposes.)

Libraries may also form peer-to-peer relationships in which they grant each other remote access to their collections, by redirecting queries and responses to and from each other. An ADEPT system is, minimally, a network of one or more autonomous libraries, each of which provides a uniform interface to one or more collections, each of which manages metadata for one or more items.

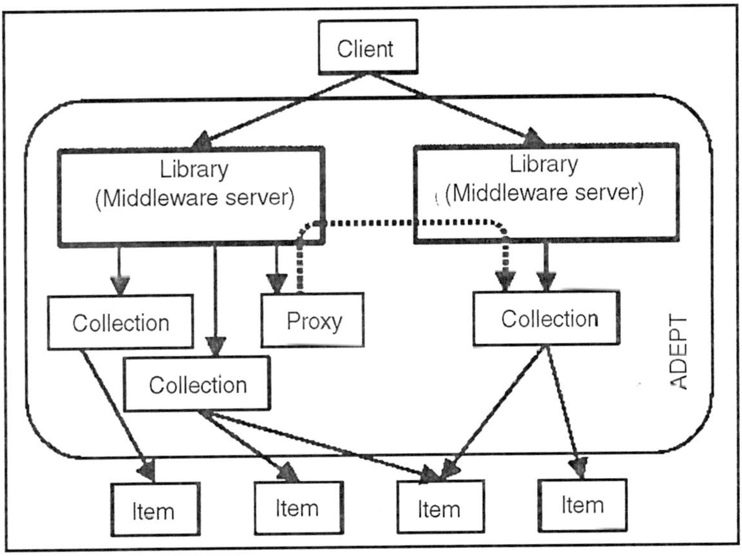

Fig. Basic ADEPT Architecture.

As in the CRADDL architecture, a collection is the fundamental unit of organization, being responsible for the metadata for both its items and itself. A library is, in effect, a "collection broker," mediating standardized access to its collections.

In terms of a standard three-tier architecture, collections correspond to the server tier, and libraries to the middleware tier. Any application that can access the middleware's client interfaces can be an ADEPT client there is no specific client defined (or required) by the architecture.

Information

The ADEPT architecture supports three kinds of externally-visible information: metadata, queries, and result sets.

Metadata

Metadata is information about items or collections. In the ADEPT architecture, metadata moves between objects as *reports,* which are documents pertaining to single items or collections. The following kinds of metadata reports are defined by the ADEPT architecture, specifically as XML DTDs (i.e., each report is an XML document):

- *Collection* reports pertain to collections as a whole. They include descriptive information about the collection (e.g. its origin), as well as summary information derived from the collection's items.
- A *bucket* report contains the item's metadata mapped (insofar as is possible) into the ADEPT bucket framework.
- A *scan* report contains a brief view of the item's metadata mapped (again, insofar as possible) to the ADEPT core buckets.
- A *full* report contains as much of the item's metadata as the collection is willing to provide. There are no constraints on the semantics of a full report; the DTD merely specifies a generic hierarchical encoding suitable for a wide variety of metadata content standards.

- A *browse* report contains references (e.g., URLs) to one or more reduced-resolution representations of the item's contents (e.g., a thumbnail image). These are typically used by graphical user interface clients as iconic representations of the item, and also to help human users qualitatively evaluate the item's suitability for a particular purpose.
- An *access* report contains references (e.g. URLs) to one or more representations of the item's content. Multiple representations allow an item's content to be made available in a variety of formats, packagings, compressions, etc. Note that the access report is the only means by which an item's content is exposed by ADEPT. Furthermore, access reports are optional the ADEPT architecture does not require that an item's content be accessible; or, if it is, that it be accessible in any particular standard format. This allows an ADEPT collection to refer to an item that it does not own or cannot access.

Queries and Result Sets

An ADEPT *query* is a predicate directed at one or more of a library's collections. A *result set* is the (possibly empty) set of identifiers of the items that satisfy the query. ADEPT clients issue queries to find items of interest, and use the identifiers from result sets to obtain metadata reports about the items.

ADEPT queries have standard semantics, defined by the ADEPT bucket framework.

ADEPT BUCKET FRAMEWORK

Our experience with various collection-providing groups (including MIL, the Earth System Science Workbench, and the UC Berkeley Digital Library Project) is that collection development is difficult, laborious, understaffed, and underfunded.

Constraints imposed by the group's mission, customer requirements, idiosyncrasies associated with the collection content, etc. typically require the group to focus most of its effort on providing customized, content-specific access to their collections.

To succeed as an alternative, universal means of access, ADEPT must minimize the requirements it places on already-burdened collection providers. It is also our experience that, despite the availability of many well-known metadata standards, collection-providing groups often work with (or are forced to work with) locally-defined, idiosyncratic metadata.

Even government agencies such as the U.S. Geological Survey and its affiliates, which are nominally mandated to use the FGDC Content Standard for Digital Geospatial Metadata, use many different standards, ranging from the published and documented to the entirely undocumented.

ADEPT must therefore allow collection providers to use *source metadata* metadata unprocessed and untransformed from its native state as employed by the collection to the greatest extent possible. It is ADEPT's goal to provide uniform client services across heterogeneous collections, and in particular, to provide:

1) common high-level search and description services,

2) structured means of discovering and exploiting lower-level, collection- and/or item-specific search and description services.

These two considerations placing minimal requirements on collection providers, and providing uniform client services lead to the *ADEPT bucket framework*: a specification governing semantics, mapping, and representation of metadata for the specific purpose of providing certain search and description services. The framework is predicated on the following assumptions:

- Collection items have metadata.
- Item metadata is of relatively high quality, with known, welldefined semantics.
- Item metadata is mappable to "core" buckets.

Although these assumptions clearly do not apply universally, in our experience enough collections satisfy these assumptions to make the ADEPT architecture of value. The current bucket framework reflects extensive changes from the original specification, including unification of search and description functionality and semantics, completion of the semantic definition of the buckets and delineation of bucket types, and support for metadata source tracking and qualified searches.

Bucket Definition

A *bucket* is an abstract, strongly typed metadata category with defined search semantics, to which source metadata is mapped. The ADEPT bucket framework specification defines the semantics, syntactic representation, and functional behaviour of buckets, as well as the mapping of source metadata fields.

We use the term "metadata category", as opposed to "metadata field," to emphasize that the framework is *not* a metadata content standard. Collection providers need not use buckets directly or internally; rather, the framework includes support for explicitly representing the mapping of source metadata to buckets. Consider an item that has FGDC source metadata, by which we mean that the item directly associates values with FGDC metadata fields, for example:

Citation/Originator = "U.S. Geological Survey"

In the ADEPT bucket framework, buckets are populated with tuples indicating the metadata value, the source of the metadata, and its appropriateness for discovery. (Metadata marked as inappropriate for discovery is ignored during searches but still returned as part of the item's description.) The mapping of the above example to the "Originator" bucket would be represented conceptually as:

Originator = {(FGDC, 1.1/8.1, "Citation/Originator", "U.S. Geological Survey", searchable)}

We say that buckets are *abstract*, or high-level, because they are intended to aggregate semantically similar metadata fields. Buckets elide small semantic and syntactic differences in favour of providing uniform, high-level search and description services.

The aggregation may occur across the items in a collection: for example, one item in a collection may populate the

Originator bucket with the FGDC Citation/Originator field, while another may populate it with the MARC

Main Entry— Personal

Name field: Or, a single item may populate a bucket with multiple values from the same or different metadata sources, as in this example:

Originator = {(FGDC, 1.1/8.1, "Citation/Originator", "U.S. Geological Survey", searchable), (USGS DOQ, PRODUCER, "Producer", "Photo Science, Inc.", searchable)}

Combining metadata mapping and aggregation allows a client to operate at two levels. A client can search for items, and a collection can describe items, by a high-level category like Originator without the client having to understand source metadata fields or their content standards. At the same time, a client can view the lower-level, source metadata if desired.

The ADEPT bucket framework also supports "drilling down" into buckets; that is, searching by specific metadata fields. For example, a client can search a collection's Originator bucket, but match on only the FGDC Citation/Originator field where it has been mapped.

Buckets are strongly typed, and thus restrict data type and representation of the values they may be populated with. For example, the Originator bucket specifies just an unstructured text type, but the Date bucket declares that it can be populated only with calendar dates, and ranges of calendar dates, expressed in ISO 8601 format.

A bucket also defines its search semantics by specifying its allowable query operands and operators, as well as the semantics of matching against items that have mapped multiple values to the bucket. For example, the Date bucket specifies that it can be searched by specifying a range of calendar dates and using one of the operators intersects, contains, or within.

Multiple values mapped to the Date bucket are treated severally; i.e., the constraint is applied to each value independently and the results are then logically OR-ed together. Search semantics are typically left slightly under-specified to accommodate multiple implementations.

For example, the Originator bucket defines a contains-all-words query operator, but the exact definition of what constitutes a "word" is left to the implementation. The advantage of combining (semantically loose) metadata aggregation with (semantically rigorous) strong typing is that the ADEPT bucket framework achieves rich search functionality while remaining flexible enough so as to have broad applicability. Buckets have simple names such as Date and Originator.

Although there is no mechanism for qualifying names, we intend that there be relatively few commonly agreed-upon buckets, with collections defining only a limited number of more domain- and item-specific buckets, and so we do not anticipate name clashes.

Buckets are generally independent and orthogonal, but there are cases where two buckets have a relationship to each other. For example, the Title bucket is a sub-bucket of the Subjectrelated text bucket, meaning that the values mapped to the Subject-related text bucket must include the values mapped to the Title bucket, and therefore every match against the Title bucket is a match against the Subject-related text bucket. Such relationships are defined by convention only; the ADEPT bucket framework provides no formal means of expressing such relationships.

Role of Buckets in the ADEPT Architecture

The ADEPT bucket framework plays three specific roles in the ADEPT architecture of the ADEPT core system: describing items, searching for items, and characterizing collections. The bucket framework provides an XML format for encoding an item's source metadata mappings. The format is capable of representing mappings to any buckets that adhere to the ADEPT bucket types. A collection returns a document in this format as the "bucket" view of the item-level metadata for an item.

The framework also provides an XML format for the ADEPT query language. The query language is capable representing Boolean combinations of constraints against arbitrary buckets, and arbitrary source fields mapped to buckets, again subject only to their adherence to the ADEPT bucket types. A query submitted to the ADEPT middleware is a document in this format.

Finally, the XML format for the ADEPT collection-level metadata includes structures for recording statistical overviews of the collection's metadata mappings. For example, a collection can record that it supports the Originator bucket, and moreover that a given number of its items have an FGDC Citation/Originator field and map that field to that bucket. In this way a client can gain substantial information regarding a collection's support for buckets and the nature of the underlying, source metadata.

Comparison with Other Approaches

In any system in which information flows from provider to consumer, it is instructive to look at what knowledge about the underlying information is captured and exploited by the system itself, for this is indicative of how much functionality the system can provide over that information.

To take an extreme example, a system that treats all input as bit streams affords relatively little functionality (copy bits, compress stream, etc.), whereas a system that recognizes that inputs are word processing files can provide much richer functionality (e.g., repagination).

To look at two examples in the realm of digital libraries, consider first the World Wide Web, which for the purposes of this discussion we define as HTML documents delivered via the HTTP protocol. Although one can express all sorts of things in HTML, the actual *semantic* content of HTML tags and HTTP headers is extremely low.

As a consequence, the functionality afforded by basic Web technology is limited to delivering documents and rendering them for direct human consumption. By contrast, in a traditional library cataloging system, Machine- Readable Cataloging (MARC) records prepared according to the Anglo-American Cataloging Rules (AACR2) are queried and delivered via the Z39.50 protocol. This system explicitly captures extremely fine-grained distinctions (e.g., "date of publication" versus "date of treaty signing").

So, in theory (though admittedly, not in practice) such a system affords much richer functionality. These two examples represent extremes of the tradeoffs between structure and standardization (or, more negatively, complexity and "heaviness") on the one hand, and flexibility and generality (or, simplicity and "lightness") on the other. This tradeoff graphically represented in Figure is:

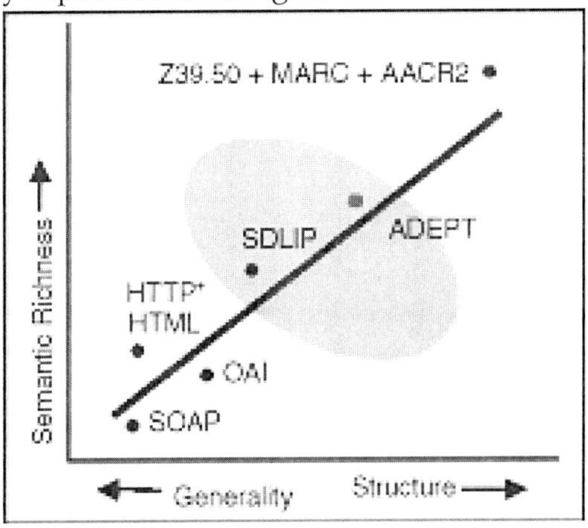

Fig. Interoperabilty Tradeoffs.

We believe there is a "sweet spot" in this figure: a set of architectural design tradeoffs that provide sufficient structure so as to afford rich functionality, and yet retain sufficient simplicity and generality so as to be flexible, broadly applicable, and easily implemented.

The Simple Digital Library Interoperability Protocol (SDLIP) represents one effort to attain this sweet spot. The ADEPT architecture represents another, with ADEPT providing slightly greater structure so as to afford richer functionality.

As a concrete example of the differences between SDLIP and ADEPT, consider how the two systems treat query languages. SDLIP does not specify a query language; it provides only a means of identifying query languages. Thus an SDLIP client wishing to query will get no support from SDLIP itself; query languages are effectively part of the underlying information flow, i.e., something to be interpreted and negotiated on a collection-by-collection basis. By contrast, ADEPT provides a standard query language.

The language is generic and extensible, and there is some flexibility in how collections may implement the language, but nevertheless, there are sufficient structures in the language, and there is sufficient commonality across collections, that it is possible for an ADEPT client to query arbitrary collections with no a priori analysis or agreements required.

IMPLEMENTATION ISSUES

Middleware

The ADEPT middleware server has been the basis for the Alexandria Digital Library's operational system since 1999, and as such it is relatively robust and reliable. Newer features such as intra-bucket searches, personal collections, and the collection discovery service are still under development at this writing.

The current ADEPT middleware server is written in Java and Python and can be run as a web application inside a servlet container, as a standalone RMI server, or both. Personal collections are supported by an embedded Berkeley DB database. External collections are supported by a generic relational database connection. The middleware currently supports the following public client interfaces, each as an HTTP-addressable servlet:

- *Configuration*: Get a list of the collections the middleware is currently connected to.
- *Collection*: Get the collection metadata document for the specified collection.
- *Query*: Pass a query to one or more collections. Queries are asynchronous. Running queries may be terminated with the *Cancel* interface. Query result sets accumulated by the middleware are retrieved with the *Results* interface.

- *Metadata*: Get a standard metadata report for the specified item from the specified collection.

The middleware also supports maintenance interfaces that report its status, and manage its connections to local and remote collections. The middleware also supports maintenance interfaces that report its status, and manage its connections to local and remote collections.

Support for Relational Databases

To date, most ADEPT collections have been implemented with relational technology (i.e., metadata fields stored in tables in relational database management systems). We have therefore developed a generic software component, the "Bucket99 driver", which accesses a relational database over a JDBC connection and which translates bucket-level search and description requests into appropriate SQL statements.

The Bucket99 driver makes an arbitrary relational database look like an ADEPT collection. The crux of the driver is a generic query translator, implemented in the Python scripting language, which converts Boolean combinations of query constraints into an SQL query. The translator works from an abstract model of a relational bucket implementation (an extensive configuration file supplies the necessary specifics), comprising, for each bucket:

- A table *T* whose rows correspond to items in the collection that have value(s) for the bucket, and a column within *T* that holds item identifiers.
- Zero or more *auxiliary tables:* That are related to *T* by given relationships and that are required to implement bucket semantics.
- A *table cardinality* that indicates how many table rows are potentially associated with each collection item. Possible values are: exactly one; zero or one; zero or more; one or more.
- An *implementation paradigm*: A set of rules that describes how an atomic constraint against the bucket is translated into a constraint against *T* and *T*'s auxiliary tables. Specifically, a paradigm is a

coordinated set of functions that translates a constraint into an SQL WHERE clause fragment.

ADEPT supplies over a dozen paradigms for commonly-encountered implementation strategies. For example, for textual buckets ADEPT supplies paradigms that support the Verity and Excalibur text engines as well as two paradigms that use VARCHAR columns.

For spatial buckets ADEPT supplies paradigms for two Informix spatial DataBlades (MapInfo and Geodetic) as well as a paradigm implementing bounding boxes with numeric columns. An optional *field selection condition*. If drill-down capability for the bucket is implemented using multiple rows per item, one row per mapped source field, then this condition selects the appropriate row.

The real power of ADEPT's query translation system is that *any* relational structure matching the Bucket99 abstract model can be treated as a bucket. The model is semantically rich enough to enable the query translator to translate arbitrary boolean combinations of bucket query constraints into SQL.

Access Control

The ADEPT architecture provides *access control points* (ACPs) at each middleware service and at each interface between a middleware service and a collection's implementation of the service. At each ACP a *gatekeeper* may be installed.

Functionally, a gatekeeper accepts the parameters of a proposed service request and returns a boolean allow/disallow response. The current middleware implementation includes several "generic" gatekeepers, which examine only the generic attributes of a request (e.g., the client's IP address).

- *ConstantGatekeeper*: Always allow or disallow.
- *IPAddressGatekeeper*: Allow if client IP address matches preconfigured patterns.
- *BasicPasswordGatekeeper*: Allow if HTTP "Basic" username/password authentication is satisfied.
- *CombinationGatekeeper*: Allow if a Boolean combination of other gatekeepers is satisfied. (E.g.,

"Allow all requests from IP address set *S1*, or all requests from IP address set *S2* that also specify a valid username/ password from database *D1*.") Gatekeepers not yet developed (but fully supported by the ADEPT architecture) could support finer-grained access control. For example, a collection-level gatekeeper to the middleware's Metadata service might allow access based on both the client making the request and the specific report being requested. Gatekeepers can be installed and independently configured at any ACP. Gatekeepers are installed by dynamic class loading, so new gatekeepers can be developed without modifying ADL in any way.

Collection Statistics

We have also developed a software package for gathering, processing, and rendering the statistical portion of the collectionlevel metadata (the spatial and temporal histograms and the counts of items) for collections implemented in relational databases.

The package requires only a command-line SQL interface to the database, and hence is largely independent of database vendor, but it is otherwise highly Unix-specific and relies on numerous third-party packages (NetPBM, Gnuplot, etc.). We plan to rewrite this package to be more in line with the middleware server, and to be more easily configured.

COLLECTION DISCOVERY SERVICE

A client wishing to access ADEPT must first know what libraries and collections exist. For this reason the ADEPT architecture has been extended with a central *collection discovery service*: a registry of known collections and a search capability that allows clients to find relevant collections.

Central Registry

Any distributed system must provide some kind of entrance or starting point for clients. Completely decentralized systems such as the World Wide Web and Gnutella eschew any central architectural artifact in favour of non-architectural mechanisms (e.g., word-of-mouth).

For ADEPT's purposes, we believe it is simpler, and sufficiently manageable and scalable, for there to be a central registry of known collections. The ADEPT collection discovery service (CDS) provides such a registry. A middleware server coming online registers itself with the CDS, at a well-known address.

Thereafter the CDS periodically (e.g., daily) retrieves the collection-level metadata for each of the middleware server's collections. (The "update frequency" field in the collection-level metadata might be used someday to suggest appropriate polling frequencies.) A middleware server that fails to respond after some interval (e.g., a week) is considered defunct.

There can be more than one CDS we anticipate collection discovery services oriented around domains or user communities such as the National Science Digital Library (NSDL).

A middleware server may register itself with any number of collection discovery services. The CDS registry is sufficient for finding collections, but as a complete solution it scales very poorly. Given little or no information about collections, a client wishing to find information in the system can do so only by querying every collection every time.

The unworkability of this approach was demonstrated by an early version of the FGDC Clearinghouse. Visitors to the Clearinghouse website in 1999-2000 were presented with a simple list of collections (*sites* in Clearinghouse parlance) with no context other than a name (e.g., "Southwest Data Centre Clearinghouse"). Additional information about sites could only be obtained manually and individually. (The Clearinghouse has since improved its interface to include a preliminary collection identification phase.)

Collection Relevance

The CDS harvests, stores, and indexes collection-level metadata for each known collection. ADEPT has specified a content standard for this metadata. The portions of the standard relevant to this discussion include:

- Spatial histograms indicating the geographic

coverage of the items in the collection. A spatial histogram is a two-dimensional histogram whose domain is the Earth's surface, and in which a cell value indicates the number of collection items that.

- Have a value for the Geographic location bucket, and
- Whose value overlaps the cell. A graphic rendering of a spatial histogram is shown in Figure. The data structure computed and stored is an Euler histogram, which is a slight variation of a simple histogram that supports range searching.

- Analogous to the spatial histogram, temporal histograms indicating the calendrical coverage of the collection. Specifically, a temporal histogram is a one-dimensional histogram whose domain is calendrical time, and in which a cell value indicates the number of collection items that.
  - Have a value for the Date bucket, and
  - Whose value overlaps the cell. Again, the histogram is an Euler histogram.
- The controlled vocabularies used to categorize items in the collection, and, for each vocabulary term, the number of items in the collection relevant to the term.

If a vocabulary is a thesaurus (that is, supports broader/ narrower relationships between terms), the counts reflect the specificity of the terms. So, for example, if "images" is a broader term for "photographs", then the number of images includes the number of photographs. The CDS allows clients to rank collections by each of the above three quantities. For example, a client specifies a spatial or temporal query in the form of a geographic region or time period, and the CDS returns a (possibly truncated) list of the known collections ranked by the number of items each collection has that spatially or temporally overlap the query region.

A vocabulary query takes the form of a single vocabulary term, and ranking of results is by the number of items associated with the term. Conjunctions of queries are discussed under Limitations, below.

It should be noted that the CDS's query language is essentially a subset of middleware's query language, i.e., the query language used to query individual collections. Thus a client can formulate a single query that can be used to, in effectively one step, both identify relevant collections and subsequently search for items within those collections.

Scalability

Evaluating a query region against an Euler histogram takes constant time. The histograms and item counts amount to only a few kilobytes per collection, and thus can all be stored in primary memory. We therefore anticipate that the CDS can easily accommodate tens of thousands of collections, and answer queries with reasonable speed, without having to resort to more sophisticated indexing and querying techniques.

Limitations

There are several limitations to our approach to collection discovery. First, the CDS, as described above, cannot perform joined queries. For example, consider the query "Find collections that are likely to contain aerial photographs of Southern California taken in the 1930s."

The CDS can rank collections by the numbers of items relevant to Southern California; by the numbers of items relevant to the 1930s; and by the numbers of aerial photographs. But it cannot rank collections on the joint condition because the underlying statistics are gathered independently.

Currently we approximate joint conditions by assuming that the statistics are linked. Under this heuristic, a collection with lots of aerial photographs and good coverage of the 1930s is presumed to contain relatively many aerial photographs taken in the 1930s. We are exploring new data structures that explicitly capture joint statistics and yet are still compact and easy to compute. Second, the CDS relies on binary statistics: an item is either relevant or it is not.

A world map drawn on the back of a napkin thus has the same spatial relevance as a high-resolution, multiterabyte dataset with worldwide coverage. We are working on incorporating resolution (specifically, minimum feature size) as a way of approximating information density. (I.e., the dataset has much higher information density than the napkin, and thus would rank higher.) Ideally, one could constrain both minimum feature size *and* information density after all, there are times when one indeed wants the napkin and not the dataset.

Third, the CDS is not especially effective for collections that are not well discriminated by geographic space, calendrical time, or controlled vocabulary terms, or which contain items that lack the metadata supporting such discrimination. A possible solution may be to augment the CDS with an approach based on word frequency, such as that used in STARTS.

Acknowledgements

We thank Larry Carver, Linda Hill, Mary Larsgaard, Terry Smith, and David Valentine for their contributions to the design and implementation of the ADEPT architecture. The work described herein was supported by the National Science Foundation under cooperative agreement IIS-9817432.

Chapter 5

Cornell Digital Library Research Group

The CDLRG (Cornell Digital Library Research Group) is investigating the architectures, protocols, and supporting mechanisms to create *component-based digital libraries*. This paper describes the nature of that research programme.

Any description of a research programme should begin by broadly defining the subject of research. Attempts to define the term *digital library*, however, sometimes resemble the fabled "blind men and the elephant". I can only claim to be one of those blind men and offer the particular definition on which this research programme is built.

A digital library is a managed collection of digital objects (content) and services (mechanisms) associated with the storage, discovery, retrieval, and preservation of those objects.

Management has three components:

- It begins with selection of the digital objects that are constituents of the collections from which the library is composed. These objects are selected from a global information space (e.g., the set of all published books, or the set of all digital objects on the World Wide Web), and become constituents of the library collections based on criteria applied by collection managers (which may be human, automated, or some hybrid).
- Management also entails the definition of the services included in the digital library. Some common examples of services are indexing, which

allows discovery of content in the collections; preservation, which assures longevity of the objects in the collections; and awareness, which alerts users to changes in the collections.

- Finally, management includes the development and enforcement of policies for tasks such as controlling access to collection contents and preserving items in the collection.

The use of the term *component-based* to refine this definition is a reflection of a belief that the architecture of digital libraries should be based on modularity a well-known software engineering principle. That is, digital library services should be constructed as independent modules, or components, that may be distributed across the Internet and which communicate with each other through open protocols.

The advantages of this modularization include *customizability*, the configuration of services in an individual digital library can be tailored to meet the requirements of the intended user community; *ease of refinement,* the functionality of individual services (e.g., new search engines) can evolve independently; and *extensibility,* new services can be developed and integrated into the service infrastructure, and take advantage of the functionality of existing services.

The notion that digital library architecture should enable multiple communities and individuals to tailor information content and information spaces for particular needs is a theme that extends throughout our research programme.

This reflects the fact that technical solutions are but one facet of digital library research, and that complex social, political, and economic factors must be considered.

The remainder of this paper describes the research programme of the CDLRG in the following areas:

- *Digital Library Infrastructure*: Creating the service infrastructure on which distributed digital libraries can be created.
- *Digital Object Models*: Providing the mechanisms for storing and combining multi-format content and disseminating it in multiple fashions.

- *Policies*: providing the mechanisms for the creation, administration, and enforcement of policies that manage content and services in digital libraries.
- *Metadata Standards*: Allowing individual communities of expertise to formulate and administer metadata vocabularies and combine them in descriptions of digital objects and digital library services.
- *Publishing Models*: Examining new paradigms for sharing and disseminating scholarly information.
- *Devices*: investigating the interaction of disconnected devices and mobile networks in an information environment.

RESEARCH AREAS

This section describes each of the major research areas of the Cornell Digital Library Research Group.

Digital Library Infrastructure

Historically and conceptually the core work of the CDLRG lies in the formulation and investigation of infrastructure to facilitate component-based digital libraries.

Work on infrastructure within the CDLRG began with the CS-TR (Computer Science Technical Reports) Project, a DARPA (U.S. Defence Advanced Research Projects Agency) funded effort to examine tools for electronic publication of Computer Science Technical Reports.

This early digital library project was a collaboration of the "top five" computer science institutions in the United States: Berkeley, Carnegie-Mellon, Cornell, MIT, and Stanford.

Cornell contributed the mechanism for interoperability in the project, a system called Dienst (Distributed Interactive Extensible Network Server for Techreports). (Dienst, pronounced dçnst, is also the Dutch word for "service".)

In the context of our research, the word "Dienst" refers to a number of things:

- A conceptual architecture for distributed digital libraries.

- A protocol for service communication in that architecture.
- A software system that serves as a reference implementation of the protocol and architecture.

Broadly speaking, Dienst is a system for configuring a set of individual *services* running on distributed *servers* to cooperate in providing the services of a digital library.

The *open architecture* of the Dienst system exposure of the functionality through a defined protocol makes it possible to combine Dienst services in flexible ways and augment the existing services with other *mediator services*, which build on the functionality of the existing services.

A complete description of Dienst is outside the scope of this paper, but a brief listing of the features of the architecture is as follows:

- A document model that incorporates unique naming, multiple versions, logical structuring, and multiple content-type disseminations. This document model is fully exposed through the protocol, allowing multiple *disseminations* objects stored in Dienst repositories.
- A set of individually defined services that expose their operational semantics through an open protocol.. The interaction between a set of core Dienst services User Interface, Query Mediator (QM), Name Server (NS), Index, and Repository is illustrated in Figure.
- A mechanism for combining services and content into multiple collections.
- A mechanism for distributing collections among regions to facilitate global distribution.

Over the past several years, Dienst has provided fertile ground for both practical deployment and as a testbed for research into distributed digital libraries.

The most notable deployment of Dienst is as the technical infrastructure for NCSTRL (Networked Computer Science Technical Reference Library), a globally distributed digital library that incorporates content from over 100 institutions. Dienst also provides technology for a number of other collections including CoRR (the Computing Research Repository) and ETRDL (ERCIM Technical Reference Digital Library).

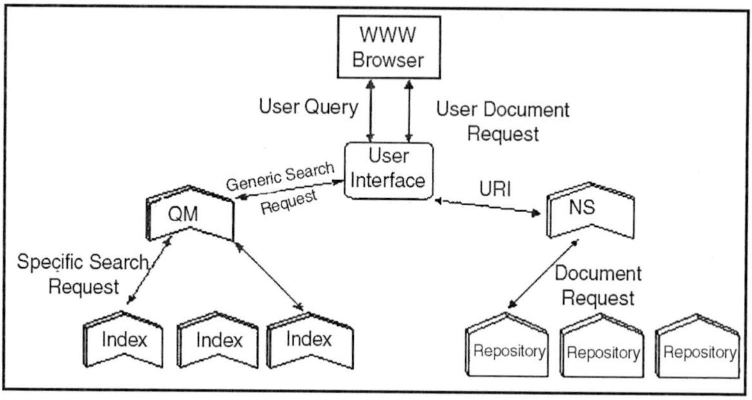

Fig. Dienst Service Interaction.

Within the CDLRG, we have exploited the Dienst system and implementation for a number of research investigations. One particular area is distributed searching; mechanisms for determining query routing among distributed search engines. Another research area is the mechanism for creating collections in globally-distributed digital librarie.

Work on the Dienst architecture, protocol, and implementation is ongoing. We are, at the time of writing of this paper, in the final stages of producing a new software release that supports a new version of the Dienst protocol.

These new versions considerably enhance the functionality of the Dienst system (e.g., a more powerful document model for structured documents, increased metadata functionality) and improve the modularity of the system. This not only facilitates administration of a Dienst server, but makes the system more amenable for research experimentation (by making it easy to improve and replace service modules).

Digital Object Architecture

Digital libraries have the potential to represent new types

of content and deliver them in innovative ways. Existing digital library research projects and deployed systems give a glimpse of this potential by providing access to digital content in a variety of forms including text, images, video, audio, maps, datasets, and software.

The utility of these single medium digital resources is indisputable. However, the rich potential of digital libraries is fully demonstrated by multimedia content that aggregates multiple single medium content streams that are inter-related semantically, structurally, and temporally. The result is digital content that is more informative and more accurately represents physical reality.

Across this diversity of content there is the need for a layer of *uniformity* among digital resources; a *digital object* model that provides common high level functionality among all resources regardless of their content. This common functionality includes *deposit* in and *access* from repositories, *discovery* by users and agents, *dissemination* or *presentation* of content, and *access control* for protection of intellectual property.

Such high-level operational uniformity allows multiple objects, each with their own idiosyncratic composition and content, to be combined in distributed digital library collections.

While generic uniformity of digital objects is essential to the (inter) operation of digital libraries, there is also the need for functionality that exposes and exploits object *specificity*. For example, at the most generic level, dissemination from a digital object is simply the output of a stream of bits.

At the object specific level, however, disseminations take on unlimited forms unique to the semantics of the specific digital object; for example, the output of a frame from a "video" digital object, a page from a "book" digital object, or a subroutine from a "programme" digital object.

In the FEDORA (Flexible and Extensible Digital Object and Repository Architecture) project, the CDLRG is investigating a general digital object model and repository architecture for encapsulating and securing digital library content of all forms and genre.

Mechanisms for extensibility are built in to the architecture, thereby allowing individual communities to develop new content types and rights management schemes, yet interoperate in a broad digital library framework.

The key challenges we are addressing in FEDORA include:

- The creation of complex objects that aggregate heterogeneous types of data, which may be distributed in location,
- The ability to endow these objects with sets of behaviors that pertain to any global or domain-specific notion of content (such as a book, a journal, an article, a movie, or others), irrespective of the object's underlying structure,
- Client access to multiple views, or *disseminations,* of the object's data through the transparent activation of external mechanisms that execute these *content type* behaviors,
- Association of external rights management schemes with any dissemination of an object's contents.
- Extensibility for content types and rights management schemes.

FEDORA defines a container abstraction known as the DigitalObject that encapsulates multimedia content in typed byte stream packages called DataStreams. The actual byte stream in a DataStream may be local (or internal) to the DigitalObject, or it may be a reference to data external to the DigitalObject (e.g., a result of a GET transaction from an HTTP server). This allows a DigitalObject to be act as a value-added surrogate for other content; a capability which is exploited in our policy enforcement work.

All DigitalObjects have a set of generic behaviors (the PrimitiveDisseminator methods) to create and access DataStreams and to manipulate the structure of the Digital object. The Digital object also has an extensible interface layer that provides views, or *disseminations,* of encapsulated data in a contextually meaningful manner.

A dissemination can be a direct transcription of stored data (e.g. a page of a book), any computable derivation of stored content, an interactive object (e.g., a book viewing applet), or any mixture of these. A Disseminator is a FEDORA component that associates an extended set of service requests with a DigitalObject to produce disseminations.

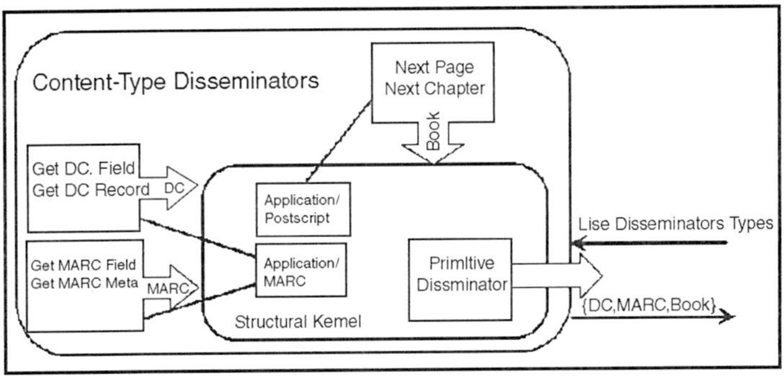

Fig. FEDORA Digital Object.

The architectural segregation of structure, extensible interfaces, and mechanisms for executing extensible behaviors is key to the FEDORA DigitalObject model. Many types of Disseminators can be associated with a DigitalObject to extend its behaviour beyond the generic methods.

For example, a DigitalObject can have a Disseminator that endows it with a set book-like behaviors, allowing a client to interact with the DigitalObject through a set of requests such as "get next page" or "get next chapter." Each Disseminator references a Signature which is a formal definition of the set of methods that pertain to a particular Disseminator Type.

It also references a Servlet which is a mechanism (a programme) that executes the methods defined by the referenced Signature. Both Signatures and Servlets can be stored in DigitalObjects and registered with a global naming service (e.g., the Handle System).

This creates a de facto registry of Disseminator Types Signatures and Servlets become "known" when their names (e.g., URNs of their DigitalObject containers) are registered with a global naming service. A FEDORA Repository provides an environment for activating and running Servlets.

A simple FEDORA DigitalObject is depicted in Figure. It

contains a *structural kernel* with two DataStreams (a Postscript stream and MARC metadata) and the Primitive Disseminator, which is the set of *generic* service requests. There are also three Disseminators (BOOK, MARC, and DublinCore). Clients can obtain various disseminations of the DigitalObject by invoking the methods of each Disseminator.

For example, a client can obtain a Dublin Core record by invoking the getDCRecord() request. Although there is no Dublin Core data inside this object, the DC Disseminator activates an external mechanism that derives Dublin Core from MARC data. This is one simple example of how the underlying structure of a DigitalObject is distinct from the disseminations it can produce.

Over the past year, the CDLRG has been developing and experimenting with a prototype implementation of the FEDORA architecture. This prototype is implemented in Java and uses the CORBA distributed object model. In our research, the prototype has been used for a range of interoperability experiments with colleagues at CNRI (Corporation for National Research Initiatives).

FEDORA will also be used as the basis for experiments with policy enforcement. In addition, a research packaging of FEDORA is available for other researchers who wish to use the implementation for digital library experimentation.

Policy Enforcement

This paper began with a definition of digital libraries that contains the notion of *management* layered on top of *infrastructure*. In particular: a digital library *infrastructure* provides the service definitions, protocols, and digital object model; digital library *instances* exploit this infrastructure by selecting services and content and administering policies on those selections.

It is illustrative to compare these digital library instances to the current notion of a portal on the Web, for example Lycos, Yahoo, and AltaVista. These portals offer access to distributed content and provide some services over this content (e.g., searching). Yet, there is little argument that these current portals do not provide the level of curatorial responsibility undertaken by existing libraries.

The model of a digital library instance proposed here can be thought of as a *hybrid portal*. It not only expands the traditional portal concept with enhanced services and content, but recognizes the need for *integrity maintenance* (curatorial responsibility) ranging from casual (a distributed e-print archive) to strict and broad ranging (a research library).

The effect then is that content and mechanisms may be shared among multiple digital libraries, but the policies applied to that content and services are tailored to the requirements of the organization administering the digital library instance.

Digital library integrity requirements for security, preservation, or otherwise – can be expressed through formal statements called *policies*. The issue of policy formulation and enforcement for digital libraries is a major focus of the research of the CDLRG.

Policy enforcement mechanisms need to be constructed that permit enforcement regardless of the level of control the digital library (the policy formulator and enforc-ement agent) has over the distributed objects and services. In this context, we are examining the implementation of a *policy layer* through which each digital library can enforce its policies on the range of content and services and range of control over that content and services.

Libraries, digital or otherwise, formulate and enforce a number of policies. In our research we have chosen to focus on two:

1) *security*, management of access to content,

2) *preservation*, the long-term archiving of content. Research in preservation is addressed.

The many forms of content in digital libraries offer new challenges for the formulation of security and preservation policies.

Two examples from the security domain are illustrative:

- Raw databases are likely candidates for inclusion in a digital library, so consider an electronic document that encapsulates an opinion survey (database) with software to access the data. The document's publisher-to protect its investment-might stipulate that the database, though readable in its entirety, never be copied; the survey participants—to protect their privacy—may have stipulated that only certain (personally uncompromising) sets of queries against the database be allowed.

- The provider of an image database might wish to make low-resolution renderings of database images generally available and higher-resolution renderings accessible only under certain conditions.

In order to understand the effect of these many forms of content in digital libraries, one thrust of our research will be a thorough analysis of security and preservation requirements in the digital library context.

This analysis will take into account the diversity of stakeholders that need to be served – for example, traditional and non-traditional publishers, authors, and the established research library community.

It will also consider the impact of the portal model, in which content is distributed and therefore lies outside the *control zone* of organizations trying to formulate and enforce policies.

In addition to the formulation of security and preservation policies for these new genres of content, there remains the problem of enforcing the policies in a digital library. The mechanisms for policy enforcement in existing computer applications for example the read, write, and execute access to files and programs that most operating systems implement are some distance from those required to enforce the complex policies we envisage in digital libraries.

The prudent course in designing a digital library architecture is to provide support for an extremely wide variety of security policies. Our intention, therefore, is to take *enforceability* as the only hard constraint on what policies are allowed, and build mechanisms based on a formal notion of enforceability.

We base our research in this area on a formal definition of *enforceability* for a class *EM* (for *Execution Monitoring*) of policies that can be enforced using mechanisms that work by monitoring (any aspect of) system execution. The execution steps monitored may range from fine-grained actions (such as memory access) to higher-level operations (such as method calls) to operations that change the state of an object and thus restrict subsequent execution.

The formal definition of *EM* is outside the scope of this paper. As a substitute, a few examples will suffice. All known hardware and operating system-based mechanisms, such as those alluded to earlier that restrict access to files, are in *EM*.

The policies discussed above for the survey database are instances of such *EM*-enforceable access control policies. Rights management policies discussed in connection with electronic documents also fall into this class.

A few examples outside the scope of *EM* are also illustrative. Policy enforcement mechanisms that use more information than becomes available only from observing the steps of a target's execution are, by definition, excluded from EM. Information provided to an EM mechanism is thus insufficient for predicting future steps the target might take, alternative possible executions, or all possible target executions.

Given this notion of enforceability, our research is then proceeding on two tracks:

- Developing notations for expressing security and preservation policies and developing methods and tools for formulating as policies the requirements of authors, publishers, and library customers.
- Developing practical enforcement mechanisms for those policies.

In addressing the two issues, we will exploit on-going work at Cornell in new policy enforcement mechanisms. All *EM*-enforcement mechanisms can be viewed as implementing an automaton that makes a transition each time the target system does and that causes the target system to halt if ever an action is being attempted that does not comply with the policy being enforced. Practical realizations of this abstraction are thus based on three mechanisms:

- There must be a way to identify the transitions in the target system. A transition may correspond to accessing a memory location, to executing a machine language instruction, to executing only certain specific machine language instructions (e.g., supervisor or kernel calls), or to executing certain procedures, functions, or methods. The level of granularity of transitions depends on what events are being constrained by the policy.
- There must be a way to keep track of the enforcement-automaton's current state and for the automaton to change state in response to transitions made by the target system.
- There must be a way for the enforcement mechanism to trigger events in the target system (e.g., when the security policy is about to be violated access to a digital object should be terminated).

We are currently experimenting with these policy enforcement mechanisms in the context of our FEDORA digital object model. The assumption is that we can build digital library specific "policy enforcement layers" by creating digital object surrogates for distributed resources.

As described earlier, the DataStreams "contained" in a DigitalObject may, in fact, be remote data disseminated by other digital objects or, in fact, from any other protocol transaction (e.g., HTTP).

Thus, it is possible to, in a sense, "impose" policies on external objects. For example, we can build a surrogate digital object that serves as a *preservation monitor* (that implements some preservation policy) for some external content and that triggers notification events in defined cases (e.g., when conversion of an object is necessary due to a new software version).

FEDORA digital objects then become *policy carrying* containers, in addition to *content* and *behaviour* carrying containers. This concept is illustrated in Figure, which shows a simple digital object containing a policy statement and reference content available through an HTTP GET. A disseminator is associated with these DataStreams that enforces the policy on the remote content (e.g., sends an alert when a preservation state change occurs).

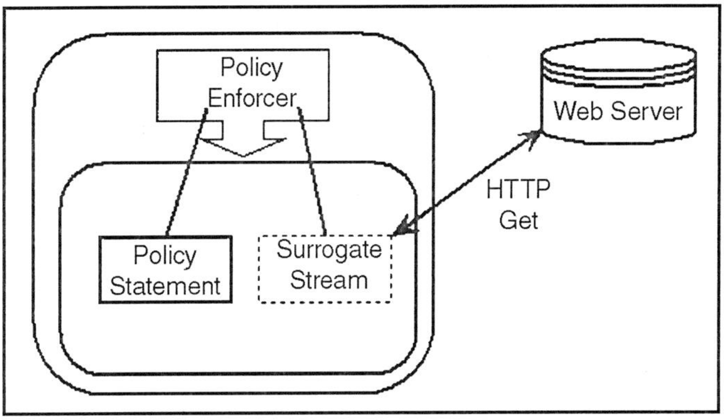

Fig. Policy Carrying Object.

An important related issue of this research is the tension between varying levels of control over distributed content and services and the types of policies that need to be enforced. For example, it may be necessary to "assert" full control over an object in certain situations in order to achieve certain policies (e.g., copy the object locally to ensure its full preservation).

Metadata Interoperability

The work of the CDLRG in metadata interoperability builds on several years of active participation in the DCMI (Dublin Core Metadata Initiative). Our primary interest in DCMI has been the role of the Dublin Core Element Set in a broader metadata fabric.

This is the issue addressed by the WF (Warwick Framework), which describes a container architecture for associating multiple metadata vocabularies (packages) with digital objects. We note that this container architecture and subsequent work on it provided the foundation for the FEDORA architecture.

The motivation for the WF is the belief that metadata should be modular – individual communities should create and maintain metadata vocabularies appropriate to their areas of expertise. For example, whereas bibliographic metadata should be created and administered by the information management (library) community, metadata governing terms and conditions for access should be the jurisdiction of the rights management (legal) community.

This modularity encourages metadata communities to scope their individual efforts and encourages them to avoid attempts at developing a universal ontology. Instead, individual metadata commu-nities should concentrate on classifying and expressing semantics tailored toward distinct functional and community needs. Warwick Framework-like modularity underlies the design of the W3C's Resource Description Framework (RDF), which is a modeling framework for the integration of diverse application and community-specific metadata vocabularies.

While the Warwick Framework proposes modularity as fundamental to a workable metadata strategy, it recognizes a number of challenges in the implementation of such. An outstanding one is the interoperability of multiple metadata packages that may be associated with and across resources.

These packages are by nature not semantically distinct, but overlap and relate to each other in numerous ways. Achieving interoperability between these packages via one-to-one *crosswalks* is useful, but this approach does not scale to the many metadata vocabularies that will inevitably develop.

A more scalable solution is to exploit the fact that many entities and relationships for example, people, places, creations, organizations, events, certain relationships and the like are so frequently encountered that they do not fall clearly into the domain of any particular metadata vocabulary but apply across all of them.

We are currently investigating a logical model for metadata interoperability with the rather insipid title ABC that is examining the nature of these common entities and relationships.

ABC is an attempt to:

- Formally define these underlying common entities and relationships;
- Describe them (and their inter-relationships) in a simple logical model;
- Provide the framework for extending these common semantics to domain and application-specific metadata vocabularies.

The concepts and inter-relationships modeled in ABC could be used in a number of ways.

In particular:

- Individual metadata communities could use these underlying concepts (the ABC vocabulary) to guide the development of community-specific vocabularies. These individual communities could use formalisms such as RDF to express the possibly complex relationships between the ABC model and their community-specific vocabularies.
- The formal expression of the relationships between community-specific vocabularies and the ABC model could provide the basis for a more scalable approach to interoperability among multiple metadata sets. Rather than one-to-one mappings among metadata vocabulary semantics, a more scalable basis for interoperability could be achieved by mapping through this common logical model.

This research is in its early stages but will be the subject of a workshop held at the end of January 2000. This workshop will bring together a small number of experts from the metadata and data modeling community and will produce a document that refines a conceptual model that could be used and refined by individual metadata initiatives and application developers.

Scholarly Publishing

These are tumultuous times for scholarly publishing On the one hand, there is a sense of serious economic imbalance as subscription prices for scholarly journals rise at a rate far exceeding inflation and put tremendous pressure on flat research library budgets. On the other hand, the rapid pace of advances in a number of disciplines (e.g, computer science, physics, law) conflicts with the relatively slow turn-around of the traditional scholarly publishing model.

A number of exciting initiatives are responding to these pressures. Several scholarly disciplines, especially the hard sciences, have launched ambitious e-print efforts. The most notable example is the physics archive (arxiv) hosted by Los Alamos National Laboratory. We at Cornell have been active in e-print initiatives within the computer science community both with NCSTRL and CoRR (the Computer Resource Repository).

In addition, a number of scholarly publications have been started that are only available in digital form. For example, Cornell and CNRI jointly publish D-Lib Magazine, a monthly publication documenting digital library research. Finally, many members of the traditional publishing community now make their publications available in electronic form (for example, the ACM digital library).

A prevailing meta-question in these digital publishing efforts is what is the proper model for interoperability amongst them? Researchers, who often cross disciplinary boundaries, will suffer a loss if the traditional single point of access offered by the print library catalog transitions in the digital age to a plethora of individual entry points.

These questions of interoperability are fundamentally those that we are examining in the context of our infrastructure research. As part of this research, we are involved in the OAI (Open Archives Initiative).

OAI developed at a meeting held in October 1999 in Santa Fe that was attended by a number of people already running digital scholarly archives or actively interested in the issue.

The purpose of the meeting was to develop standards for interoperation. The meeting ended with agreement on a *harvesting* model of interoperability, whereby participating sites will follow a standard for making common and specific metadata available.

This metadata can then be used by *mediator services* that build additional layers of functionality using this information. Some examples of these additional layers are federated searching, abstracting and indexing services, and so-called "overlay journals" (which combine documents from multiple resources into a virtual journal). One area of special interest in our research is *reference linking*.

The OAI agreement contains the following components:

- A very simple common metadata standard for coarse granularity resource discovery purposes.
- A simple protocol for harvesting this metadata, site-specific metadata, and other basic information from participating archives. This protocol is a subset of the Dienst protocol.

The OAI is still in very early stages but it has already attracted a significant amount of attention from the scholarly community.

From the standpoint of the research of the CDLRG it provides a number of benefits:

- It raises awareness of the Dienst protocol as a vehicle for richer interoperability.
- The success of the OAI and the adoption of the harvesting standard by a number of content provides will increase the number of collections for our work on policy enforcement.

Nomadic Devices

In general, digital library technology assumes that the user has a networked personal computer that is used to access server computers, which store content and provide information services. In practice, people increasingly use a variety of computing devices in their daily lives not all of which are continuously connected to a network.

This growing proliferation of palm devices, hand-held computers, disconnected laptops, and embedded processors (*e.g.* "smart" mobile telephones) offer exciting opportunities for the creation of *personalized information spaces* – digital libraries with collections and services that correspond to targeted needs and situations. Increasingly, we expect that individuals will want to exploit the mobility of these devices and use them for storage, access, and update of selected information resources when network access is impractical or impossible.

Developing and deploying these nomadic digital libraries will require technology that is sensitive to two critical dimensions of these devices:

- *Device capability*: Each computing device has unique hardware characteristics, including display capability, input mechanisms, presentation software, and hardware capacity.
- *Device Connectivity*: The connections of these devices to the networks vary in both permanence and speed.

These two dimensions can be characterized as *device appropriateness*. The CDLRG is currently undertaking a research and implementation project to investigate a number of the salient problems in realizing nomadic digital libraries that are sensitive to device awareness. This research programme has the following components:

- *Synchronization of Personal Information Spaces*: This research is addressing what constitutes a coherent *collection* in a digital library distributed among multiple device types. We are extending the collection abstraction that we developed for "attached" digital libraries to nomadic devices with varying connectivity and hardware characteristics. This raises fundamental issues related to the synchronization of the collection among devices.
- *Remote Reference Linking*: We are investigating issues of reference linking in the context of disconnected devices. This involves investigating a number of questions in this area. What is the appropriate partitioning of reference linking mechanisms between the mobile device and participating servers? How can this partitioning be done in a device-aware manner? How can this model be extended to a set of occasionally connected mobile devices – for

example, how might a group of individuals at a meeting share references through their infrared ports?

- *Disseminations*: The capability of an individual device must be considered when disseminating digital library content to that device. For example, a user of a desktop workstation with a fast network connection may want to see a richly illustrated dissemination of a book, but the user of a palm device may find an abbreviated text-only summary appropriate. We are investigating the mechanisms to allow matching of device characteristics with dissemination capabilities of an individual digital object. This work builds on the FEDORA dissemination characteristics.

FUNDED RESEARCH PROJECTS

This section briefly summarizes the funded research projects of the Cornell Digital Library Research Group within which research on the above topics is being carried out.

Project Prism

Project Prism is project funded as part of the U.S. multiagency Digital Library Initiatives Phase 2. Prism is a collaboration between the CDLRG, the Cornell University Library, and the Cornell Human Computer Interface Group. The project is investigating integrity issues and policy enforcement in distributed digital libraries.

A particular focus of Prism is digital library preservation. The media has alerted the American public to the loss of valuable materials maintained only in electronic form. As described in, there are no currently agreed-upon processes or model programs for preserving digital collections over time. Most existing digital preservation projects approach the problem from the narrow perspective of specific media or issues related to content alone. The Prism project is taking a broader approach that is examining preservation issues from both the policy and technical perspective.

Policy work on preservation within Prism involves librarians, archivists, and information specialists working together to develop formal functional requirements for digital preservation.

This requirements definition work is focusing on factors related to digital object vulnerability and issues pertaining to preserving digital objects and associated services in a distributed environment, with the attendant "control zone" issues. Technical work within Prism on preservation is focusing on the design and implementation of a *Preservation Service* as part of a wider component-based architecture.

This service interacts with other digital library services to detect vulnerable objects and initiate preservation actions based on individual preservation policies. Among the tasks that such a service might perform are: broadcasting a preservation alert or a set of conditions that require preservation action, detecting objects that satisfy the conditions of the alert or a set of conditions that require preservation action, detecting objects that satisfy the conditions of the alert, disseminating object state information, or initiating a range of possible actions for preserving vulnerable objects.

One challenge is how to implement preservation tasks in the context of distributed content and services with varying levels of cooperation from the content and service providers.

Harmony

Harmony is a funded as part of the Joint NSF-JISC International Digital Libraries Project. The project is an international collaboration involving the CDLRG and researchers from the United Kingdom and Australia.

Harmony is investigating the issue of metadata interoperability. Description of single-medium atomic digital resources has advanced in the past several years due to the development of metadata standards such as Dublin Core, which provides a framework for describing simple textual or image resources, and MPEG-7, which will provide the same for audio, video, and audiovisual resources.

While such single medium documents are certainly useful

and prevalent, the potential of digital libraries lies in their ability to store and deliver complex multimedia resources that combine text, image, audio and video components. The relationships between these components are multifaceted including temporal, spatial, structural and semantic and any descriptions of a multimedia resource must account for these relationships.

The Harmony Project is investigating a number of key issues in describing such complex multimedia resources in digital libraries with the following key goals:

- Collaborate with metadata communities to develop and refine developing metadata standards that describe multimedia components.
- Investigate a conceptual model for interoperability among community-specific metadata vocabularies. Such a conceptual model should be able to represent the complex structural and semantic relationships in multimedia resources.
- Investigate mechanisms for expressing such a conceptual model, including technologies currently under development in the W3C (XML, RDF, and their associate schema mechanisms).
- Develop mechanisms to map between community specific vocabularies using such a conceptual model.

The ABC workshop, is being organized as part of the Harmony project.

OpCit

OpCit, The Open Citation Project, is a three-year project funded as part of the Joint NSF-JISC International Digital Libraries Project. The project is an international collaboration involving the CDLRG with researchers from the United Kingdom.

OpCit is investigating the issues of reference linking, a generalization of citation linking, which is well developed in the traditional information professions, and a refinement of hyper-linking, used on the Web. The goal of reference linking is to enable access to content which may be a digital object, a collection of digital objects, or a portion of a digital object – from a reference to that content. The reference may be a URN, a URL, a formal citation in the form of a formatted bitliography entry, or an informal phrase that referes to a work – for example, "Bill Arms' latest book on digital libraries".

The OpCit project is following two inter-related paths:

- Our U.K. partners are examining reference linking within the context of the Los Alamos e-print archive.
- The CDLRG is examining linking issues among several archives. This involves investigating generic linking issues such as the nature of a "linkable API" for a digital object and the architecture of a "linking service" that could co-exist with other digital library services.

D-Lib Test Suite

The D-Lib Test Suite is a group of digital library testbeds, funded by DARPA, that are made available over the Internet for research in digital libraries, information management, collaboration, visualization, and related disciplines. The Test Suite currently includes six testbeds, one of which is the NCSTRL collection developed and administered by the CDLRG.

NCSTRL (pronounced "ancestral") is an international collection of computer science research reports and other materials made available for non-commercial use from over 100 participating organizations worldwide. By and large these organizations are Ph.D. granting computer science departments, e-print repositories, electronic journals, and research laboratories.

The NCSTRL collection is continually growing as new institutions become participants and as existing institutions add new documents. Documents in the NCSTRL collections are almost all textual ranging in size from 100-plus page doctoral dissertations to short technical reports.

NCSTRL is a federated digital library; content, and services that provide access to the content, are distributed over sites in North America, Europe and Asia. Interaction between services and access to documents is via the Dienst protocol, an open service-based protocol for distributed digital libraries.

Nomadic Digital Libraries

The Nomadic Digital Libraries Project, recently begun, is a small Intel-funded project to investigate the application of distributed digital library technology to nomadic (disconnected or randomly connected) devices (e.g. palm devices, hand-helds, and roaming laptops). This project is one component of a developing nomadic computing research focus in the Cornell Computer Science department.

This is an exciting time to be involved in digital library research. Initial successes in research projects and prototypes in the 1990's set the stage for major advances in the field over the next few years.

This paper has described research of the Cornell Digital Library Research Group in a number of areas that are important to this future progress. Work on architectural components lays the groundwork for moving digital libraries from local to diverse and broadly distributed systems.

Work on digital object architectures provides the mechanisms for rich and varied content in digital libraries. Work on policy enforcement investigates the key issue of extending information integrity, which is so well established and important in "brick and mortar" libraries, to the distributed digital domain.

Work on new publishing models examines information distribution techniques that exploit these new architectures. Finally, work on nomadic devices investigates extending these techniques to the latest developments in hardware and networking.

We look forward to these projects contributing valuable results and generating intellectual energy for future research efforts.

Chapter 6

Data Stream Management into Digital Library

Recent trends in ubiquitous and pervasive computing, together with new sensor technologies, wireless communication standards, powerful mobile devices and wearable computers strongly support novel types of applic-ations.

An example is tele-monitoring in healthcare which makes use of this new technology in order to improve the quality of treatment and care for patients and the elderly. In particular, if we consider our aging society, the amount of elderly people suffering from one or more chronic diseases is increasing.

Tele-monitoring applications enable healthcare institutions to take care of their patients while they are out of hospital, which is especially useful for managing various chronic diseases as well as for measuring the effects of treatments under real-life conditions.

A similar but even more comprehensive application is the support for the elderly and for people with cognitive disabilities living at home. Here, not only physiological sensors and data are relevant for tele-monitoring but also context information, e.g., information on the current activities of a person, where she or he is located, etc. In the DELOS task Integration of Data Stream Management into a Digital Library, different stream applications will be considered, yet with particular focus on eHealth.

RESEARCH OBJECTIVES

Continuous data streams generated by (wearable) sensors

have to be processed online in order to detect critical situations. This is important for instance for traffic or network monitoring, but also for eHealth applications. For this purpose, usually different streams (generated by different types of sensors) have to be combined (e.g., jointly consider oxygen saturation, ECG signals and blood pressure).

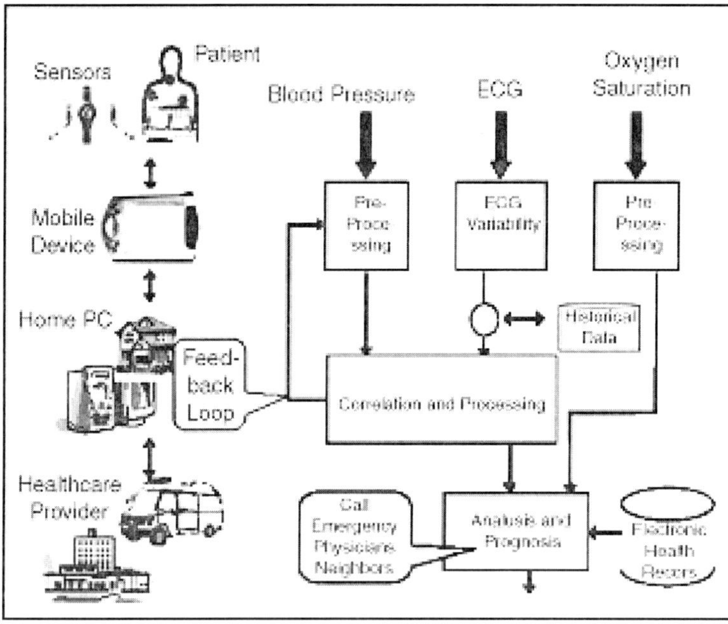

Fig. A Sample Data Stream Process for Health Monitoring.

This is done by making use of specialized operators (e.g., signal preprocessing, filtering, joining different streams, aggregating stream data, and feedback looping etc.). In Figure, a concrete setting taken from tele-monitoring in eHealth is depicted. Such an infrastructure has to be able to combine these operators in an applicationspecific way.

However, in addition to the stream operators, also traditional discrete (web) services, e.g., services that do not operate on continuous input data, have to be integrated.

These services are needed, for instance, in order to notify emergency physicians in very critical cases, to notify neighbors about abnormal situations, but also to write information aggregated from stream data back to the electronic health record of a patient.

The latter is very important to integrate data stream management into an eHealth digital library. Reliability of the eHealth digital library infrastructure is of utmost importance. In order to achieve a high degree of reliability, the task addresses failure handling a various levels from message level, Preprocessing operator or activity level, to process level. In particular, at operator level the task provides sophisticated and efficient operator checkpointing in order to allow for application-transparent operator migration.

Expected Results

The main goal of this task is to identify, design, and build demonstrators for data stream operators, i.e., the continuous processing of combined streaming data generated by different types of sensors. Appropriate web services are also needed in order to process and store the results and aggregates of stream operators. Finally, appropriate notification mechanisms are needed in order to inform a patient as well as healthcare providers on critical deviations of her/his health state. These operators and services will be combined in an infrastructure for stream processing.

While in the first year of this task, the focus has been exclusively on eHealth applications, its scope has been generalized. Currently, also other application domains (e.g., traffic management) are being addressed. In particular, this task started with an evaluation of applications where the combination of data stream operators (continuous processing of streaming data) and web services (discrete invocation of application functionality) is an inherent requirement.

Based on this evaluation, selected streaming operators (e.g., for searching outliers in a data stream or for joining parallel data streams) are currently being implemented and notification mechanisms will be provided. In addition, a prototype implementation of an infrastructure for workflow processes including stream processing supporting the integration of stream operators and web services will be provided. This allows for the insertion of the results of data stream processing into a DL, thereby tightly integrating data stream processing and Digital Library Systems.

Project Organization

The authors of this extended abstract are the members of this project. The partner institutions are: National and Kapodistrian University of Athens, Greece; Swiss Federal Institute of Technology (ETH) Zürich, Switzerland; University of Konstanz, Germany; University of Basel, Switzerland.

Chapter 7

Library Support For e-Learners

E-RESOURCES, E-SERVICES, AND THE HUMAN FACTORS

The growth of e-learning or online learning, in which education is delivered and supported through computer networks, is transforming academic libraries. E-learners and traditional learners have access to a universe of digital information, which frequently removes the need to visit a physical library.

New information and communications technologies, as well as new educational models, require librarians to re-evaluate the way they develop, manage, and deliver resources and services. Historically, librarians have provided services to distance learners that are equivalent to those available to on-campus learners; this aspiration is grounded in the philosophical frameworks of the Canadian Library Association's *Guidelines for Library Support of Distance and Distributed Learning in Canada* and the Association of College and Research Libraries' *Guidelines for Distance Learning Library Services.*

Both the Canadian and American *Guidelines* recognize that distance learners frequently do not have direct access to the full range of library services and materials, and that this necessitates equitable services that are more personalized than might be expected on campus.

The library literature provides a rich record of service models and best practices; as such, there has been an explosion of publications as librarians consider ways to support learners in a networked environment.

What do e-learners need from librarians? Suggestions advocating changes to librarians' roles, in support of distance learning in the information age, appear throughout the literature.

Librarians "must assert themselves as key players in the learning process thereby changing their roles from information providers to educators"; they have become providers of technical support; and they have been transformed from "information gatekeepers" to "information gateways". Lippincott advocates librarian involvement, as teachers and learners, in learning communities:

"The librarian can shift the focus from explaining library resources to meeting the ongoing information needs of the students in the broad information environment". In responding to the need to provide ongoing online library support, librarians have worked at translating what they do in a traditional library into virtual or digital environments, while customizing their services and resources for e-learners. Traditionally, libraries offer circulation services, interlibrary loans, course reserves, an information desk, a reference desk, and library instruction.

To serve learners connected to their institutional library primarily through a computer network, librarians provide remote access to, and electronic delivery of, library resources, and use communication technologies to deliver electronic reference services and instructional support. When we speak of providing support to e-learners, we are referring to a wider community of learners than the term "student" suggests.

An academic library's learners may include students, faculty, staff, researchers, and others. The library is seen as a source of training and guidance to a community of learners concerned with navigating the complexities of locating and using digital resources and services.

Moreover, the move toward an online environment has resulted in a shift from the systematic one-to-one information flow of the past to a new model in which the users and the providers of information are able to relate in a many-to-many, dynamic relationship.

For example, in the traditional model, a librarian provides a bridge between learners and information providers by selecting and cataloguing resources and by providing assistance with these resources.

In the new model, the librarian serves as a facilitator by offering ongoing support which enables learners to interact and exchange knowledge with others, to communicate directly with the publishers and vendors of information resources, and to participate in a collaborative endeavour to make available rich collections of online scholarly information resources.

This chapter examines how libraries are responding to the challenges of delivering core services and library resources to e- learners. We look at library practices and technologies being applied in the development and maintenance of virtual libraries. We also consider the challenges and opportunities that virtual libraries bring to the support of e-learners, as well as the importance of providing support within a collaborative environment which stresses human factors, such as communication and interaction.

DEFINING THE VIRTUAL LIBRARY

Gapen defines the virtual library as the concept of remote access to the contents and services of libraries and other information resources, combining an on-site collection of current and heavily used materials in both print and electronic form, with an electronic network which provides access to, and delivery from, external worldwide library and commercial information and knowledge sources. Additional terms for the virtual library include the digital library, the electronic library, and the library without walls.

Many libraries are hybrids, providing virtual access to electronic resources and services, while maintaining and supporting the use of a physical collection housed in a library building. With the tremendous growth of the Internet, e-learners have access to an overwhelming range of information sources, available at the click of a mouse, including library and academic resources, the sites of governments, non-governmental organizations, corporations and professionals, mainstream and alternative news, and an immense blogosphere.

Librarians have traditionally selected and organized limited collections of resources with great care and provided assistance and instruction to their patrons in accessing and using these collections.

Their task in the information age is to rescue e-learners from information overload, and to foster the competencies and critical reflection required to navigate an information environment characterized not by scarcity but by abundance and a multiplicity of formats and voices.

A virtual library links e-learners to library catalogues, licensed journal databases, electronic book collections, selected Internet resources, electronic course reserves, tutorials, and to opportunities for communication and interaction with librarians. The virtual library permits e- learners to access and use library and networked resources and services anytime and anywhere that an Internet connection and computing equipment are available.

THE LANDSCAPE OF LIBRARY RESOURCES

Technology offers opportunities to be innovative, as the following discussion of electronic resources and services demonstrates, but it is important to bear in mind inequalities such as access to computing equipment, the availability, speed, and stability of Internet connections, and the information skills required to make optimum use of virtual libraries.

Access to print-based library materials continues to be important, because not all of the information resources that e-learners need are available in electronic format; many of our most valuable research materials are still print-based.

Although there has been a shift away from purchasing print materials to be housed in a physical building, and toward providing access to licensed digital resources made available over a computer network, librarians continue to work to resolve issues pertaining to distance delivery of resources that are unavailable in digital format.

Online catalogues, indexing, and abstracting systems

provide e-learners with convenient access to bibliographic information about valuable scholarly documents. When those documents are not available in full-text form online, demand is generated for delivery from a library's print collection or from the collections of other libraries through interlibrary loans.

Typical solutions for delivery of non-digital formats include the use of mail and courier services, the establishment of collections at designated sites, and the negotiation of agreements with other libraries through consortia. Given that a growing number of learners are accessing library collections online, librarians are working to develop an integrated approach to providing access to electronic resources that facilitates retrieval and reduces confusion.

A library web site can function as an information portal and an entry point to a range of online resources, with the library catalogue and journal databases as key components. Most online catalogues permit the integration of electronic books and electronic journals, enabling users to locate items from digital and physical collections with one search.

User services – such as the ability to check due dates, renew materials, and request materials online – are also provided. A number of electronic tools have come into play recently in the provision of distance library services. Federated search tools such as *WebFeat*; *dbWiz,* an open-source product created at Simon Fraser University Library; and *Google Scholar* allow users to search a number of electronic resources simultaneously, using one interface. Libraries have the capability to customise the federated-search tool so that it searches a given set of electronic resources.

Federated-search solutions offer e-learners a faster and easier way to search multiple resources, but they can also be a good starting point for researching a topic, in that they can help to identify the most suitable databases, a task which is often extremely challenging in the world of ever-expanding digital resources. *Google Scholar* searches for scholarly articles, books, and other resources. Indexed items come from a variety of sources, including "academic publishers, pre-print societies, universities and other scholarly organizations".

These items may be available online, or they may only be available in print. While having the ability to search for multiple resource types in one place is beneficial to the user, what makes *Google Scholar* so important is that it allows users to choose which libraries they want to search. *Google Scholar*'s Library Links programme allows libraries that use *link-resolving software* to make their library holdings available in *Google Scholar*'s results lists.

An e-learner, wishing to access a particular article, clicks on the link to the library to retrieve a list of databases that hold the article; the e-learner must then provide identifying information to enter the database via the library's authentication process in order to access the article. *Google Scholar*'s Library Links programme also makes it possible to search library catalogues for items held by local libraries.

Through a partnership with Online Computer Library Centre (OCLC)'s Open WorldCat project (http://www.worldcat.org/whatis/default.jsp), it is possible to search the collections of libraries whose holdings are in OCLC. A more recent addition is the ability to search AMICUS, the catalogue of Libraries and Archives Canada.

Link-resolving software products, such as *SFX* from *ExLibris,* and *WebBridge* from *Innovative Interfaces Inc.*, allow users to *link out* from one database to another to retrieve full-text articles. Link resolvers or *link servers* work with open URL-compliant databases, and pass the user's library authentication information from one database to another, thereby allowing seamless access to full-text content without requiring the user to log in again.

If an item is not available from an open URL-compliant database, link resolvers can direct users to search other library resources, including library catalogues and A-Z serials lists. All learners benefit from these products because they allow greater access to full-text materials without needing to search a number of databases; however, for online learners – and in particular those who are internationally based – the immediacy of retrieval is especially important.

Providing easy online access and reducing the need to request print copies of articles enables libraries to provide better service to e-learners, and increases the e- learners' sense of connectedness to their library. Personalized digital libraries have become another way to increase the connectedness of e-learners.

While the tools mentioned above provide e-learners with greater access to resources, personalized digital libraries "streamline access to frequently used resources and create a friendlier online environment by permitting users to build their own digital collections in a personal workspace". One of the earliest instances of a personalized digital library was *MyLibrary NCState,* which was released in 1998 as a way to combat the information overload that learners were facing, due to the library's recent expenditures on electronic resources.

The system requires learners to choose an area of academic interest during the account creation process and was developed in a way that can assist librarians in making collection management decisions, as it is possible to study the usage patterns of subscribers.

The Open University of the UK has developed a pilot project called *MyOpenLibrary,* a personalized environment for their learners that uses the *MyLibraryNCState* software, which was made public in 2000. According to the web site, *MyOpenLibrary* is "a personal library page, which knows who you are, what you are studying and presents the relevant electronic library resources.selected from Open Library".

It allows learners to select their own resources, as well as having resources supplied to them, based on the courses which they are registered in. Other examples include *MyCybrary* at the University of Winnipeg Library, which offers learners opportunities to check their library account, keep up to date on new resources, and manage personal information services.

Librarians have become increasingly creative in enhancing their web sites. Because not all e-learners have physical access to reference tools quick fact-finding tools that are the staple of library collections libraries can perform a valuable service by providing learners with pointers to online versions.

Athabasca University Library's Digital Reference Centre, for example, offers a digital version of an academic library's reference collection, including almanacs and directories, atlases and maps, data and statistics, and dictionaries and encyclopedias.

Librarians select quality Internet resources to help e-learners navigate the Web. For example, the Open University Library's *ROUTES* database contains quality-assessed, courserelated Internet resources. It is impossible to ignore the phenomenon called "Web 2.0." There has been an explosion in the number of web users who are creating social content through weblogs, wikis, social bookmarking, podcasting, and other means.

Librarians are increasingly cognizant of these tools, and have been investigating how they can be used within the library to provide services and instruction to learners, as "Library 2.0." Weblogs are used by librarians in a number of ways.

Blogs, such as *The Distant Librarian* and *The Shifted Librarian* are designed as professional development tools for librarians. In other instances, blogs are used by librarians to keep patrons up to date on issues in the library, and to answer frequently asked questions.

An example is *Frequently Asked Questions* a blog maintained by the distance education librarian at Southern Connecticut State University. Weblogs can also be used for instructional purposes. Georgia State University Library has created subject-specific blogs that provide information about new resources in particular subject areas.

Social bookmarking, or social tagging, is a way for users to classify and share resources with others. Users assign tags, or keywords, to the sites that they bookmark, and these tags are then used in finding materials. This *folksonomy*, or informal classification, has exploded in popularity on the Web.

Some scholars and librarians are choosing to use these tools as a way to classify materials in their area of interest. Social tagging is used in academic libraries as a way to allow users to add content to the library web site. These resources may be in the form of web sites, bibliographies in specific content areas, or other items.

The University of Pennsylvania Libraries created *PennTags*, a service that can be used by members of the University of Pennsylvania community. In addition to allowing users to tag web sites, *PennTags* allows users to tag resources from library catalogues, magazines, journals, and newspapers.

It is possible to annotate resources, which can increase the pedagogical benefits associated with the use of social bookmarking. Integrated library system vendors are also beginning to explore the possibilities created by social tagging. For example, Innovative Interfaces Inc. is in the process of developing a new product called *Encore*, which allows librarians and patrons to tag resources found in library catalogues, including e-resources.

As libraries work to enhance their presence on the Web, a growing number have incorporated electronic course reserves (*e-reserves*). The traditional course reserves desk of an academic library, with its limited copies, short loan periods, and high late fines, can be a considerable source of frustration for students.

In the e-reserves model, the library makes available, through the Web, items that faculty have selected and "placed on reserve" for students in a particular course. San Diego State University (SDSU) pioneered e-reserves in the early 1990s. SDSU uses *Docutek ERes*, a system that provides access to course readings, chat rooms, and bulletin boards.

Many other libraries have initiated their own projects, using commercially available products or systems developed in-house.

The library literature points to a diversity of approaches. Athabasca University Library's Digital Reading Room (DRR) is an e-reserves system developed in-house at Athabasca University, using open-source software.

Scanning and mounting hardcopy materials is time consuming and requires securing of copyright permissions. The DRR encourages optimizing the value available from the library's electronic subscriptions through direct, persistent linking to content from the subscribed databases.

Each course in the DRR has a *digital reading file*. The licensed contents, such as journal database articles, require authentication through the library's proxy server, permitting only Athabasca University's community of users to access them; non-licensed resources, such as web sites, are freely available to the public.

A search engine permits e-learners to search across courses, providing a multidisciplinary approach to course reserves. By encouraging the inclusion of resources in a variety of digital formats, such as video, audio, and simulations, the DRR supports a wide range of learning objectives and styles.

Managing the remote access and authentication issues involved in making digital resources available has become a significant area of support to users of virtual libraries.

Librarians may be called upon to respond to questions concerning login and password information, browser configuration, software installation, and a range of troubleshooting needs. Access problems are hugely frustrating for e-learners and must be resolved quickly.

Ensuring that front-line library staff is adequately trained, providing clear instructions on the library's web site, and coordinating support activities with computing services personnel can contribute to effective technical support. E-learners also benefit from having a variety of means to contact the library, including email, web forms, and a toll-free telephone number.

LIBRARY SERVICES: CHALLENGES AND OPPORTUNITIES

The provision of appropriate and meaningful reference and instructional services to e-learners is fraught with both challenges and opportunities.

E-learners require more than access to e-resources. Traditionally, a reference librarian acts as an additional resource, someone who can be counted upon to provide expertise in making sense of library systems and research tools, and to offer a helping hand along that often slippery path known as the research process.

Virtual library users face additional challenges in mining relevant information out of a computer system that "obstinately" returns zero hits in response to a query that does not match the character strings in its database files.

The most common means of providing electronic reference services to remote users has been email, the advantages and disadvantages of which have been well documented in the literature. The around-the-clock and around-the-world accessibility of email enables e-learners to connect with librarians beyond the walls of library buildings and outside the usual hours of operation.

Email provides a written record of requests and responses, permits the electronic transmission of search results, and allows librarians time to reflect on requests. One of the most serious concerns about email reference services is their impact on traditional face-to-face reference interviews, particularly the absence of verbal and non-verbal cues, which typically assist a librarian in effectively responding to a question.

A well designed reference web form, such as that provided on the Athabasca University Library's "Ask about a Research Topic" web page, encourages e-learners to include full identifying and course information.

This web page encourages users to clearly describe their research problem and search terminology, and to state the parameters of their assignment. The feature also clarifies requests for librarians and reduces the need for email. Automated email replies sent out in response to the receipt of a message reassure e-learners that their messages have been received and lets them know what to expect in terms of service.

Email reference service can be enhanced and supplemented with additional technologies that raise the level of interaction via real-time communication. Chat technology allows e-learners and librarians to send text messages back and forth instantly, using a form of communication that is familiar to most Internet users.

A number of issues surround the use of chat in the

provision of reference services to remote users. Choosing the appropriate programme for the library's specific needs and resources is essential if the virtual reference initiative is to be successful.

Available programs range from vendor-based systems that offer features such as "co-browsing, patron queuing, sharing files, and the ability to keep more extensive statistics", to instant messaging programs, which are freely available. Some chat programs require downloads on the part of users, which can be problematic and may also discourage e-learners from using the service.

In an effort to reach more e-learners, some libraries have begun using instant messaging programs such as AOL's *AIM* product, MSN's *Messenger*, and *Yahoo! Messenger*, primarily because many e-learners are already using these systems.

More recently, libraries have begun experimenting with programs such as *Trillian* and *Pidgin*, which log into a number of instant messaging accounts simultaneously and allow librarians the flexibility to respond to instant messaging questions coming into the library, no matter which system the e-learner is using.

This reduces the need to monitor several different instant messaging programs at the same time. Virtual reference consortia have the potential to expand the library's abilities to serve its community of users effectively.

Libraries in the consortia answer questions from e-learners in other parts of the consortium service area. Traditionally, chat reference services are only available during specified hours, so virtual reference consortia are beneficial for e-learners in different time zones than their home institution, because they increase the likelihood of a librarian being available to answer questions immediately.

Even if the initial reference transaction is received through chat, however, it may ultimately prove difficult to provide a complete answer using this method. If a user requires assistance in learning how to use a particular library resource, it may be possible to provide a complete response via chat.

However, if the user is requesting assistance to find

information on a complex topic, the librarian may need time to determine appropriate search strategies before responding. In these cases, the follow-up response is often done by email. Providing e-learners with a toll-free telephone number remains an effective and convenient reference services strategy, particularly for intricate inquiries. The telephone reference interview works best when both librarian and e-learner are working in front of computers connected to the Internet.

Instruction

E-learners are frequently silent and invisible as they search and explore a library's online resources, and they do not have the same access that oncampus learners have to formal library instruction sessions.

With the array of digital resources available to them, the many different interfaces and search tools, and the need for evaluation and critical thinking when using the Internet for research, information literacy skills are essential. Information literacy has been defined in relation to competencies, with information sources in a variety of formats. According to the Association of College and Research Libraries, an information-literate student

- Determines the nature and extent of the information needed.
- Accesses needed information effectively and efficiently.
- Evaluates information and its sources critically and incorporates selected information into his or her knowledge base and value system.
- Individually, or as a member of a group, uses information effectively to accomplish a specific purpose.
- Understands many of the economic, legal, and social issues surrounding the use of information, and accesses and uses information ethically and legally. Supporting the integration of information literacy skills training into the core curriculum has become an important issue for libraries.

A discussion is also emerging around the need to promote critical reflection in relation to information and knowledge, to conceptualize a *critical information literacy* that goes beyond a focus on competencies.

Critical information literacy draws on scholarship in critical theory and critical education to provide librarians with a theoretical framework that acknowledges their responsibility to help students see that knowledge is not neutral but socially constructed and contested.

Teaching the value of incorporating peer-reviewed journals in research papers, for example, need not preclude a discussion about how alternative voices may be silenced by the peer-review process and how to find alternative literature.

As an extension of their traditional role in providing library instruction sessions and developing instructional materials, librarians design online tutorials and courses that promote information literacy and encourage active learning. Particularly fine examples are the University of Texas System Digital Library's TILT – Texas Information Literacy Tutorial; and Utah Academic Library Consortium's Internet Navigator, a multi-institutional online course developed by a team of librarians and web developers.

The Open University Library created SAFARI, a freely available interactive tutorial, as well as an information literacy course called Making Sense of Information in the Connected Age or, more commonly, MOSAIC. Athabasca University offers the undergraduate course, Information Systems 200: Accessing Information. Many libraries provide instruction to e-learners by making information available on their web pages, including research guides and "how-to" pages. for example, Athabasca University Library's Help Centre.

An awareness of the importance of context-specific help has grown and it is quite common to find links to tutorials at the point of need. Software packages for developing animated tutorials, such as ViewletBuilder, Camtasia, and Captivate enable librarians to demonstrate effective database searching techniques asynchronously.

Brief tutorials that incorporate voice-over and demonstrate database features within the context of real searches are particularly effective. Joining an existing, collaborative initiative reduces workload and removes the need to "reinvent the wheel." The Council of Prairie and Pacific University Libraries (COPPUL), a consortium of twenty university libraries located in Manitoba, Saskatchewan, Alberta, and British Columbia, is responsible for the *Animated Tutorial Sharing Project* (*ANTS*).

Participating libraries, including libraries outside of COPPUL, access a wiki where they can adapt databases for tutorial development, upload tutorials, and download tutorials developed by other libraries. Online tutorials usually operate on a model in which the e-learner interacts in isolation with a computer.

Their effectiveness can be enhanced by the addition of more interactive forms of instruction. The librarians at the Florida Distance Learning Reference and Referral Centre, for example, have experimented with chat software to simulate a virtual classroom and open a "live" group instruction to e-learners. Librarians can be incorporated through the learning management system, participating in online courses as teaching assistants, co-instructors, or co-designers.

This 'embedded librarian' approach increases learner awareness of the value of the library in research and scholarship, and improves access to the expertise of librarians within the context of course needs and assignments. In addition, podcasting and video clips have become a popular choice in the delivery of instructional materials to remote users, as libraries recognize the popularity of mobile devices such as the *iPod.*

According to a Pew Internet and American Life survey, "more than 22 million American adults own iPods or MP3 players, and 29% of them have downloaded podcasts". These methods allow e-learners to access the materials "anytime, anywhere," while still providing them with the type of instruction that their on-campus counterparts may receive.

Tutorials range from a simple orientation to the library and its services to more in-depth tutorials on the research process or searching specific databases. For example, Mount Allison University Library makes audio *libcasts* available. These libcasts can be downloaded or subscribed to and listened to, using *iTunes* or a similar product.

THE SUCCESSFUL VIRTUAL LIBRARY

PARTNERSHIP AND COLLABORATION

In reviewing definitions of the virtual library, Sloan identifies an emphasis on the technological and informational building blocks, and a neglect of the human components, such as the service tradition and human interaction.

The continuing changes in technology have been truly astonishing, and the scope for building new information services and new ways of representing content seem unlimited. Although technology is the key infrastructure of the virtual library a tool used to support library goals human factors are the most important determinant of the success of the virtual library.

As noted by Colgate, Buchanan Oliver, and Elmsly, technology could cause problems in building relationships because of the difficulty in developing a successful rapport between people via remote contact.

One of the major challenges that virtual libraries face is the lack of opportunity for face-to-face reference service and communication. Combine this with a lack of awareness of library services and the end result is poor communication between library staff and e-learners.

The digital library serves mainly as a facilitator in organizing and providing knowledge and resources to its users. Sharing knowledge and information among library staff, researchers, faculty, students, and other departments within the institution encourages them to work together, develop their skills, and form strong and trusting relationships.

One method which can be effective in the development of strong relationships with faculty is the librarian-liaison role, where a librarian liaises with specific departments regarding resources, library services, and the provision of instructional support for students in those departments. When the liaison focuses on building effective channels of communication and understands the effects of technology on communication, it becomes easier to share knowledge and information among institutional stakeholders.

In addition, the focus on collaboration between the library and the faculty promotes a responsive approach to course design and supports teaching and learning objectives, particularly when this collaboration incorporates student contributions and feedback.

This approach considers the library as an active partner of the learning community, helping e-learners to become "information literates" by integrating information literacy skills into the curriculum.

The library can help e-learners to think critically about information, offer reference and instructional support, mentor their work by offering one-to-one communication and interaction, and work collaboratively with them to achieve a deeper level of understanding of what e-learners need.

A number of models can be involved in creating an environment that is responsive to the scholarly information needs of a diverse group of e-learners. Librarians select, describe, and ensure access to quality digital resources, providing e-learners with content from a wide range of resources and publications, including peer-reviewed journals.

Within this framework, the library works with faculty, researchers, scholarly societies, and publishers to develop and manage a collection of enriched online scholarly resources. Such a partnership enables researchers to interact with others, exchange experiences, and publish their works online.

The library role is thus transformed from simply providing library resources to meeting the ongoing support needs of the parties involved. The library also fosters research skills by encouraging e-learners to search, investigate, discover, and take advantage of these valuable online resources.

Further, senior management support and involvement is as much a key to success in developing the virtual library as in any other project.

They need to work closely with the library staff to understand the nature of services, values, and support the library should be offering, and to adopt successful communication and interaction strategies.

An institution providing distance and online education has an ethical obligation to ensure that its learners have access to appropriate library support. The Canadian Library Association *Guidelines* categorize responsibilities in terms of funding, administration, personnel, facilities, resources, services, publicity, and professional development of librarians.

The *Guidelines* note as essential advance planning by the library in consultation with faculty, programme administrators, and other appropriate campus personnel, and with librarians at unaffiliated libraries. The *Guidelines* also advocate that leadership should come from all levels of the institutional administration, but particularly from the library. All staff involved in providing library support to e-learners must be included in the partnership. Technological changes have been the dominant force reshaping library services.

Instilling a culture of sharing, motivation, equity, and active partnering encourages library staff to respond positively to the changing roles, responsibilities, and skills that the integration and use of technology requires.

A well-designed, ongoing training programme enables library staff to upgrade their skills to their new assignments, and helps them to understand and control fear of change. The home institution has primary responsibility for library support, but can benefit from external partnerships, collaborative efforts, and consortia in supporting e-learners.

Within Canada, university libraries extend in-person borrowing privileges to students, faculty, and staff from across the country, through the *Canadian University Reciprocal Borrowing Agreement.*

There are also initiatives to share virtual reference desks, such as the Library and Archives Canada's Virtual Reference Canada, through which e-learners benefit from the range of information resources and staff expertise available at a variety of participating institutions. Consortia approaches to database subscriptions enable libraries to expand the scope of the electronic resources they are able to offer their e-learners in a time of shrinking budgets and escalating journal costs.

The Lois Hole Campus Alberta Digital Library (LHCADL) initiative, through funding provided by the Government of Alberta, provides participating post-secondary institutions in Alberta with digital information resources for teaching, learning, and research.

LHCADL includes an information literacy and awareness component dedicated to sharing expertise and training resources with participating libraries.

In summary, library services are an essential component of a quality online learning experience. As access to online courses grows, an increasing number of e-learners are dispersed around the globe, often in parts of the world where physical access to the collections of large academic and research libraries is impossible or severely limited.

These learners are largely dependent on the quality and academic usefulness of services that the library can offer electronically.

The strength of virtual libraries and digital collections depends on the relationships libraries develop and maintain with the creators, publishers, and aggregators of e-resources, as well as with those who use, learn from, and evaluate these resources. Providing ongoing technical, reference, and instructional support to e-learners requires that libraries redefine their values and services, collaborate with their users and other partners, and approach their tasks creatively.

Chapter 8

Information Management in Digital Libraries

The Self-Organising Map (SOM) has been proposed as an alternative interface for exploring Digital Libraries (DL), in addition to conventional search and browsing. With advanced visualisations assisting the user in understanding the contents of the map and its structure, as well as advanced interaction modes as zooming, panning and area selection, the SOM becomes a feasible alternative to classical search and browse interfaces.

Several applications show the SOMs utility for this task. However, there are still shortcomings in helping the user understanding the map there are insufficient methods developed for describing the map to support the user in the analysis of the map contents.

In this paper, we give an overview of existing techniques and applications of SOMs in Digital Libraries, and present recent work in assisting the user in exploring the map by automatically describing maps using advanced labelling and summarisation of map regions. Therewith, the SOM becomes an attractive tool for Information Management.

The Self-Organising Map (SOM):

- Is a popular unsupervised neural network model that provides a mapping from a high-dimensional input space (for example text documents described in a vector space model) to a low, often two-dimensional, output space. The mapping of the SOM is topology preserving – elements close in the input space will also be close in the output space. Due to its interesting properties, the SOM has been used in several applications to automatically organise documents in a Digital Library by their content. Examples are text, as in the SOMLib Digital Library system.

- Or in a map of news texts.
- Or music in the SOMeJB system.
- As a recent example also the Digital Library Management System (DLMS) developed by the DELOS Network of Excellence.
- Reckons the possibilities of using the SOM as an interface to a Digital Library's content, as it offers the user support in analysing and exploring the content. With advanced visualisations and interaction possibilities, the user can exploit the full potential of the SOM. However, we still lack techniques to adequately help the user in analysing the contents of the map. For large maps, containing several tens of thousands documents describing various different topics, it becomes increasingly difficult to quickly analyse the map.

In this paper, we give an overview of existing applications of the Self-Organising Map in Digital Libraries and techniques to explore and interact with the map. Furthermore, we present recent work in making the SOM more usable for Information Management by automatically describing regions in the map through adding semantic labels to the SOM, using clustering methods to identify topical areas and selecting representative labels for those regions. Moreover, we present work on automatically summarising the content of those regions on the SOM.

The remainder of this paper is organised as follows: Section II gives a brief overview of the Self-Organising Map and its application in the context of Digital Libraries. Section III describes our work in labelling and summarising regions, while Section IV presents the experiments conducted. Section V presents conclusions and future work.

SELF-ORGANISING MAP

The Self-Organising Map (SOM) has been successfully used for clustering various kinds of data. It provides a mapping from a high-dimensional input space to a lower-dimensional output space.

In the context of Digital Libraries, the input space is mostly a vector-space model representation of the documents the Digital Library holds, may it be text, images, audio, video, or any other media that can be represented in vectorial form.

Although many different architectures exist, the output space is in many applications organised as a two-dimensional rectangular grid of units, a representation that is easily understandable for users due to its analogy to 2-D maps. Each of the units on the map is assigned a weight vector, which is of the same dimensionality as the vectors in the input space.

During the training process, vectors from the input space are presented to the Self-Organising Map, and the unit with the most similar weight vector to this input vector is determined.

The weight vector of this unit, and, to a lesser extent, of the neighbouring units, are adapted towards the input vector, i.e. their distance in the input space is reduced.

At the end of the training process, the output space will be arranged in a way to represent the input space as closely as possible.

For more details on the SOM training process, please refer e.g. to. An important property of the SOM is that the mapping is topology preserving - elements which are located close to each other in the input space will also be closely located in the output space, while dissimilar patterns will be mapped on opposite regions of the map.

The SOM therefore provides a sort of clustering of the data, however, without explicitly assigning data items to clusters. It neither identifies cluster boundaries as opposed to, e.g, the k-Means method.

The generated map can help the user in getting a quick overview of the patterns in the input space. With fitting visualisations highlighting boundaries, it also allows an easier interpretation of the cluster structures and correlations in the content.

A. Self-Organising Maps in Digital Libraries

The Self-Organising Map as an interface to digital document collections has already been proposed in the WEBSOM project., where the contents of a newsgroup collection containing a million of articles was clustered on the map. The application provides the user with a map of the document collection which she can zoom into by pre-defined levels and navigate in.

- On the most detailed zooming level, a list of the documents mapped onto that region of the map is provided. The map itself, and the exact position of the documents on the map, is not available anymore. To add semantic meaning, the map gets automatically labelled by the names of the most dominant corresponding newsgroups, which is a feasible approach when some kind of categorisation is available for the documents. The labels are however not determined by topical clusters, but rather on a unit basis. The SOM as an interface to Digital Libraries has further been demonstrated in the SOMLib Digital Library System
- The SOMLib system utilises the SOM and other techniques to support the user by employing as many concepts as possible which she already knows from a conventional library. Similar to a map of a conventional library, depicting the arrangement of the shelves where books on certain topics are located, the SOM gives the overview over the contents of the Digital Library. Similar to finding related books in the same shelf, once the user has found a specific document of interest, she can find documents that are related in content in the neighbourhood of that document. A symbolic visualisation of bookshelves using the LIBViewer method further supports this

metaphor. The SOMLib system utilises a labelling algorithm to automatically add semantic descriptors to the single map units, without having the need for any category information being available.

- The SOM is used to create a web-based knowledge map of news articles. The application supports hierarchical zooming into the map in pre-defined levels of zoom. However, the map layout changes on different levels of zooming. Besides the map, also a hierarchical list of topics is displayed as an alternative for users who prefer a onedimensional visualisation. uses clustering on the map to apply labels to regions, which are generated based on term and document frequencies, using a tf × idf-based approach.

The focus in this work is on the visualisation, which tries to resemble geographical maps as closely as possible. This is achieved using a separate GIS software system.

The interaction possibilities for the user are limitedzooming is in predefined levels, the labels cannot be changed interactively, and only one type of visualisation is available. Based on the concept of the SOMLib system, a sophisticated desktop client software has been developed, which allows for various ways of user interaction with the Digital Library content.. With zooming and panning functionalities, the user can analyse the content at any desired detail level, from viewing the whole map at once down to viewing single documents.

Tools for selecting rectangular regions or units along a path allow the user to select several documents at once, and open them for example in a text viewer or in an audio application for playlist generation. One important aspect of SOMs as interfaces to Digital Libraries is that they should not be meant to replace traditional query and retrieval techniques, but rather be complementary to it. This approach is presented in., where a Self-Organising Map is integrated into the popular open source system Greenstone as a new service, based on the existing query services such as search or list browsing.

That way, the user can still use all the basic functionalities provided by Greenstone, but she will also be able to use the wealth of additional information the SOM mapping provides about the documents matching the query results and the whole collection itself.

A screenshot of the system is depicted in Figure, where the left side figures the traditional Greenstone search interface, the lower part the document result listing, and the right part holds the map. The map can be used in two different ways. First, results of the Greenstone search will be highlighted on the map by markers.

The user can immediately see which documents have a topical similarity, as these documents will usually all be located close to each other and form a cluster on the map. This way, distinguishing between different topics found on an ambiguous word as e.g. 'jaguar' becomes easily – the documents referring to the sports car will be clearly separated from those talking about the animal because they appear in a different context together with other words.

Additionally, outliers found via the search become visible as isolated spots on the map. Secondly, the user can explore the map – she can select nodes, upon which the documents lying on that nodes will be added to the result list of the Greenstone search.

This allows the user to retrieve potentially relevant documents for a specific information need, even if they were not initially retrieved by the (usually rather short) query issued. Documents that have been matched both by the map selection and the search result will be marked especially, as they may be of higher importance.

The user can get additional information on the content of the collection by mouse-over popups displaying terms that best describe the documents on a certain node. A small user study suggested that this interface is suitable for Digital Libraries once the user has become a bit familiar with the map.

The SOM has also been used for other types of media besides text. In the SOMeJB project, the concept of the SOMLib system has been extended to audio and music documents.

Similar to the SOMLib system, the SOMeJB arranges musical pieces, described by a set of feature vectors extracted solely from the audio content, into topical clusters by the sound characteristics, as the user is familiar with from a traditional record store. In the PicSOM project., the SOM has been used for Information Retrieval in image databases, incorporating methods of relevance feedback.

III. DESCRIBING THE SELF-ORGANISING MAP REGIONS

In this section we present our work on identifying and describing regions in the mapping generated by the Self-Organising Map. As the SOM does not generate a partition of the map into separate clusters, we utilise another clustering algorithm on the weight vectors of the units to identify the regions.

Applying the LabelSOM method, we create semantic labels for those regions that assist the user in getting a first glance overview of the contents of the map. To further support the analysis phase, we additionally provide summarisation of documents of the regions using Automatic Text Summarisation methods.

Clustering

Clustering is an unsupervised process of finding natural groupings amongst unlabelled objects. The members of a cluster are similar in some way, and are dissimilar to members of other clusters.

To identify topical regions, we are clustering the units of a SOM applying an agglomerative, hierarchical clustering algorithm on the units' weight vectors.

In the beginning of an agglomerative clustering process, every unit lies in its own cluster. In each subsequent step, the two nearest clusters are merged, until finally only one cluster remains. Specifically, we use Ward's linkage (also known as minimum variance clustering) as one of the most performant within the linkage clustering families.

In this algorithm, the distance of each pair of clusters is defined by the increase in the "error sum of squares" (ESS) if the two clusters are to be combined. The ESS of a cluster X of |X| values is defined as:

$$ESS(X) = \sum_{i=1}^{|X|} \left| x_i - \frac{1}{|X|} \sum_{j=1}^{|X|} x_j \right|^2$$

and the distance D between two clucters X and Y is defind by

$$D(X,Y) = ESS(X,Y) - [ESS(X) + ESS(Y)]$$

where XY is the union of clusters X and Y. The result of the Ward's algorithm is a hierarchy of clusters which the user can browse through. Increasing the number of displayed clusters means splitting existing clusters into two new ones, while reducing the number of clusters is achieved by merging two clusters into one.

This is advantageous over a non-hierarchical clustering algorithm, where changing the number of clusters might completely change the layout of clusters, which obviously is not a desired behaviour when we want to allow the user to interactively analyse the map contents by changing the number of clusters.

Moreover, hierarchical clustering allows us to at the same time display multiple layers with a different number of clusters. In contrast to other clustering algorithms, the clusters of a layer with more clusters can never be cut by clusters of a layer with less clusters.

Labelling Units with LabelSOM

To assist the user in interpreting the regions of the SOM, we automatically generate labels for the clusters we identified previously.

The cluster labels are based on the units labels generated by the LabelSOM method, which assigns labels to the units of the SOM describing the features of the data points mapped onto the respective unit.

This is done by utilising the quantisation error qik of the vector elements, which is the sum of the distances for a feature between the unit's weight vector mi and all the input vectors xj 2 Ci, i.e. the vectors mapped onto the unit i.

$$q_{i_k} = \sum_{x_j \in C_i} \sqrt{\left(m_{i_k} - x_{j_k}\right)^2} \quad k = 1...n$$

This means that a low quantisation error characterises a feature that is similar in all input vectors to the weight vector. Thus the assumption is made that this feature describes the unit well. If the input vector however contains features which are non existent and therefore have the value of 0, those attributes often also have a quantisation error of almost 0 for a unit.

Such features are in most cases not appropriate for labelling the unit, since this would describe what the unit does not contain. Therefore, we require a feature to also have a minimum average value, calculated from all the input vectors mapped to the unit.

Labelling Regions

To choose a label for a region, we consider only the unit labels present in that cluster, as the unit labels are already a selection of features describing the contents of each unit. This method is faster in computation than checking all possible features. Depending on the data, it is preferable to choose the region label based upon a low average quantisation error, a high mean value, or a combination of both.

Therefore we offer the user the possibility to interactively assign priority weights for those two measures, to achieve more meaningful labels.

Making use of the properties of the hierarchical clustering as described in Section III-A, we can also display two or more different levels of labels, some being more global, some being more local. In the visualisation of the SOM, the labels are placed in the centroid of the cluster, which may result in some overlapping labels.

To achieve a clear arrangement, the labels can be manually moved on the map, or adjusted in their size and rotation. For some labels, it might also be useful to edit their text, for example if the label text is only a word stem as in our experiment described later in this paper.

Region Summarisation

Even though labelling the map regions assists the user in quickly getting a coarse overview of the topics, labels can still be ambiguous or not conveying enough information. Therefore, we also employ methods from the Automatic Text Summarisation field.

Based on the regions identified from the clustering process, we automatically provide a short summary of the contents of the documents mapped onto those regions, allowing the user to get a deeper insight into the contents.

Automatic Text Summarisation tries to automatically generate a summary of one or more texts to present the main ideas of the contents in a short and compact form. It can in principle be divided into two areas: single and multidocument summarisation.

Single document summarisation deals with providing a summary of a single document, may it be by extraction of the most relevant sentences, or the more sophisticated approach of generating an abstract of the text. Multi-Document summarisation, on the other hand, deals with generating summaries of a whole collection of documents. Simple approaches would just treat each single document separately, generate the summary of it, and then present all the summaries to the user.

This approach of course does not consider redundancy in the extracted sentences. More advanced techniques would treat the whole document collection at once, and extract the sentences which are most important concerning all documents. Redundant sentences are eliminated first by applying a measure for overlapping words, and remove sentences with too high similarity.

Although we also provide summaries of single documents in our application, the main focus is to assist the user in analysing the contents of the Digital Library by providing summaries of the previously identified regions using multidocument summarisation. The application allows the user to select whole regions, or manually any other rectangular shape or units a long a path.

For the chosen documents, the user can choose from

several different summarisation algorithms using different weighting schemes to determine the importance of sentences for the summaries, and can also specify the desired length of the summary, measured in per cent of the original sentences.

EXPERIMENTS

The following experiments were performed using the 20 newsgroups data set1, a big benchmark corpus which has become very popular for text experiments in the field of machine learning. The data set consists of newsgroup postings from the 20 newsgroups listed in Table.

Each newsgroup contains 1,000 articles from the year 1993; each text consists of the message body and in addition the 'Subject' and the 'From' header lines.

Table. The 20 Newsgroups Data Set.

alt.atheism	rec.motorcycles	soc.religion.christian
comp.graphics	rec.sport.baseball	talk.politics.guns
comp.os.ms-windows.misc	rec.sport.hockey	talk.politics.mideast
comp.sys.ibm.pc.hardware	sci.crypt	talk.politics.misc
comp.sys.mac.hardware	sci.electronics	talk.religion.misc
comp.windows.x	misc.forsale	sci.med
rec.autos	sci.space	

In our experiments we used a standard bag-of-words indexing approach. Porter's stemming algorithm was applied to remove prefixes and suffixes to obtain word stems. From the remaining word stems, the features for the input vectors were selected according to their document frequency, and the weights are computed using a standard tf × idf weighting scheme.

This resulted in a 3151 dimensional feature vector for each document, from which the maps were trained. The specific map we will use in the remainder of this paper to illustrate our results is of 75 × 55 units in size.

Cluster Hierarchy Browsing and Labelling Regions

In our application it is possible to explore the clustered SOM interactively: to view the different levels of clustering and to zoom into the map to view the single postings. The user can browse the clustering levels either viewing only the cluster borders, or also highlighting each cluster in a different colour.

The former is shown in Figure, illustrating the steps from one to eight clusters. There is a special cluster in the lower right-hand corner with the a label also used on other clusters – 'god' in the fourth step, and 'gun' in the steps five to seven.

This cluster is, however, not a separate one when viewing the clustering with colours, it becomes apparent that this area is part of the disjoint clusters 'god' and 'gun', respectively, in the upper part of the map. With this interactive exploration of the clusters, the user can gain valuable information about the structure of the documents in the collection.

The upper image in Figure shows nine clusters with larger labels, and in addition 67 clusters with smaller labels.

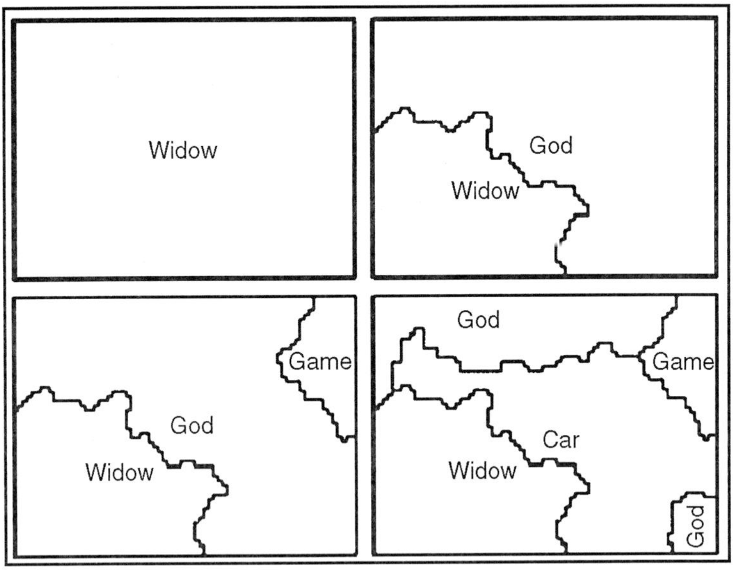

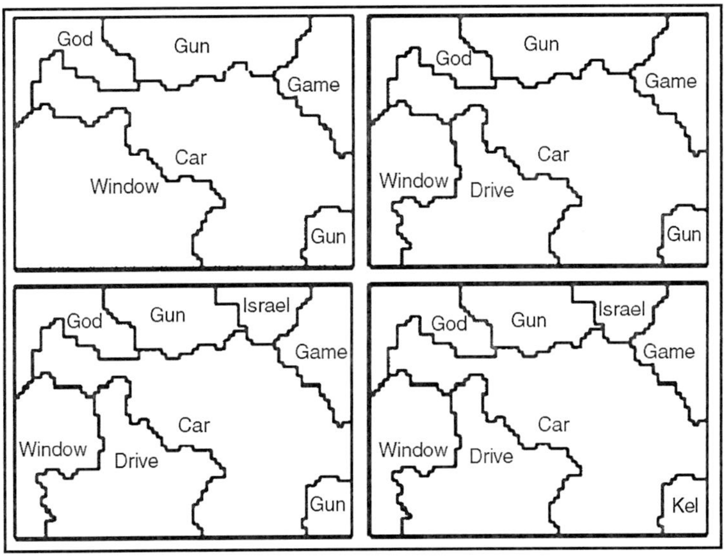

Fig. Clusters With Labels.

The two clusters labelled 'david' are in fact one disjointed cluster. As a result of the stemming algorithm, words ending with an y now end with an i, for example the labels 'kei' (containing most of sci.crypt) or 'batteri' (various postings e.g. from sci.electronics or rec.motorcycles). There are also some labels where obviously the suffixes of the original words have been removed, as in the labels 'imag' or 'insur'.

The labels were not edited to show the terms based on which the map has been created. In the top right-hand corner is a large cluster labelled 'game' containing most postings from the two sports related newsgroups.

The large cluster next to it labelled 'israel' contains mainly postings from talk.politics.mideast. In the upper left-hand corner there is a cluster labelled 'god' containing all the newsgroups dealing with religion, i.e. alt.atheism, soc.religion.christian and talk.religion.misc.

It is interesting to note, that in contrast to the newsgroup hierarchy, where these groups lie in three different top level hierarchies, they are combined into one cluster here. The large cluster in the middle labelled 'book' contains many of small clusters of which only a few have meaningful labels.

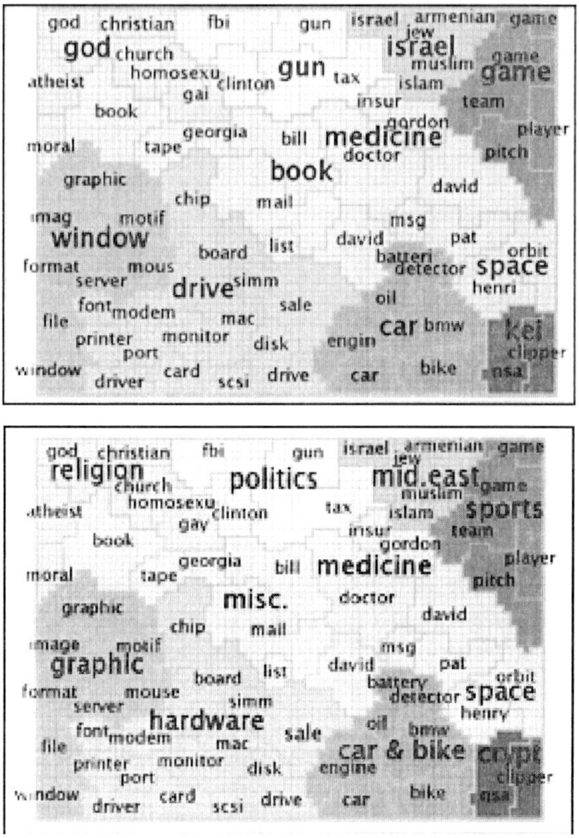

Fig. Nine Coloured and Labelled Clusters and 67 Smaller Clusters with Labels.

The small clusters labelled 'insur' and 'doctor' suggest that they contain postings from the sci.med newsgroup and the cluster label 'orbit' relates to the newsgroup sci.space. The labels containing names such as 'gordon', 'david' or 'bill' do not help in identifying the underlying topics in those areas of the map.

However, names cannot be easily automatically removed, as some common names as Mark or Bill are also a verb or noun respectively. Furthermore names can sometimes be useful labels, for example if they refer to a famous person. The small cluster labelled 'drive' lies in the cluster with the hardware topics but also directly next to the cluster labelled 'car'.

It imples that in this area lies an transition of the word drive being used in the meaning of hard disk drive or in the meaning of to drive a car. To enhance the comprehensibility of the map some labels are manually edited, which is shown in the lower image of Figure: word endings have been added and the labels of the larger areas have been edited to better suit the diverse topics.

For example the cluster automatically labelled 'car' is extended to 'car & bike' to point out both newsgroups contained in this cluster.

The cluster previously labelled 'gun' containing the newsgroups talk.politics.guns and parts of talk.politics.misc and talk.politics.mideast is adapted to 'politics'. The large cluster in the middle is manually described with three labels to point out the various topics inside.

The map thus created can now be used to interactively present the contained information of the Digital Library in an intuitive way.

In this paper we presented the usage of the Self-Organising Map as an interface to Digital Libraries. On top of this well-known approach, we presented recent work on methods to assist the user in interacting with the map. We employ clustering of the SOM to reveal hierarchical structures which can be explored by the user to get a rough overview of the structure of the data on the map.

The clustering identifies regions, which we describe on the one hand very concisely by single descriptive words extracted from the document contents, and secondly by applying automatic text summarisation techniques to generate executive summaries of the contents. All methods are integrated into a single application, that provides additional features such as visualisations and advanced interaction via zooming and panning, and selection of arbitrary regions of the map.

With these tools available, the user can be greatly assisted in analysing the SOM generated from the contents of the Digital Library, and therefore getting a quick overview of the contents of the Digital Library itself, and the structure and relationship of the documents it contains, even if the number of documents is huge and their topics diverse.

Therewith, the SOM becomes an attractive tool to support Information Management. Future work will focus on user studies on the region identification, labelling and summarisation, and the interaction possibilities with the map.

Chapter 9

Management of Digital Library Education

The concept of digital library has several differing interpretations, derived from different communities involved in digital library research, practice, organization, and commerce. Educational offerings followed these activities.

The major aim of the paper is to present results from a survey on the current state of digital library education in academic institutions. But we also examine the rationale and orientation for digital library education. We suggest several models that have emerged in the teaching of digital libraries and in incorporation of relevant topics into various curricula.

Digital library is a term and concept that serves as an umbrella for a great many of diverse activities. Virtual library, electronic library, library without walls and a few other terms have also been used to carry a similar connotation, but the term 'digital library' seems to be here to stay.

But what does this concept cover? A number of differing interpretations exist, as formulated by sharply different and divided communities that have something to do with digital libraries.

In this paper we are concerned with education for digital libraries. Clearly, the differing interpretations of what is meant by digital library, as well as what topics or activities are covered provide necessary educational context(s) and perspective for choices and orientation from curricula to courses to topics.

The classic educational questions, asked about teaching

in all educational areas, are being asked in great many institutions in relation to digital libraries:

- Why teach digital libraries?
- What to teach about digital libraries?
- How to teach about digital libraries?

The first question relates to specification of a rationale to incorporate teaching of digital libraries in a given educational perspective, framework, curriculum, or even course there is much more to a rationale than pragmatically saying: "It is there, thus we teach."

The second question deals with selection of content from a myriad of topics from general to specific that are directly connected with digital libraries and are based on the chosen rationale. The third question gets to choices not necessarily only of pedagogy, but more importantly, of ways and means to incorporate and organize the chosen topics into given curricula, courses, and offerings.

In this paper we explore the three questions in an analytical way and with the 'real world' as a primary source. Our goal is not to be prescriptive. For the question on rationale, we briefly explore the nature and growth of different activities related to digital libraries. Their existence is forcing educational choices.

For the second question, we explore the different conceptions of digital libraries as perceived in different communities. The third question constitutes the bulk of the paper: we provide results of a survey on digital library education from a number of academic institutions, mostly, but not all, from the U.S. Based on results we discuss differing models that have emerged in the teaching of digital libraries.

This is a work in progress. We plan to continue and expand this work with further analyses, covering more institutions, disciplines, and efforts, both nationally and internationally, and present the results in comprehensive reports.

A similar survey was conducted in 1998. This report could be considered as a continuation of that effort. This is also an outgrowth of interest in teaching and research in digital libraries at our institution, the School of Communication, Information and Library Studies, Rutgers University.

A course Digital Libraries was first offered in the Fall 1998 and continues to be offered. Along with the course, we established D-Lib Edu: Resources for Education in Digital Libraries, a web-based, collaboratively constructed compendium of sources useful for education and study in this area.

Multidisciplinary research in digital libraries at Rutgers University is covered by the Rutgers Distributed Laboratory for Digital Libraries (RDLDL), involving participants from several university departments and schools, as well as others holding seminars on digital libraries covering a wide array of research topics. All of these have contributed to our thinking and work reported here.

Digital library as a concept and a reality

Digital library as a concept and a reality is defined in a number of ways; at times it is even treated as a primitive, undefined concept. In other words, there is no agreed upon definition of digital libraries. We will reflect more about this in the review of definitions in the next section.

In order to develop a rationale for teaching, we interpret digital libraries and all the associated activities in a broad sense as to encompass great many variations on two general themes of:

(i) Organizing and accessing human knowledge records in

(ii) Digital and networked environments.

More often than not, this understanding is an implicit rather than an explicit assumption in the majority of works claiming to deal with digital libraries. The first of the two underlying themes is not new, of course.

Collecting, organizing, preserving, and accessing human knowledge records were themes of many efforts from the dawn of civilizations, across time, cultures, geographic boundaries, and societies.

It is a permanent theme, because the evolution and

functioning of any advanced society is connected with creation and use of a societal memory through records. And the first theme was always connected with the second one, reflecting the technology of the time, and thus, the types of implementations over time.

The permanence of these themes and the connection to the new technology is subtly reflected and summarized in the title of a recent book about digital libraries: "From Gutenberg to the Global Information Infrastructure: Access to information in the networked world.".

The assumption is that the new digital technology and networks will affect and even revolutionize the handling of human knowledge records, and through it, the society as a whole, as much, if not more, than the technological invention symbolized under Gutenberg's name. Although it is too early to tell, this seems indeed to be the case.

Given that understanding and the advances in capabilities of digital and network technologies, it is not surprising that digital libraries draw a lot of interest. The history of digital library is short and explosive. A number of early visionaries, such as Licklider, had a notion of libraries in the future being highly innovative and different in structure, processing, and access through heavy applications of technology.

But, besides visionary and futuristic discussions and highly scattered research and developmental experimentation, nothing much happened in the next two decades. By the end of the 1980s, digital libraries (under various names) were barely a part of the landscape of librarianship, information science, or computer science. But just a decade later, by the start of 2000s, research, practical developments, and general interest in digital libraries has exploded globally. What a decade for digital libraries!

Several trends affected this digital library explosion.

- *First,* advanced societies in the Western world kept evolving into a new form variously referred to as information-, knowledge-, or post-industrial society. Managing knowledge records became an ever more important part AND problem of that evolving society, especially since the phenomenon of information explosion, the unabated growth of knowledge records of all kinds, kept accelerating.

- *Second,* the digital and networked technology reached a certain level of maturity and spread rapidly, which provided for more involved, varied, and broader opportunities and problems at the same time.
- *Third,* in most, if not all fields, the nature of scholarly communication changed drastically, creating problems and fueling exploration for new approaches for supporting and sustaining it.
- *Fourth,* substantive funding became available for research and for practical developments and explorations on a variety of solutions to these problems. Digital libraries have been embraced as one (but not the only one) of the more advanced and more encompassing conceptual and practical solutions.

The impetus for explosive growth of activities associated with digital libraries came from two sides: a wide recognition of the enumerated social and technical trends and associated problems, and more importantly, availability of substantial funding to address the problems.

The amount of funding for digital libraries in the last decade is hard to establish, however, it is in the range of several $100 millions internationally. Here are some examples as to highly diverse funding sources, illustrating at the same time a variety of efforts and approaches:

- Funding for research on digital libraries came from a variety of governmental organizations. In the U.S., digital library research is guided and even defined through the projects supported by Digital Library Initiatives (DLI). The Initiatives are funded by a consortium of government agencies under the leadership of the National Science Foundation (NSF). DLI-1 (1994-1998, ~$23 million), funded by three agencies, involved six large projects. DLI-2 (1999-

2003, ~$55 million), funded by eight agencies, involves some 60 large and small projects.

- Funding for practical developments from government and organizational sources. A major leader in the U.S. is the Library of Congress through a number of projects, such as the American Memory Project, funded by public and private funds. Many such projects are reflected in the efforts of Digital Library Federation. In the U.K. purpose of funding for the eLib projects is "to stimulate and enable the cost effective exploitation of information systems and to provide a high quality national network infrastructure for the UK higher education and research communities." A number of other European initiatives, most with practical aims, are surveyed by Raitt.
- Funding for operations from academic and public institutions. An example is our own institution, Rutgers University Libraries, which has a long range plan (as do many other universities) for academic digital libraries. Other notable examples are University of California, Berkeley Digital Library SunSITE and Oxford University, U.K. Bodley Library.
- Funding for new implementations in their realm from professional and scientific societies and subject-specific institutes. A society-based example is the Digital Library of the Association for Computing Machinery. A subject based example is the Perseus Digital Library at Tufts University.
- Funding from publishers to enter the new age of digital publications and access. An example is Elsevier Science which developed an array of resources for digital libraries and funded also exploration of various economic models.
- Funding for putting their treasures in the digital domain from historical societies, archives, and museums. An example is a collaborative effort The

Museum Educational Site Licensing project (MESL) at Cornell University (now completed).

- Funding from collaborative contributions to provide for common good in the new Internet tradition of 'free' information. An example is the Virtual Library, (Switzerland, US, UK & other countries)

Clearly, much more funds and efforts have been spent on digital libraries in great many countries and world regions, way above the few examples provided above. The Library of Congress on its web pages provides an impressive set of links to various digital libraries internationally, and so does the journal D-Lib Magazine.

These efforts produced a large number of practical developments, a considerable amount of professional experiences, a number of new practices, a score of new methodologies, many new technology-based applications, considerable research on a number of complex problems, and an evolving body of (as yet widely scattered) scholarly knowledge. All these exist and they provide choices for establishing a rationale for education in digital libraries. But the array of choices is wide.

Unfortunately, education has had little direct or organized connection with any of these rapid and substantive developments. There was little or no funding for education in digital libraries, as related to any of the multitude of the diverse activities. True, a number of research leaders in digital libraries have also been connected with some or other course in digital libraries, but the whole connection is sporadic rather than organized and systematic.

Overall, education is not a leader by any stretch of imagination, but a follower in digital libraries. Mostly, the existing rationale for digital library education, if offered at all, is reactive, meaning that education reacts with a time lag to both research and practical developments in digital libraries.

TEACH ABOUT DIGITAL LIBRARIES

The answer depends, to a large extent, on having a relatively clear idea about what are digital libraries. As mentioned, no agreed upon definition exists, which is fine, because the same constructs can be viewed from a number of viewpoints or perspectives. Let us explore some of these perspectives through definitions offered. Of course, a choice of a given perspective dictates the choice of the content.

Different perspectives about digital libraries, together with competing visions and associated definitions, come from several communities that are involved in digital library work. We are concentrating here on two communities: research and practice.

While they work and proceed independently of each other, they can be considered on two ends of a spectrum, which as yet have not met in the middle. To use another metaphor: the research and practice communities are in the same planetary system, but one is on Mars, the other on Venus.

The research community grounded mostly in computer science, on one end of the spectrum, asks research questions directed toward future vision or visions of digital libraries, or rather of their various technology oriented aspects and components, unrestricted by practice.

On the other end of the spectrum, the practice community, grounded mostly in librarianship and information science, asks developmental, operational, and use questions in real-life economic and institutional contexts, restrictions, and possibilities, concentrating on applications on the use end of the spectrum.

In research, DLIs did not define 'digital library.' In order to incorporate a wide range of possible approaches and domains, the concept is treated broadly and vaguely. Thus, the projects, particularly in DLI-2, cover a wide range of topics, stretching the possible meaning of digital library to and even beyond the limit of what can be considered as being digital and at the same time recognizable as any kind of a library or a part thereof.

This is perfectly acceptable for research frontiers need to be stretched. But at the same time, it makes choices for educational content diffuse and difficult.

The closest to the definition applicable to the approaches

taken by the research community is the one given by Lesk in the first textbook on the topic:

- "Digital libraries are *organized collections* of digital information. They combine the *structure and gathering of information*, which libraries and archives have always done, with the *digital representation* that computers have made possible." (Emphasis in this and following definitions is added to illustrate possible choices for educational content).

Arms in a newer text on digital libraries, also from a research community and technology applications perspective, provides what he calls an "informal definition:"

- "A digital library is a *managed collection* of information, with associated *services*, where the information is *stored in digital formats* and *accessible* over a *network*."

The practice community, whose majority is residing in operational libraries, concentrates on building operational digital libraries, their maintenance and operations, and providing services to users. The approach is developmental, operational, and eminently practical, with relatively little or no research involved.

As a result, hundreds, if not thousands of digital libraries have emerged worldwide, with more becoming operational every day. The efforts are diverse. Many approaches are being used. Many types of collections and media are included and processed in many different ways. Many are located in libraries, creating a hybrid library (combination of a traditional and digital library); others are not bound to brick and mortar libraries at all.

In the US, the Digital Libraries Federation (DLF) (formed in 1995) is an organization of research libraries and various national institutions. The stated goal of DLF is "to establish the conditions necessary for the creation, maintenance, expansion, and preservation of a distributed collection of digital materials accessible to scholars and the wider public." The organization represents libraries and practitioners.

After considerable deliberation, DFL agreed on a

"working definition of digital library," representing the definition of the practice community:

- Digital libraries are organizations that provide the resources, including the specialized staff, to select, structure, offer intellectual access to, interpret, distribute, preserve the integrity of, and ensure the persistence over time of collections of digital works so that they are readily and economically available for use by a defined community or set of communities.

Borgman provides a more complex definition (including an extensive discussion) of digital libraries, a definition that may be considered as a bridge between the research community definition and practical community definitions:

- Digital libraries are a set of electronic resources and associated technical capabilities for creating, searching, and using information. They are an extension and enhancement of information storage and retrieval systems that manipulate digital data in any medium The content of digital libraries includes data, [and] metadata Digital libraries are constructed, collected, and organized, by (and for) a community of users, and their functional capabilities support the information needs and uses of that community.

Following these perspectives, the content choices fall into categories that are based on: systems, networks, and technology; collection and resources in various media; representation, organization, and operability; storage and searching; functionality, access and use; institutions and services; and user communities and related applications.

The educational choices are among technology, resources, organization, access, institutions, and use, or a mix thereof. A balanced and at the same time a comprehensive mix is difficult, if not impossible, to achieve.

SURVEY OF APPLICATIONS

In order to go beyond generalities and into observation

of existing educational practices we conducted a survey. The survey consisted of two parts: a *Web survey* of curriculum and course information as posted on the sites of a number of schools and an *Email survey* of answers to invited questions posted on several listserves. We report the results of each survey separately.

Each of the survey methods has strengths and definite limitations. Deriving conclusions about the content of education of given institutions through an examination of information provided on their own Web sites is fraught with peril. It is similar to the well-known peril of examination of catalogs.

However, Web listings are more current and inclusive; they provide, by and large, much more information than catalog listings, up to inclusion of syllabi; and they are updated more often. As a rule, general email surveys have a small rate of self-selected returns.

But the answers tend to be specific to the questions. Both surveys complement each other. The methodology was considered appropriate for a general (rather than detailed) assessment of the emerging approaches to what is taught and how these approaches are positioned in the existing teaching practice.

Web Survey

Method

In the first part we examined the Web sites of 56 accredited programs listed in the directory of the Association of Library and Information Science Education (ALISE) as found on their web site.

The schools housing these programs are generally known as schools of library and information science (LIS), but in reality a good number of them have changed from this designation to several classes of different names. For brevity, we will use the LIS label for the programs.

The accreditation is by the American Library Association (ALA) and covers the professional degree programme on the master's level. It does *not* cover doctoral or undergraduate education, offered by a number of these schools. Geographically, it covers schools in North America the U.S. and Canada. Thus in this part no other countries were included.

We looked at course titles, course descriptions and syllabi when available. In line with the broad definition of digital libraries (or lack of definition) as discussed above, we cast the net widely. We concentrated on courses where *digital libraries* or *digital librarianship* were mentioned as a term, but we also included courses that used synonymous concepts, exemplified by terms such as *electronic library*, or *library of the future*; we also included *virtual museums*, as having a strong connection with digital libraries.

On a broader level, we included courses that mention processes that are closely related to digital libraries, such as management and preservation of electronic records, electronic text design, metadata for digital collections, production of network multimedia, designing accessible web based materials, and electronic text.

Finally, on the broadest level we included courses that are oriented toward *information technology* and address the technological bases of digital libraries, such as *network architecture, managing networks, digital tool kits, Internet applications*, and the like. We used these gradations and distinctions as tools for classification as incorporated in tables below.

Inclusion

Of the 56 LIS programs, 47 (89%) include digital library in some form or another or to some degree in their curriculum; for 5 (9%) programs, this cannot be determined and 4 (7%) programs show no presence of digital library education.

This analysis shows that digital library education is included in the curriculum of most LIS programs. However, the degree of inclusion varies widely. When considered closely, the inclusion ranges from a full course or courses on digital libraries to metadata standards being covered in organization of information courses to cases in which digital library focus is relegated to continuing education. Participation of the students in a local digital library project is another way of including the digital library topics within LIS education.

Integration

To what degree are digital library courses offered as independent or full-blown courses? To what degree are digital library topics integrated in other courses? Table addresses these questions.

Table. Course Integration in Digital Library Education in ALA-accredited Library and Information Science Programs. (N=47 Programs that Include Digital Library Education from 56 Accredited Programs).

Digital library content in relation to the curriculum	No. of LIS programs
1. Independent DL courses	15 (32%)
2. Combination of independent DL course and DL content integrated in other courses	8 (17%)
3. DL content integrated in other courses (without independent DL courses)	23 (49%)
4. Other (DL content integrated with continuing education)	1 (2%)

Note: Two major types of courses are

- Tndependent digital library courses (typically titled "Digital Libraries" or a similar version), and
- Digital library content integrated in other courses.

As shown in Table, half of the schools have significant digital library content in the curriculum. They include schools with specialized digital library courses on the books; we call these independent courses, although we cannot tell to what degree these are also segregated courses, with little or no connection to the rest of the curriculum.

Such an independent course is either an elective or special topics course offered either as the only course with digital library content in the school's programme or a course offered in addition to other digital library topics that appears elsewhere in the curriculum.

The other half of the schools have some level of digital library content integrated in their programme, but no course specifically focusing on digital libraries. The programs that integrate digital library topics in their courses vary in the level of inclusion and strategies for inclusion.

LIS programs

LIS programs at the masters level are *professional* programs; this defines the context for digital library education in such schools. An examination of digital library course descriptions from Web sites reflects that education for digital librarianship in many cases does not reflect a systematic view or programme of education. Presumably, digital library content is simply an acknowledgment of an emerging field of practice and institutional realities. Even schools with a full course devoted to the problem area of digital libraries show variation in their approaches.

The courses offered under the umbrella term 'digital libraries' range from theoretical and survey courses to project-focused courses. Some are broader and some narrow in focus. A combination of theory (highlighting multiple facets of digital library research) and application (giving an overview of existing practices and providing hands-on experience) seem not to be practiced in such courses.

Weighing one against the other, theory against hands-on experience, it seems that theoretical and survey courses provide a more flexible framework to be expanded with an on-the-job training and apprenticeship in the changing digital library practical environment. An ideal would be the integration of practice-based with survey and theory-based approach to digital library education.

As mentioned, we have been inclusive rather than exclusive in defining what constitutes integrated content. We have considered courses in networking, topics in telecommunications, metadata standards, courses integrating topics on the preservation of electronic-born information as integrating digital library content and digital libraries as developmental form in the history of knowledge records and therefore contributing to digital library education.

In many cases, from brief course descriptions and sparse online syllabi, the degree to which digital library problems were truly addressed is not always clear. In our conservative estimate, in more than half of the schools.

The degree of inclusion cannot be determined with certainty with the methodology used here. The question is whether information technology course addressing the *'library of the future,'* a course dealing with social roles of information organization that includes traditional and digital libraries, archives, network architecture, or the concern with 'structures, processes, dynamics and applications that determine the effective use of motion imagery in multimedia, on-line, and other digital media,' all relate to the problem area of digital libraries.

Together, the approaches represent a pandemonium typical of the general uncertainty toward digital library education. The choices result from an undisciplined mix of the pressures of the libraries as market for graduates, ten years of research and development in the area of digital libraries, and varying degrees of faculty expertise and perceptions of what constitutes a meaningful approach. Multiple and often overlapping approaches in different schools are symptomatic of that general uncertainty.

Because the schedule and frequency of offering is a determinant of impact of specific courses or a mix of courses on digital library education in specific LIS programs, clearly one cannot make sweeping statements. Several schools that integrate digital library content into other courses, or offer courses that do not have digital libraries in their title but focus on the creation of distributed electronic repositories of information, are taking an integrated rather than independent approach.

The "independent" (segregated) vs. "integrated" approach and the "combined independent with integrated" approaches reveal an underlying philosophy of digital library education. Integration is the ideal, but it may suffer from superficiality. Segregation is also fraught with peril of a different sort of offering a view of compartmentalized technology.

A smaller fraction offers a combination of independent and integrated approach to digital library education (17 per cent). There may be a number of reasons for this, one of which may be a reflection of competing perspectives within a given programme. We did not detect that any school has a organized course of study in digital libraries, such as a specialization or track.

Email Survey

We also invited email answers to a list of questions posted on several listserves oriented toward audiences as individuals (rather then institutions) in different areas.

They included: listserve JESSE in library science, the member list of the American Society for Information Science and Technology (ASIST), listserve of the Special Interest Group on Information Retrieval, Association for Computing Machinery (ACM SIGIR), listserve of the Humanist Discussion Group, and ETEXT-L.

We sought answers to the following questions:

- Does your institution offer course(s), seminars or institutes in digital libraries and/or related areas? If so, please provide as much information as possible, particularly including URLs.
- Does your institution teach digital library topics within (or as a part of) other courses, seminars, or institutes? If so, please provide as much information as possible, particularly including URLs.
- In what department or school are the digital library course(s) offered?

- On what level undergraduate, graduate, doctoral, professional development?

While the listserves reach great many recipients, we received only a total of 27 responses, of these 20 were relevant. The small number of responses was very disappointing, but then responses to general surveys are always low. We know that in reality there are many more programs and courses related to digital libraries, and that this is but a very small sample. We cannot tell how representative it is. Still it is worthwhile to analyse this sample.

Given the nature of the sample and the size of the returns, about all that could safely be concluded is that there is an interesting and broadening array of disciplines other than LIS in which digital library courses are being taught and such courses are at a variety of levels, undergraduate and graduate.

Digital Libraries Taught

To answer the question on how were digital libraries taught we did not look at pedagogy. Instead, we have looked at broader issues: How did various programs address the basic and connecting areas for digital library education?

What models have emerged? This illuminates the contexts of digital library education within the programs; more specifically it shows area clusters where digital library education has gravitated.

Method

Here we deal only with 47 ALA accredited LIS programs that have presence in digital library education to some degree or other. We undertook a detailed examination of presented curricula, course descriptions, syllabi, and other information as provided.

The level of available information differs greatly from programme to programme, thus our conclusions are only as good as the information available on the programs' Web sites. The analysis is qualitative, with all the strengths and weaknesses of such methods.

In a grounded theory approach, we derived classes from

data, and then grouped the data in these classes. Subjective? Of course. But the derivative approach also enables to show clusters in the greater body of data, which are otherwise not visible. To provide consistency, we applied the same analysis criteria to all programs.

Results

We identified several dimensions or models of digital library education emerging in the programs examined. Various approaches that LIS programs are taking in conceptualizing the digital library education, with regard to areas of application. Of the 47 LIS programs that were identified as including digital library education in their programs, six have digital library content contained within a single course, one programme shows digital library content to be integrated across the curriculum; and for six programs we could not determine the area of application.

The derived classification is divided in two classes. The first or general class identifies four broad areas of application, i.e. the general domain of emphasis and orientation for digital library education that could be identified as predominant in a given programme.

These are:

- T-tools (technologies and technology based processes);
- Environments (the context in which digital libraries operate),
- Objects (representation, structure and life cycle of documents in various formats), and
- Combined (several areas of applications present without any one being distinctive).

The second, or specific class, identifies perspectives within the broad areas. It shows a more detailed or specific orientation of programs.

In the perspectives the'basic' and'advanced' tools refer to the level of technological sophistication. The'compartm-entalized' approach is one in which digital library is conceived as a contained phenomenon.

These models show how digital library education is conceptualized and focused within a particular programme. The approaches are not exclusive and many schools combine several of these approaches. We presume that this is either as a result of competing discourses within the schools themselves or because of the uncertainty that the notion of digital library entails.

EXAMPLES

The following schools have been identified as representing the various emerging approaches to digital library education:

University of British Columbia

School of Library, Archival, and Information Studies (Vancouver, British Columbia) combines an approach through digital continuity with tools (multimedia authoring) approach. Although there is no identification of digital library as such, a number of courses deal with metadata standards and include courses which address the status of digitally-born information and the role of digital libraries in managing cultural heritage.

University of California, Los Angeles

Department of Library and Information Science reveals a combination of approaches focusing on tools, administration, standards, and preservation.

Florida State University

School of Information Studies (Tallahassee, FL) reveals (within a compartmentalized approach) an interesting multidisciplinary perspective on digital library design.

University of Illinois

Graduate School of Library and Information Science (Champaign, IL) introduces a combination of museum informatics and more traditional approaches to digital library education, including courses in electronic text creation. Some focus is on content within a museum informatics course and project-oriented coursework.

The information technology is introduced at the undergraduate level, and electronic text design on the graduate level. The focus is on project-based learning and application, accessibility, and electronic publishing. The content and structured text approach is combined with an advanced tools approach.

Kent State University

School of Library and Information Science (Kent, OH) presents an interesting case in that the graduate school offerings and continuing education offering reveal a completely opposite approach.

While the first is a traditional programme, various continuing education topics introducing metadata for digital collections with courses on XML and content management. This is a tools-approach that is segregated into continuing education programme.

University of Michigan

School of Information (Ann Arbor, MI) is by far the most developed programme of study for digital librarianship. It combines practical and skill-based programme with a focus on advanced tools, content, format migration, digital continuity, the digital library as community building agency, and even an emerging theoretical approach that identifies the general laws of infrastructure development with attention to differing national cultural styles of structuring of knowledge.

One of the strengths of this programme is that it does not single out one route, such as found in other instances, when it is combined with tools approach. The education for digital libraries combines proficiencies with critical analysis of digital library as cultural form.

The technological proficiency courses are included in the Digital Tool Kit module; advanced proficiencies are included in graduate coursework. In addition, a number of digital library courses explore specialized areas related to digital libraries.

This school is defining the emerging area of digital

libraries through its curriculum. An important component of teaching is related to research and development. It may be useful to ask what is not included in this developed programme? The archival aspects are present but not overwhelmingly.

While usability is included in the information infrastructures general course, use and user studies focus is not obvious. There is no evidence of representational (metadata) aspects of digital libraries but this may be due to the limitation of website analysis as data collection tool.

The traditional library organizational aspects and issues of access are weak in conceptualizing digital library education at Michigan, in spite of its bursting innovative energy with focus on social informatics.

Université de Montréal (Ude M)

École de bibliothéconomie et des Sciences de l'Information (Montréal, Québec, Canada) is one of the programs that addresses important theoretical aspects in which digital library education is conceptualized through a focus on structured documents which, for example, is lacking in the otherwise strong Michigan approach.

This school includes technological proficiency courses (tools-approach) to continuing education and probably computer science. The strength in document representation, usability of systems for document presentation, and organization of information in general as well as information retrieval is a definite strength in this programme that could serve as a model for development of other programs.

University of North Texas

School of Library and Information Sciences (Denton, TX) is unique in building the concept of digital library from the context of networked environment. One may identify this as syntetico-analytic approach, which does not start with the digital library as an isolated phenomenon but focuses on indirect effects of that phenomenon.

It is invoked as a process of cultural transformation in the social environment of information work which is dependent on technology.

University of Pittsburgh,

School of Information Sciences (Pittsburgh, PA) combines an integrated approach with focus on document structure, digital preservation, and digitizing library and archival research collections for access, as well as introduction to SGML/XML standards, usability studies of digital libraries, and other topics.

University of Rhode Island

Graduate School of Library and Information Studies (Kingston, RI) reveals an interesting attempt to integrate digital library technology through an understanding of media perception and interpreting the emerging environments of the digital libraries in terms of development of new visual media.

This programme presents a departure from tools approach often practiced as a response to market pressures. All programs might not have resources to offer special courses in digital libraries or those that are developing a specialization track (such as Pittsburgh with the focus on the archival aspects) or a full-blown programme like Michigan's.

The approach taken by this school may be narrow in focus, but it also reveals an interesting aspect often neglected in other approaches to digital library education, focusing on visual information.

Rutgers University

Department of Library and Information Science (New Brunswick, NJ) provides access to digital library education through a master's level courses including a regular offering of digital libraries course as one of the central courses within the information systems theme, with specialization courses including organization of information and multimedia production.

Rutgers Distributed Laboratory for Digital Libraries (RDLDL) enables doctoral student participation in university-wide interdisciplinary programme of research. The new undergraduate programme in Information Technology and Informatics will provide a new context for digital library education.

University of California, Berkeley

School of Information Management and Systems provides a model for digital library education closely tied to research and development, especially through its Digital Library seminar series. The LIS programs focus primarily on the interpretation of research and development coming out of the computer science community to fit the LIS discourse.

In many cases, this means repositioning the digital library within established social purposes of LIS programs. Berkeley, while it symbolically repositioned itself outside of these approaches by not seeking ALA accreditation, expands the problems related to digital environments beyond but not excluding the library settings.

In this model, the functioning of a system is a dominant component of the curriculum. The content component is hidden and so are the human agents and digital library as social and cultural agency.

At this point, we may agree with David Levy's statement from his keynote address to the ACM Digital Libraries'99 conference in which he pointed that "the current digital library agenda has largely been set by computer science community and clearly bears the imprint of this community's interests and vision."

In our survey, the focus on tools and information technology that underlies the tools approach identified as the prevailing one among the LIS programs in their approach to integrating digital library content in education shows the traces of this agenda.

Levy identifies the omissions from the agenda of the first decade of digital library research and development in the area of attention to preservation. Related to this is our finding that although an emerging model as seen in Michigan, the University of British Columbia, and Pittsburgh, focuses on various aspects of preservation, there is a relative absence of attention to content.

In LIS programs, the current educational approach for digital library education places it within information technology context. This is not surprising because digital library is easily interpreted to epitomize the promises of technology and progress, an acceptable ideological position in LIS programs.

Integration of digital library education in the context of foundations, knowledge representation, and archives is not surprising either. It is driven by the concerns of research and practice communities. The schools with least developed programs of digital library education (as indicated by the number of courses offered) typically contain this education within information technology or foundations context.

However, there are alternative homes for digital library education with no connection whatsoever with LIS programs. Our email survey provided a glimpse only. They reside in: departments of computer science, medical informatics (Oregon); and at the University of Virginia, in the new Master's Degree in Digital Humanities.

In particular, computer science departments provide a strong educational component through research in digital libraries. Our survey did not reach that area. However the degree of involvement of the computer science community with digital libraries is huge.

We can see that from even a cursory examination of the programs of the First ACM/IEEE-CS Joint Conference on Digital Libraries and the predecessor conferences on Digital Libraries organized separately by the two societies. In hundreds of presentations given at these conferences, overwhelming numbers were from computer science faculty. This must be reflected in educational offerings, formal or informal at their institutions.

Digital library education in the two areas, library and information science on the one hand and computer science on the other, do not have any relation that we can see.

This exactly follows the practice of development and

operation of digital libraries in library institutions on the one hand, and the research in digital libraries as funded by programs identified in the section on rationale, on the other hand. While they are in the same planetary system, one is from Venus and the other from Mars.

Now to the'big' picture: The problem of purpose of digital libraries, seen in the communications' circuit of creation, organization, distribution, preservation and use of knowledge records and knowledge itself, needs to be considered in digital library education. This includs an attention to the societal purposes of digitally available information.

If we are to have:

- Collections with "associated services", persistent collections of digital works "readily and economically available for use by a defined community or set of communities"(cf. definition of Digital Libraries Federation (DLF)), or collections "constructed, collected and organized, by (and for) a community of users,"and functional capabilities of digital libraries to "support the information needs and uses of that community", then digital library education needs to spend more time on understanding the collections, usability of current digital libraries, and their social and cultural purposes.

As yet, library education does not really deal with the questions such as:

- What is the digital library made for?
- What is the meaning of collection in a digital library context?
- What issues are faced in access? How are digital libraries used?
- Should and could be used?
- How are they evaluated?
- What are the effects on the communities of users and their tasks?

Or "Digital Rights Management:

- What Does This Mean For Libraries?

"(This is the title of the keynote address at the Digital Libraries conference by Pamela Samuelson, Professor of Information Management and of Law, UC Berkeley). These issues are above and beyond the technology and they need to be included in education in some detail. We suggest that digital library education does require integrated and comprehensive programs and attention of its own.

If we accept Levy's assessment, research and development community and those involved in the education for digital libraries suffer from the same lack of purpose. Moreover, it might be expected that as the field develops, that there will be less compartmentalization and more integration of all approaches with what we have identified here as tools approach. The educational needs differ significantly from education for library and information science proper or computer science proper.

Education for digital libraries is a complex proposition, in part because it involves so many layers of technology and at the same time so much that is new in creation, content, representation, organization, access, and use, and in social, legal, and cultural issues. The importance of paying attention to digital library education lies in this: as all other areas, the quality of education will eventually determine the quality of the whole enterprise.

Chapter 10

Digital Library from "Project" to "Production"

The author explores the characteristics of a production digital library operation. He suggests that for digital libraries to mature, production organizations must be developed and that these production organizations must have certain characteristics.

These production digital library operations must:

- Be fully integrated into their parent organizations;
- Have moved beyond a focus on "projects" to one of deploying and supporting classes of systems;
- Reflect a high level of investment consistent with the institutional mission;
- Undertake *long-term* maintenance and development of the collections and access systems they support.

Using as his example the University of Michigan Digital Library Production Service, Price-Wilkin examines production organizations and explores three areas of collection support that exemplify these characteristics.

Digital libraries are in a period of exploration and rapid development. While our sense of what they are or should become varies, for the sake of this discussion we assume a definition consistent with that articulated by Don Waters, the Director of the Digital Library Federation:

Digital libraries are organizations that provide the resources, including the specialized staff, to select, structure, offer intellectual access to, distribute, preserve the integrity of, and ensure the persistence over time of collections of digital works so that they are readily and economically available for use by a defined community or set of communities.

While experimentation and research are essential to the development of effective digital libraries, it is ultimately formally defined and institutionally supported *organizations* that will ensure the viability of digital collections.

Wendy Lougee, the University of Michigan's digital library programme director, has suggested that we can apply a kind of human developmental model to the four distinct stages of digital library development, beginning with Infancy and culminating in Maturity.

Infancy is marked by learning through projects. Projects not only facilitate learning, but test resistance to ideas, find opportunities and resources and barriers, and eventually create stable building blocks. In Adolescence, we see peer modeling and the exploration of best practices: here, the digital library has begun to look outward both to other institutions, but also to methods and formats that will ensure longevity and interoperability.

The third stage of development, which she calls the digital library as Young Adult, is where we find the organizations that I wish to explore in this paper.

In this stage of development, we find an increasing focus on collaboration, especially for the establishment of standards and architectures for interoperability. Maturity is marked by the presence of a fully functioning digital society, a market economy, and rich collaboration and knowledge environm ents such as those found in UARC.

The relatively intense focus on digital libraries in the last few years has resulted in a handful of well-developed production support organizations. Although experimentation for materials such as video continues to be important, these organizations have all successfully moved beyond the early stages marked by projects, work in isolation, and developing support for basic formats and methods.

In fact, these stable digital library production organizations exhibit a new set of characteristics that are an important part of their productivity and livelihood.

- They are not only engaged with the digital library community, but are fully integrated into their larger organizations (such as university libraries).
- These relatively mature organizations have moved beyond a focus on "projects" to a mode where they are deploying and supporting classes of systems—systems into which more content can be added.
- The production organizations reflect a high level of investment by the larger institutions in which they are situated. This investment is consistent with a recognition by the institution that the digital library is critical to its mission.
- Finally, and significantly, these organizations undertake *open-ended* maintenance and development of the collections and access systems they support. While it is a certainty that the methods and strategies for maintenance will evolve, setting a term on the duration of responsibility for a collection can only contribute to a process of trivializing the collections of the digital library: these digital library collections are, in effect, our perpetual responsibility.

The University of Michigan's Digital Library Production Service is an operation that exhibits these characteristics. The discussion that follows is one that attempts to illustrate the value of these characteristics by exploring the organization of DLPS and three model systems that it uses to provide a high degree of functionality and cost-effectiveness in building the digital library.

BACKGROUND

The Digital Library Production Service is part of a larger University of Michigan Digital Library Initiative, led by one of the University Library's three Associate Directors. The catalyst for the UM Digital Library Initiative was the 1991 Information Symposium, an effort to address campus issues with regard to networked information.

That Information Symposium, involving a broad cross-section of the University faculty, culminated with a number of recommendations.

The campus should attempt to:

- Bring together library and technology expertise
- Develop visible projects
- Create an "Information Community" (i.e., principles of access and support)

Eventually, in support of these goals, the heads of the three principal information organizations on campus, the Information Technology Division, the School of Information, and the University Library, committed joint funding for a Digital Library Initiative. This funding included support for the creation of a programme director position and funding for projects that would have campus impact.

Even this commitment was situated in a set of larger accomplishments, which allowed the formalization of goals for campus digital library initiatives. Prior to the Information Symposium, the University Library had begun to embark on some preliminary and perhaps formative efforts to build digital library components.

Wide area access to non-bibliographic information sources-i.e., to the data themselves, rather than metadata-became a focal effort of the University Library in the late 1980's. The University of Michigan Library put in place a modest programme of support for statistical data files, began exploring delivery of GIS data, and then ultimately put in place a formal access system for text encoded in SGML. The Library had begun to build systems for storing and accessing library collections in electronic formats.

After the Information Symposium, beginning in 1992, the University Library undertook a number of initiatives that laid the groundwork for future work and future relationships. Some of these, like the Library's Gopher server, were unremarkable in their use of technology, but played important roles in information provision and partnerships.

Others, like the UM implementation of TULIP, put in place significant pieces of infrastructure that would later prove instrumental in the University's development of digital libraries. The Library's Gopher server was remarkable in at least one respect, its aggressive approach to putting collection material online. Although it had previously undertaken similar efforts prior to Gopher, the new mechanism allowed Library staff to mount collections like statistical information from the Commerce Department in ways that reached extremely broad audiences.

The strong presence of the Library's Gopher on campus also contributed to early cooperative efforts with the University's computing organization, ITD. TULIP's contributions were even more profound, if less visible. Although Michigan's was one of several Elsevier TULIP implementations, at the University of Michigan TULIP spawned a development effort that saw the creation of FTL, the search engine now used by JSTOR, and tif2gif, Doug Orr's optimized GIF generator for TIFF G4 images, now used by the University of Michigan Making of America system.

A broad, campus-wide partnership has played a powerful role in moving the concept of digital libraries forward at the University of Michigan. As mentioned earlier, the Library's Gopher project played an important role in establishing a partnership between the University of Michigan's Library and the Information Technology Division.

Like Gopher, the TULIP effort contributed to bringing the Library together with another campus entity, the School of Information. These partnerships were formalized in 1993, and Wendy Lougee was appointed the director of campus-wide digital library efforts. That partnership is a powerful presence today in the University of Michigan's digital library work, with management and advisory committees composed of representatives from each of the organizations, and multi-organizational funding for initiatives.

A number of significant UM digital library efforts began in 1994. Among these is the now organizationally independent JSTOR, which grew rapidly in size and scope, and now plays an important role in shaping our expectations about archiving and retrospective conversion.

Another major initiative appearing in 1994 was the UM Humanities Text Initiative, which served to expand the earlier UMLibText effort and provide a significant WWW presence for the University's SGML-based text collections. Also appearing in 1994 was the University of Michigan's NSF/ NASA/ARPA-funded digital library effort, focusing not on production technologies, but on the role of agent technologies and distribution of responsibility for the digital library.

The breadth of these 1994 initiatives provides some indication of the fruitfulness and variety of the evolving environment at Michigan. This growing proliferation of significant digital library activities—activities that had moved well beyond the "experimental" and had begun to reach wide audiences—that contributed most to the recognition of a need for a digital library production organization. Between 1994 and 1996, while the activities mentioned above continued to grow, new efforts at Michigan were introduced, and along with them new models and formats.

Among the significant efforts undertaken were UM's local image system developed for the Museum Education Site Licensing Project (MESL), the UM Making of America development, and negotiation of the Elsevier journal content that would later go into the PEAK system. These initiatives will be discussed in greater detail later, but they brought to the digital library environment at Michigan a variety of significant new elements.

Not only were new formats or methods introduced (continuous tone images in the case of MESL, and preservation-oriented monograph conversion in the case of MOA), but several of these efforts helped to highlight the absence of a formally defined organization to support the effort. In 1996, the partnership's support expanded and the resources were identified to create a digital library production service.

FORMATION OF DLPS

Origins

The University of Michigan Digital Library Production Service was formed in 1996 through a commitment of resources from the four organizations then guiding the campus Digital Library Initiative. The Information Technology Division allocated a substantial sum from its personnel budget (and many early DLPS staff were hired from ITD).

The newly formed Media Union, home to the University's advanced and robust Computer-Aided Engineering Network (CAEN) computing organization, provided DLPS with hardware and software, staff support for hardware, and use of a climate-controlled facility with around-the-clock support. The School of Information and the University Library provided a combination of staffing, hardware, and space (as well as funds for renovation of the space).

Additionally, the University Library fully funded all digital collections and most of resources necessary for creation of new materials. Formed from resources from the four organizations, DLPS works with each to ensure that it is meeting the goals set out by each. For example, DLPS supports major collections used by faculty and students in Schools and Colleges programmatically linked to the Media Union.

DLPS was established with clearly defined areas of responsibility. Not only would it provide long-term support to the growing array of production digital library operations (e.g., the Humanities Text Initiative) at the University of Michigan, but it would undertake a process of articulating and implementing a number of higher level goals.

DLPS was made responsible for defining near-term digital library architectures for the campus, primarily refining those mechanisms it had already put in place, and extending them to create a more fully integrated environment.

Similarly, it would work to take lessons learned in previous efforts to define appropriate document or data structures for the digital library. This goal was seen as essential for ensuring that our investments made in digitization would have enduring value.

DLPS was also made responsible for application development and maintenance in those primary areas of responsibility (e.g., bitonal page image systems, continuous tone colour image systems, and encoded text systems).

As new formats such as video evolve, it is expected that DLPS will take responsibility for them as well. Finally, DLPS was charged with responsibility for basic operations such as data loading, and ensuring that servers and software have appropriate levels of maintenance.

INTEGRATION INTO THE LIBRARY AND RELATED ORGANIZATIONS

The University of Michigan Digital Library Production Service was *not* intended to operate self-sufficiently, in isolation of the contributing organizations. There are important ties to each of the other organizations, and especially the University Library.

For example, DLPS relies on the Information Technology Division and the Media Union to provide a high level of computing support, which those organizations view as critical and enabling infrastructure. The services are provided in a manner consistent with the mission of the digital library (e.g., uninterrupted support for servers, as well as unique security and operating system configurations), ensuring that DLPS staff are devoted to building and maintaining digital library collections, rather than the hardware on which they reside.

Mainstream Library staff members provide an array of services critical to the operation of the digital library. Public service staff members provide user support for online collections, as well as end-user instruction.

Collection development staff members are responsible for selecting digital collections for local deployment and work with DLPS staff on "E-Teams" to weigh the advantages and disadvantages of alternative means of delivery. Preservation staff, with guidance from DLPS, make determinations of the most appropriate means of digital capture, and then prepare the materials for digital capture (occasionally operating equipment for the actual capture).

Mainstream Cataloging staff members create descriptive metadata for locally-converted materials, and specialized digital metadata specialists in the Cataloging Department help guide DLPS in decision-making for mapping between standards, display of bibliographic elements, and related issues.

Similarly, DLPS maintains important relationships with other areas of the Library, including the Library Systems Office, Acquisitions, and Special Collections. Although DLPS staff members have responsibilities that touch on all of these areas of library operation, the intention of this design is to ensure that the most qualified staff member performs each task; the intention is *not* to recreate the Library within DLPS. Consequently, DLPS is fully integrated into the entire Library operation.

MISSION

Like its staffing, the goals of the Digital Library Production Service are more specific than the larger organizations within which it exists, including those of the campus-wide Digital Library Initiative.

The campus-wide DLI has responsibility for creating a collaborative organization and a coherent environment for networked information, whether locally-maintained or held remotely. Further, the DLI has a broader mission in its responsibility to explore, for example, economic and policy issues for the campus and beyond.

By contrast DLPS' responsibilities are constrained to information that is held locally (either at the University of Michigan, or at other institutions where we are assisting in implementations). It is responsible for designing, creating, and maintaining the mechanisms needed to deliver library information via networked mechanisms. Where possible, DLPS works to provide coherence to distributed activities on campus, typically by federating collections "owned" by organizations outside the Library.

It is important to note that DLPS respects the autonomy of those collections, offering incentives to join in federation and ensuring (where possible) that those collections can be accessed independently through mechanisms supported by DLPS.

Also part of this larger goal is DLPS' responsibility to articulate an "information architecture" for the campus in ways that position the University to participate in inter-institutional cooperative activities. To this end, for example, DLPS has been active in a number of national and international digital library initiatives.

STAFFING

Staffing in DLPS has grown with its accomplishments. Initial staffing was set at levels necessary to provide a baseline of commitment to all of these areas, with growth expected for new formats and for extending DLPS' commitment to issues such as cross-collection/format integration.

In 1998, the University's Provost made arguments on behalf of the Library's budget request, allowing both a consolidation and an extension of funding for DLPS. Currently, DLPS is approximately twenty full-time equivalent (FTE) staff (with only two FTE in partial and student appointments). As of early 1999, there are four primary areas of DLPS:

- Two areas within DLPS are *format-specific,* with responsibility for complex and specialized decisions surrounding the selection of formats, their application, related online implementation issues, and long-term support for these formats. Currently, these two areas are encoded text (SGML and XML) and continuous tone imaging. Chris Powell, the coordinator of the Humanities Text Initiative, has responsibility for the first of these areas, and has staff and resources to ensure that texts are created in appropriate ways and that collections are mounted effectively. John Weise, the coordinator of Image Services, has responsibility for continuous tone imaging, and similarly has staff and resources for creation and conversion, as well as online systems.
- The third area within DLPS is a relatively large and well-integrated Systems Group. The programmers within this group work in close cooperation with the service coordinators (above) to ensure that systems are created to effectively support online access to collections in these and other areas. All systems are built through a team effort, drawing on staff from

across the organization, and especially those within the Systems Group. Many progra-mmers within the Systems Group have areas of specialization, including (for example) SGML and XML. This ensures a high degree of technical *and* format understanding in building the online systems.

- The fourth area within DLPS is an "infrastructure" group, including staff members who provide services that touch on most areas of DLPS operations. For example, a DLPS Interface Specialist is responsible for working with implementation teams to perform a functional "needs assessment" for each system, and then to design and evaluate the interface for that system. Also in this group are staff members who perform data loading and technical support for DLPS staff. This group is led by an assistant head of DLPS, who also has as a major responsibility for DLPS "data" management. This critical area provides an integrative oversight role for data creation and management, giving attention to questions such as what data elements are captured, where are they stored, and how can we ensure effective migration of data.

A fifth area of DLPS is the NEH-funded Middle English Compendium operation. The MEC staff members have responsibility for converting and encoding the monumental *Middle English Dictionary*, and creating the complex and authoritative HyperBibliography of Middle English Prose and Verse. The MEC, online at http://www.hti.umich.edu/mec/ represents a major effort in Middle English philology, and intends one day to add a large body of encoded text primary sources from the period.

Although the future of the MEC is still uncertain, we are hopeful that it will generate sufficient revenue to support the ongoing extension of the resources it includes.

COLLECTIONS

Currently, DLPS manages collections in three principal

areas: bitonal page images (typically with raw text to facilitate retrieval), encoded text with or without associated bitonal page images, and continuous tone image collections.

Within each of these areas are book and journal collections, and a variety of art, architecture, and artifact images. Including the pages in the PEAK collection (Elsevier journals), DLPS manages approximately eight million pages of books, journals, and reference materials online.

In 1999-2000, we will add to this approximately 2.3 million page images as part of a monograph conversion project using titles in our Buhr Storage facility, as well as several million more pages of journal material. Particularly under the aegis of the Humanities Text Initiative, approximately three million pages managed by DLPS are encoded text.

Most of this material is historical literature (fiction, poetry, philosophy, and other prose), but a significant portion of the SGML/XML material is also reference works such as the *Middle English Dictionary*. Image Services manages a diverse body of materials, ranging from high resolution images of papyri from the University of Michigan Papyrology collection, rare books and manuscripts, archeological objects from the Kelsey Museum of Archeology, and art and architecture images from several campus and off-campus organizations.

In all, it contains approximately 25,000 images, and 100,000 descriptive records for visual resource materials. It is important to note that though these resources are nearly without comparison in the digital library community, the size of these collections-approximately 1,200 journals and 20,000 monographic titles -they pale in comparison to the large research library.

ECONOMIES OF SCALE

The size and array of resources within the University of Michigan Digital Library Production Service creates significant economies of scale, making many processes less expensive and ensuring the availability of resources to systems or activities that might not otherwise have them.

We are able to capitalize on investments such as

expensive search engines (or "free" search engines that are expensive to support), using them for a variety of projects ranging considerably in size. Some examples of these sorts of economies are:

- *"Persistent" URLs*: The Internet still lacks a dominant and successful model for creating URNs, leaving digital library production organizations with a need to invent and sustain interim methods. At DLPS, these methods (based on CGI-accessible database mechanisms) are elaborated once for each type of system supported by DLPS, and are then used subsequently as collections are added.
- *Internet commerce and authentication*: Investments in methods for authentication and commerce are ultimately necessary for organizations of this sort. At DLPS, we have used several methods for per-item commerce transactions, including credit card transactions, and use Oracle databases for multi-institution authentication in the PEAK system. These mechanisms, along with SSL, are available as part of other systems or collections that DLPS builds.
- *Tools and methods*: Like the resources needed for authentication, many specialized and often expensive tools are needed for digital library support. Search engines and compression/decompression tools for on-the-fly conversion are just two examples. DLPS uses tools such as tif2gif, CPC, and wavelet compression are used in a variety of systems as dictated by need and format.
- *Expertise in complex areas*: Skills in challenging areas such as SGML/XML or support for SQL databases are an important commodity, and building a production organization by "leasing" such expertise is not realistic when the systems of access or management depend so fundamentally on them. DLPS has benefited from these sorts of investments, especially in SGML/XML skills and in imaging (formats, colour, and metadata).

DLPS ARCHETYPES: SYSTEMS, NOT PROJECTS

The University of Michigan Digital Library Production Service is working to define classes of systems, and to put in place mechanisms to support these classes. These systems represent archetypes, and each collection is assessed to determine whether and how it might fit existing systems.

We are careful not to *force* a particular body of material to fit one of the existing systems, but when it is possible, we are able to achieve those previously mentioned economies of scale much more effectively. This approach also results in other significant advantages.

- By approaching support for the digital library in this way, we are able to draw on significant format expertise within DLPS.
- We are able to deploy collections in an environment of ongoing support and planning. Each class represents a model or framework for continuing expansion rather than a standalone system that could be orphaned.
- DLPS staff members are able to participate more effectively in national or regional cooperative efforts, sharing models and expertise. These larger efforts enrich DLPS efforts at the same time that DLPS contributes to the larger digital library community.

As we continue development of these classes, we are frequently able to see opportunities for consolidation or expansion. A powerful example of this refinement process was encountered in 1998.

The HTI, in cooperation with SGML Systems, deployed each new collection in its native SGML encoding, re-using access mechanisms previously developed wherever possible. Although DLPS principles of re-use were in wide evidence, the large number of legacy systems for text collections had become a significant problem when we wanted to add new features.

Each new feature assumed a foundation of code that may or may not be in existence, depending on when the collection was put online. A strategy was articulated for encoding all such collections in a common format, and building a single piece of code to provide all of the functionality needed for all of the text collections.

If the collection was predominantly drama and HTI wished to provide searching on speakers and speeches, this subroutine would be invoked; otherwise, in cases where it was inappropriate to the collection (or speaker and speech were not encoded), speaker/speech searching would not be made available.

The approach was christened GUMS (General Unified Markup System), and early work on moving to implement collections and systems using GUMS has been very successful. There is a clear sense, however, that we must undertake an ongoing activity, parallel to the work of extending the current systems, to refine and document of the current set of classes.

THREE SAMPLE MODELS

The principles elaborated earlier are clearly visible in many of the collections or services within DLPS. Each of the following three examples benefited from previous work within DLPS, and each forms a class, as well as a system to which more content can be added.

Making of America and Encoded Text Systems

The system built for the first University of Michigan Making of America collection was designed to fully support preservation-oriented conversion methods and provide a gateway or even bridge to the high-quality access systems developed for the Humanities Text Initiative.

The history of the UM MOA development effort is documented elsewhere, and a more lengthy treatment of the technology used is also available. The UM MOA system has been extraordinarily successful, both as an architecture within the DLPS digital library efforts, and as a digital library resource for a broad range of users.

Of primary importance in the UM MOA architecture is support for the products of a Library Preservation process.

Images in the system are 600 dpi bitonal, TIFF G4 files. No derivatives (e.g., GIF or JPEG images) are created or stored, except at the time of viewing request. When a user requests a page, the system generates a GIF or PDF derivative in real time and without any appreciable delay (typically less than one second).

Four levels of resolution in GIF are made available to users, taking into account the wide range of displays and network connections; a 600dpi PDF version is also made available, primarily for printing. While the number of pages—approximately 3 million by late 2000—is relatively small compared to a typical research library collection, its large size, expected continued growth, and continuing changes in desktop technology (including networking) argue against storing anything but the master images online.

Use patterns also suggest that as long as we are able to generate appropriate derivatives in real time, based on user demand, we will significantly minimize the requirements for management. Of course there are still concerns about the appropriateness of TIFF G4 as a preservation-quality surrogate for pages, but the University of Michigan Library believes that this format provides a high quality surrogate for most printed materials.

Page images from the Preservation conversion process are subsequently treated by automated Optical Character Recognition (OCR), and the OCR is associated with the page image using a simple form of SGML.

The extensibility of the MOA system has in fact been tested through our OCR processes: two generations of OCR have been applied to all of the materials without the need to change the system architecture. Current OCR technology used by DLPS is a voting system, providing the MOA system with a significantly high quality of character representation than typical OCR.

The system exhibits approximately 99.8% accuracy for nearly all content-bearing pages (e.g., excluding pages with engravings and textual pages such as the title page and advertisements). The SGML applied to the text is XML-compliant, and provides information such as image location, page type (e.g., table of contents), "confidence" of the OCR, and page number.

The automatically generated SGML in MOA is also largely consistent with the Text Encoding Initiative (TEI) Guidelines, allowing a full integration with DLPS' encoded text efforts. While certain attributes such as those mentioned above (e.g., OCR "confidence") have been added to the MOA SGML Document Type Definition (DTD), it is otherwise entirely consistent with the TEI.

This has allowed DLPS' encoded text operations in HTI to extract individual texts and upgrade them, correcting OCR and applying fuller encoding. Because the MOA system is fundamentally TEI-compliant, it can accommodate both the loosely encoded texts and texts with more detailed encoding.

As resources are available to HTI, materials can be enhanced in MOA, ensuring better retrieval and higher levels of functionality for users. Extensibility is critical for a system of this size and importance. The UM MOA system has been designed to be augmented in a variety of ways without significant overhaul.

For example, DLPS has regenerated OCR for MOA without interruptions in service, thereby improving retrieval. Texts can be augmented by HTI, as discussed above. New texts can be added as Preservation resources allow, and all indexing and preparation of Web pages is automated.

The underlying body of materials can remain largely unchanged while work on enhanced interfaces takes place—a process that took place between November 1998 and January 1999. We believe that the MOA system is a model of scalability and extensibility.

The success of the MOA archetype has been multifold. It has allowed us to add materials, a process now underway with MOA4 (2.3 million additional pages). It has helped reduce HTI costs, providing a readily accessible surrogate for the encoding process; in 1998-1999, HTI will add 100 more texts to the American Verse Project collection.

HTI works with the MOA system and contract services to keep its overall cost down and ensure future integration of its products with a Preservation surrogate. Perhaps most significant among MOA's successes, however, is the level of use by a broad range of users.

While the printed source materials were largely unused (most had not circulated in more than ten years), in their online format they are searched some 100,000 times each month, and approximately 100,000 page images are displayed. The constant stream of positive user responses comes from genealogists, philologists, and academics alike.

Image Services

The system built by DLPS Image Services provides a high degree of functionality for a variety of images of objects ranging from art and architecture, to artifacts, to manuscripts. It is also a model for federating diverse collections, respecting the autonomy and heterogeneity of the source collection while creating a union collection for mainstream users.

Image Services uses a mapping strategy for its metadata, keeping the native field names and data but simultaneously "tagging" each field with a corresponding value in a sort of Dublin Core scheme.

This allows Image Services to provide collections in two ways: first, as a highly functional version of the database maintained by the contributing organization (e.g., the University of Michigan Museum of Art); and second, with generic field labels common to all of the images in the system.

Thus, for example, the Museum of Art might use the field label "Artist," while the History of Art Department might use the field label "Source." Having selected only the Museum of Art data online, the user would be presented with search options for "Artist," and data would be displayed accordingly.

However, if the user search across the entire collection, the Dublin Core value "Creator" is presented to the user as a search option and in the display of records. This, along with features for tailoring display and functionality ensures that a contributing organization such as the Museum of Art will enjoy the benefits of a powerful and highly functional system for their data.

Trying to bring together a wide variety of administratively separate collections on campus is challenging, but we believe that the incentive of a cost-effective, inexpensive, highly functional host service (rather than, for example, administrative mandates) has been very effective in creating a unified database managed by DLPS.

DLPS Image Services uses a unified database to ensure a high level of performance and flexibility. Indeed, many of the collection providers maintain local management systems that could be brought online successfully.

The diversity of systems, including Oracle, FileMaker, Embark, and others, would present a serious challenge to creating a distributed search feature. Instead, data are extracted from each of these systems on a periodic basis, and are then ported into the DLPS Image Services system.

Using the methods described above, Image Services is still able to provide access to each collection as if it were an isolated, separately managed collection; the federating approach does not force a lowest common denominator effect.

Instead, the significant resources of DLPS can be leveraged to provide faster search mechanisms, low-cost RAID, and around-the-clock maintenance of the database. These too are effective incentives to organizations when considering whether to mount their data through a central campus agency such as DLPS.

The Image Services system is very rich in functionality. Primarily to satisfy the variety of needs created by the diverse collections, Image Services has built its system using a template system. By specifying (and possibly even creating) a different template, one can make the system appear radically differently.

For example, the primary interface presented to users is a search interface, with results appearing as a collection of thumbnails with associated descriptive information. Each thumbnail and descriptive label is, of course, a link to a fuller resolution view and more descriptive data.

However, by invoking another template such as that for "slide shows," the system can be made to appear as a set of larger images in a pre-selected and set sequence. Another templates provides an interfaces for comparison of multiple images, critical for use of art and architectural images. Each high-resolution image is ultimately displayed with a pan-and-zoom interface.

Users can take advantage of low network speed connections or low-end displays by sending relatively small segments of high resolution images across the network, and panning directionally to view more of the image. This feature has been extremely useful to a wide variety of users, including our Papyrologists, who use the system to work with extremely high resolution images of papyri, and are rarely equipped with computing resources to be able to bring up the full resolution image.

The approach taken by Image Services is extremely scalable. Adding other collections incurs only small, marginal costs (e.g., RAID and time to process the new collection) rather than requiring us to build a new system for each.

We are also able to add new functionality easily, adding "modules" or subroutines to the current middleware rather than re-writing the programs each time. At the same time, the system provides a high degree of functionality for a wide variety of users, including those who own and maintain the collections represented.

Peak

The PEAK system is, in the simplest terms, a mechanism for delivering the entire body of Elsevier Science's journals to a dozen institutions, with varying levels of access within and across institutions.

It is, however, an excellent example of the value of a production organization in an academic research institution. The University of Michigan was able to use DLPS to leverage production technologies in support of the research mission of the University.

Although alternatives were available to using a locally-developed system, those alternatives would not have allowed us to use the Elsevier materials to learn about the economic decisions of users and institutions when using current journals.

Critical to our being able to support the research mission was our ability to use known technologies to bring the journals online. The University of Michigan had prior experience with the Effect Specifications (i.e., Elsevier's format for delivering image, OCR, and metadata) during the TULIP experiment, and as mentioned earlier, UM developed several significant tools to make the TULIP journals available.

Notably, Ken Alexander had developed the search engine, FTL, which was subsequently used and refined in JSTOR, and Doug Orr had developed tif2gif to enable real-time generation of GIF derivatives from the TIFF G4 images. The use of these tools in previous environments (e.g., TULIP and the early days of JSTOR development at UM) allowed us to look past these critical hurdles and instead to focus on supporting the research model.

The availability of the known technologies also allowed us to invest energies in putting in place database mechanisms for authentication and for subscription/purchase control information, as well as new methods for compression to handle the large amounts of material.

Material began to arrive in late summer, 1997. Within a few months, the system was ready for use at the University of Michigan, and by the beginning of 1998, it was released to the subscribing institutions.

With Elsevier's cooperation, Michigan contracted with eleven other institutions to deliver the 1,200 journals with some very unique subscription models. Using a model dictated by Prof. Jeff Mackie-Mason, four types of access were put in place:

- *Free*: Older materials (i.e., pre-1997) were made freely available to all project participants. All project participants were also permitted free access to bibliographic and full-text searches, with no charges levied for viewing citations or abstracts.
- *Traditional subscription*: As its name suggests, this model corresponds directly to the familiar

subscription by journal title. A traditional subscription to a journal title permits unlimited access to the articles within that journal for the subscriber or subscribing institution.

- *Per-article purchase*: When access to an article is purchased by a user, the user has unlimited access to that article. While at one level, this is a fairly unremarkable feature, Mackie-Mason's additional stipulation that this access should not be time-bound added the burden of using a database to associate a user identity with an article identity. This ensured that that the user who purchased access to an article would continue to have unrestricted access to the online article for the duration of the project.
- *Generalized subscription:* The generalized subscription is the most novel and most challenging addition to PEAK. A generalized subscription consists of a number of "tokens" that can be spent on articles. An institution would purchase "bundles" of tokens, or generalized subscriptions. When tokens are available, they are spent on behalf of users for articles not covered by other subscription models. For example, if a user attempted to read an article from a journal not in an institution's traditional subscr-iptions, a generalized subscription token would be spent on that article. The article would then be available, without restrictions, to all other users at the institution. Again, the PEAK system must collect information about individual article access permissions, and associate them with users from each institution.

The research model further complicates these methods for access, where all methods for access are not available to all institutions, and not all institutions choose to take advantage of all methods available to them. This creates a complex matrix of users and materials, a matrix that must be available and reliable for the system to function properly.

Please note that publications analyzing the results of this

research will follow. We have already learned important lessons, however, and are working to share data on use with the participating institutions.

In implementing PEAK, our production technologies *and especially our production organization* allowed us to extend the digital library more fully into the University's mission of research and teaching. Independence from Elsevier was critical in order for us to be able to test these models, and the body of Elsevier materials was equally important to ensure that users would have a valuable body of materials that would draw them into the research environment.

The ultimate control and flexibility of the local production environment allowed the University of Michigan to perform research that would probably not have otherwise been possible, or could not have been performed in ways that the researcher stipulated.

MODELS-CONCLUSION

These model systems help us to understand the value of a production organization in building the digital library. They also amply demonstrate each of the principles or ideals proposed as critical for the functioning of a digital library production organization.

- None of these systems would be possible without the full integration of DLPS into the Library, and indeed the University itself. Politically and procedurally, the fact that DLPS is a part of the University Library ensures a range of outcomes, including effective preservation-oriented conversion and deployment (in the case of Making of America), online strategies guided by information professionals (in all of the systems), and integration of online resources with subscription and acquisition procedures (especially in the case of PEAK).
- Each of these systems is or represents a "class" of information, with consistent characteristics and support. Each is easily extensible through the addition of features or migration of code, and each

continues to grow (in size) without revision of the underlying mechanisms. The imperatives of DLPS have ensured that we have invested in these models and long-term value, rather than hastily deploying "stovepipes" of separate and inconsistent systems without integration.

- The investments made in the systems (and support for them) reflect a high level of investment consistent with the institutional mission. The quality of the underlying resources, for example, is extraordinarily high, just as the underlying metadata are extraordinarily rich. The staff resources (20 FTE) are primarily base budget resources, and staff skills are very high.
- All of the systems were constructed so that they could be supported in an open-ended fashion (i.e., as much as it is possible to say this, in perpetuity). Capture formats are all standards-based and high fidelity; in fact, most are suitable for creating replacement copies of original publications. In nearly all cases, the "archival" version of the digital surrogate is also the online version.

These models are all cost-effective and sustainable, and represent model systems for DLPS, with a significant emphasis placed on long-term support and extension.

The progress of digital libraries will depend increasingly on the creation of production organizations, particularly within libraries.

The digital library cannot thrive on a proliferation of experimental projects, projects that will tend to undermine the viability of collections and work against cooperative architectures. In order for the digital library to thrive, we must begin to see a shift from "projects" to "archetypes." A focus on archetypes rather than projects is only possible in a production organization because of the need for continuity and re-use of resources in a coordinated, planned way.

The effective digital library production organization must be fully integrated into campus' academic mission, and especially into the mission and functions of the library. This can only be done by situating the digital library production organization *in* the library.

Too many of the processes and resources needed to support the digital library are a part of libraries; the principles for information organization and management are an essential part of librarianship.

Success in creating digital library production organizations like those I describe here will also lead to an increased probability that we will successfully federate digital library resources. The holistic approach creates not only economies of scale, but also important opportunities for integration.

At Michigan, this approach is leading to the elaboration of an architecture where every digital object is managed in highly functional ways that ensure the long-term maintenance of that object. This architecture also brings these resources together in ways that are transparent to the user, but which ensures tight integration of multimedia resources. A focus on overall architecture is essential, and again can only ensue from testing hypotheses in production organizations.

Finally, sustainability is one of the key issues of the digital library, and an issue that also argues for the presence of the production operation. Certainly, as an ideal, many of us can readily embrace the notion that decisions must be made with regard for long-term value of the digital object.

It is only through a permanent production organization—an organization with funding in a base budget, with open-ended appointments for staff, and with long-term responsibility for maintenance and migration—that this ideal can be supported.

WHAT IS OAI-PMH GOOD FOR?

The relatively high uptake of the Open Archives Initiative Protocol for Metadata Harvesting (OAI-PMH) confirms the continuing interest on the part of librarians, curators, and other scholarly content providers in resource sharing and interoperability. As of December 2005, less than 5 years after the public introduction of OAI-PMH, there are almost 900 OAI data providers known to be up and running worldwide. Collectively, these repositories provide metadata describing several million digital objects.

All manner of object types are represented, covering a broad spectrum of topic areas and temporal periods. Interest in other, overlapping and complementary protocols designed to facilitate interoperability and resource sharing (SRU/SRW, RSS, OpenSearch.) is also high.

There's clearly a strong desire to get the word out about digital information resources in ways more proactive than passively waiting to be indexed by Google. High-level sharing of resources and resource descriptions is recognized as a prerequisite to enhanced and more ubiquitous end-user access to scholarly information.

In many respects, however, recent work with OAI-PMH, RSS, ZNG (singly and in combination) and with the many content management and aggregation tools that exploit these and other protocols ContentDM, EPRINTS.ORG, D-Space, Greenstone, DigiTool. (the list goes on) has only served to whet the appetite.

End-user services based on metadata and/or resource sharing are proving challenging to do well (one would expect no less). OAI-PMH provides an essential layer of standardization and community agreement, but on its own is not enough. Additional layers of community agreement on issues critical to the shared use of harvested metadata (and eventually the resources themselves) are also required.

INFRASTRUCTURE SUPPORTING INNOVATIVE DL SERVICES

Developing the technical infrastructure for a large-scale digital library composed of disparate, physically scattered component collections and content repositories is a bit like reverse engineering an onion from the inside out with only a hazy vision of what the finished vegetable will look like.

We understand that the technical infrastructure we want will be multi-layered, with each layer simultaneously dependent on those within it and a prerequisite for outer layers. We have an idea, albeit an imperfect one, of the skin of services that will overlie the layers of technical infrastructure.

But we can't yet name or count all the layers of essential infrastructure individually. The truth is we don't yet know all the layers we need. As we design and add each new layer of technology or standardization we keep thinking (hoping) we'll be ready next for the outermost skin of robust and innovative digital library services, only to discover that there is more needed to enable the full suite of services and functions we want.

Each additional layer tends to be larger and more complex. Each new layer makes clear the need for additional layers of technology and community consensus.

OAI-PMH serves as a layer somewhere midway between the innermost and outermost enveloping and reliant on core digitization technologies, collection building policies, and the essential transport and presentation protocols of the Web but still requiring to be surrounded itself by layers of standard metadata schemas and community agreements on metadata authoring and processing.

In retrospect it is clearly a useful step in the right direction; clearly it is also not the final step. It's difficult to visualize the complete vegetable when all you have in hand are the innermost layers of the flesh, but that's exactly what we must do if we are to succeed.

This workshop provides an excellent opportunity to look at what we've learned from work with OAI-PMH to date and to prioritize the near-term technical architecture issues which have surfaced from that work and most need to be addressed to build the next layers of digital library supporting infrastructure.

In doing so we must re-examine critically and in some depth our shared understanding of the objectives of digital libraries the functions they are designed to support and begin to develop the additional community consensus and technical architecture agreements essential to support robust, high-quality, innovative digital library tools and services.

LESSONS LEARNED FROM OAI-PMH

UIUC-IMLS Digital Collections and Content Project

In 2001 IMLS convened a Digital Library Forum to "discuss the implementation and management of networked digital libraries, including issues of infrastructure, metadata, thesauri and other vocabularies, and content enrichment such as curriculum materials and teacher guides."

In collaboration with several researchers involved in the (U.S.) National Science Digital Library (NSDL), this group promulgated the first edition of the *Framework of Guidance for Building Good Digital Collections,* now in its second edition and maintained by NISO <http://www.niso.org/framework/Framework2.html>.

The Forum also recommended (among other things) that IMLS should create a registry of IMLS-funded digital collections and should encourage the use within the IMLS community of OAI-PMH (as a de facto emerging interoperability standard) by creating an item-level metadata repository for metadata describing items in IMLS-funded collections.

This led in 2002 to a grant to the University of Illinois at Urbana-Champaign (UIUC) for a project to do just that. Three years on we have learned a great deal from this project (and from several other OAI-PMH based projects) about the use of OAI-PMH and about resource metadata sharing and aggregation more generally.

For instance, practical experience has confirmed the general utility of the OAI-PMH design which divides the digital library universe into content providers and service providers. Certainly this view of the digital library universe is simplistic. But just as the client-server model remains useful in some contexts as a view of many intrinsically complex network interactions, so too is the OAI content provider-service provider paradigm useful as a model for designing digital library architectures.

Such a model encourages the creation of an architecture that attributes different roles and responsi-bilities to each participating partner. In such a model content providers can assert a measure of control over their resources and strive for a clearer, more explicit understanding of their obligations as content providers and of the expectations they should have of service providers harvesting resource metadata.

Service providers can focus on the central aggregation services they want to build and leave the content creation and primary resource management responsibilities to the content providers.

Though arguably not as "light weight" technically as originally advertised, OAI-PMH has generally proven robust and relatively easy to implement, either directly, through shareware or vended software, or through special purpose gateways such as the OAI Static Repository gateways hosted at Los Alamos and UIUC (and elsewhere) and the FileMaker Pro OAI gateway developed at UIUC and being tested and further developed for ongoing UIUC projects and for the IMLS-funded *MOAC Toolbox* project being led by UC-Berkeley. These extensions and add-ons to canonical OAI-PMH have the potential to facilitate the development of technical infrastructure for the proposed Middle East Digital Library.

More problematically, work with OAI-PMH has shown that while sharing metadata is technically easy, sharing good and useful metadata remains hard. Efforts to aggregate metadata have brought to the fore a host of inconsistencies in metadata authoring practice, ranging from general metadata quality concerns, to problems that arise with loss of context when metadata is removed from local implementation and aggregated, to problems with descriptive granularity and definitions of exactly what level of resource abstraction should be described (depends on purpose, of course, and that's difficult to predict a priori).

Add to these the additional problems associated with the cultural heritage institution spectrum of diverse descriptive traditions and practices (as apparent in the broad range of available metadata schemas and standards available), and the end result is a hodge-podge of metadata records that really don't function well collectively when aggregated.

Experience with OAI-PMH the last few years has made shareable metadata issues far more visible and has demonstrated the shared responsibilities that both service providers (who harvest, normalize, and enrich metadata) and data providers have to ensure quality metadata aggregations.

This recognition in turn, as a positive outcome and a further foundation, has stimulated work to begin the process of resolving these issues notably the *DLF-NSDL OAI and Shareable Metadata Best Practices* effort <http://oai-best.comm.nsdl.org/cgi-bin/wiki.pl?OAI_Best_Practices>, work funded in large part by IMLS and NSF.

The proposed Middle East Digital Library will do well to build on the foundation this work offers with regard to descriptive metadata (in addition, of course, to the work being done by the BA on the unique problems of Arabic-language metadata authoring and dissemination).

Recently, we've also seen a growing interest in creating digital library services that go beyond simple search and discovery. While OAI-PMH anticipated this evolution, such efforts have served to show the limitations of OAI-PMH in the absence of additional community-based agreements and standards.

The problem, of course, is less with OAI-PMH than it is with the lack of community agreement and consensus on metadata standards, crosswalks, thesauri, name and term authority, practices for normalization and enrichment of harvested metadata. (again, the list goes on).

This has led to an emerging appreciation of the critical need for additional layers of technology (e.g., vocabulary and schema registries), standardization, and community agreement.

Priorities

Given all that needs to be done, the natural question is what first? Based on my experience I would suggest three critical needs in regard to digital library infrastructure:

- The need to more clearly define information resource granularity, to understand collection identity, and to appreciate the relationship between a collection and its constituent items. The decision of IMLS to couple together both a collection registry and an item-level metadata repository in the grant to Illinois was prescient in that it has encouraged us to consider issues of collection identity and descriptive granularity as part of our work. Earlier work done at Illinois under funding from the Andrew W. Mellon Foundation, which included a focus on how EAD might fit with OAI-PMH, and ongoing work being done at Illinois in collaboration with the U.S. Midwestern research universities that comprise the CIC, also have encouraged study of these issues. Results so far make clear (not surprisingly) that users do not always query indexes or use resources at a single level of granularity. Multi-word queries frequently contain keywords found at different levels of descriptive granularity. End-user information needs variously are best met by collections, by items, or by combinations of both. Data gathered in the UIUC-IMLS DCC project confirm that questions of collection definition represent not just a theoretical problem but one that is being contemplated by practitioners and both actively and passively responded to in the daily work of digital library development. We need to understand better how collection identity will be transferred, transformed, and created and how item granularity and interrelationships will be handled in development of the proposed Middle East Digital Library, and how we can exploit agreements on these issues to provide enhanced services to end-users.

- The need to understand archetypical behaviors (views) of specific classes of resource objects and to agree on means to obtain standard views of content. The initial focus of OAI-PMH has been on descriptive metadata, but recent work demonstrates that the protocol has the potential to facilitate as well the sharing of complete resources. The demand and utility of specific views of resources for use in specialized analytical tools and to facilitate specific DL functions and services is high. Current techniques to crawl or spider information resources directly from Web servers tend to be crude, and the objects gathered by such means are not always in the form or fidelity needed for desired purpose. To effectively exploit OAI-PMH to harvest complete resources, we need better and more explicit agreements on the ways resources are disseminated. Consider a complex textual resource made up of ordered page images and OCR'd text. For some purposes an end-user (or digital library tool) might require individual page images. For other purposes, the OCR'd text. For other purposes, scanned pages suitably arranged for page-turner software. There needs to be community agreement on how each of these views (and other potentially useful views of content class members) are labeled, requested, and disseminated.

- *The need to define expectations.* In discussions about digital libraries we often make the mistake of assuming a common understanding of the functions and services that define a digital library. Indeed, there is some research about digital library defining functions. The IFLA Functional Requirements for Bibliographic Records (FRBR) model defined four user tasks, *Find, Identify, Select* and *Obtain*, and suggested a possible fifth function: *Relate*. Others have suggested additional functions that digital libraries should perform in support of end-users, e.g., *Navigate* and *Interpret*. However, current functional definitions of digital libraries are inconsistent and vary signific-antly from domain to domain. Relationships between digital libraries and applications such as institutional repositories, learning management systems, meta-search utilities, traditional OPACs remain hazy. There is not clear, explicit consensus on the essential functions and services that define a generic digital library. One can argue that this is because no complete exemplar yet exists, but nonetheless it behooves us at the start of a project like this one to reach explicit agreements on what we are trying to do. To realise essential technical infrastructure we need to understand how object properties and attributes relate to delivered functions and services. Given that many metadata elements can support multiple functions, we need especially to understand how normalization and enrichment done to support one function effects metadata usability for other functions.

Where does this leave us relative to the question I chose as a title for this brief? The answer I offer is that OAI-PMH is good for sharing descriptive metadata and possibly complete resources. But it is not sufficient onto itself. On its own, it has limited utility, or perhaps none at all.

As a layer of a robust, multi-layered infrastructure underpinning a digital library, it has great value. Obviously OAI-PMH enables nothing in the absence of quality content held in well-managed and well-maintained content provider repositories.

Perhaps less obviously, the full utility of OAI-PMH can't be realized without community agreement on a host of additional issues e.g., collection identity, descriptive granularity, common conventions for dissemination of full content, shared understanding of target digital library functions and services. Agreements, consensus, and technical conventions on such matters are essential to create an adequately robust technical infrastructure on which to build a useful Middle East Digital Library.

Chapter 11

Digital Information Preservation

In this Chapter we discuss long-term digital preservation from an information perspective, rather than the predominant approaches; the Archival and the Technocratic Approach. Our standpoint is that information is at the core of long-term digital preservation. This means that information is the object of preservation in the long term. Information lives longer than people, organizations and tools (software).

The Information Continuum Model provides support for this standpoint. However, we find that there exists no concept to support practical action in preservation from the information perspective. Existing concepts as information object, digital object, preservation object, electronic record, information package and significant properties are context dependent and focus on the object to be preserved, rather than preservation of information.

Consequently, they are not suitable for realizing the information perspective in long-term digital preservation. The concept of Digital Information Preservation Object is therefore introduced and a tentative definition of the concept is presented.

We believe that Gladney is worth to be quoted to begin this paper. He stated, "If all that information is worth creating in the first place, surely some of it is worth saving!" During the last years, the development of digital technologies has been very fast and for the most unpredictable. Consequently, the amount of information created in electronic form is growing exponentially. Records like scholarly studies, multi-media recordings, business, scientific, government and personal records convey information critical to democratic institutions and to human well-being.

Every citizen depends on some information, partly portions unique to him, for practical as well as cultural reasons. According to Runardotter et al., digital information has to be available for the future society by legal, historical and democratic reasons. For instance, archivists have as their mission the preservation of records and its continuing value and the providing access to those records.

At the same time, the development of technologies has created unforeseen problems, such as the obsolescence of hardware and software. There is no information system capable to retain and make the information accessible for more than 30 years.

Constant upgrading of operative systems and software applications in one hand and new storage technologies on other hand are leading to the very difficult access to information.

File formats are experiencing the same problem because what today is standard for some applications or platform shifts or disappears within a decade. The solutions that are today for preservations and foremost to make digital material accessible on long time are insufficient.

Archival inquiry "Archives for Everyone – Now and in the Future", called attention to these great shortcomings and argued that models, methods and platform-independent software for preservation of the digital material are omitted largely.

On one hand, the "problem" with digital preservation is the lack of proven methods to ensure that the digital information will continue to exist On the other hand, the software currently available does not include good tools for saving digital recorded information in the face of rapid hardware and software obsolescence.

It states that digital preservation is suddenly urgent because the needed technology and infrastructure are not in place. The challenges that needed to be addressed include legal, educational, and technical aspects.

Among these challenges only one difficult technical problem impeded digital archiving until recently – how to preserve information through technology changes. Within the practice of preservation, archives are still using methods developed since 1970-1980. These methods cause losing of functionalities of the records when archiving.

Archival science has not developed as rapid as information technology. Information in the digital era demands several kinds of tools for its processing. Nevertheless, there is a lowest common denominator: digital processing.

However, such processing tools are viewed as mediator for digitally recorded information. Digital material that is produced on a certain platform, with a certain application, a certain version and in a certain format, needs to be converted to other platforms, applications and/or formats in order to gain access to information over time.

Another way of retrieving stored information is to emulate the original software (and platform) in which digital material has been produced. In either way, information might be lost and the information retrieved might not be fully reliable.

According to Runardotter et al., the concepts that are fundamental in archival science, such as record, document or archival record, has not the same dignity in systems science. In information systems sciences there are not methods that in the same degree as in archival science deals with long-term, "forever" perspectives.

This has not been detected as an issue in systems science until recently. The transition between paper based mediums to digital media was not preceded by a strategy for long-term digital preservation.

This phenomenon explained in terms of lack of knowledge and experience when handling digital material. Besides, no one could foresee the speed and complexity of the evolution of computers and software.. Information and long-term digital preservation is one of the acutest questions for all kinds of preservation institutions like archives, libraries, local authorities and for society as a whole.

Society and information curators must face the challenge

of finding some sustainable solutions to ensure that digital recorded information of today become accessible and understandable in the future. Otherwise, digital material and likewise one part of society's future cultural heritage and history are in danger of disappearing forever. Consequently, legal and democratic demands cannot be fulfilled.

According to Gladney it was stated, that technology has influence in almost every aspect of long-term digital preservation and it is not widely believed these solutions can be achieved solely through technological means.

To find solutions to the problem much research was limited to technical aspects of preservation but our research has taken another view on long-term digital preservation, which puts information in focus. This paper therefore discusses the concept of information as central for long-term digital preservation.

FACING LONG-TERM DIGITAL PRESERVATION

The authors of this paper are connected to the Long-term Digital Preservation Centre (LDP Centre) in Sweden. The major activities of the LDP Centre concern research and systems development within the field of long-term digital preservation.

The LDP Centre has adopted, at this stage, migration as method for preservation. The starting point for digital preservation was the OAIS Reference Model. In this work, the LDP Centre has developed a model for structure for Information Package.

This structure was (and is) intended to be used by archive creating organizations, in order to later deliver digitally recorded information to long-term digital preservation archives. Conceptually, this model consists of a base structure, and other elements. The base structure consists of different sets of metadata according to well-established international metadata standards used in archiving.

These standards are Metadata Encoding & Transmission Standard (METS, covering technical and provenience metadata), Encoded Archival Context (EAC, covering archival metadata about the creator of the information), Encoded

Archival Description (EAD, covering structural metadata) and PREservation Metadata Implementation Strategies (PREMIS, covering technical and process metadata).

We found out that the existing models for structuring information about the object to be preserved, produces problems in implementation. As we can realise from the descriptions above, these structures are used as "wrappers" carrying metadata sometimes overlapping one another.

Consequently, dealing with all these structures causes both intellectual complications and technical implementation difficulties. We, at the LDP Centre, have experienced that all these structures have some kind of inherent philosophy which focuses on special features or attributes of digital material. Here we did three significant observations.

- The used structures do not focus specifically on information.
- Using several structures sometimes causes an intellectual "mess" due to their inherent philosophies (such as ontological confusion).
- The used structures are inherited from the archival world and, as we see, they support legislative (or authority) records more than digitally recorded information in general.

We also found out that putting a lot of efforts on these structures, made us loss focus on that we believe is important to preserve, to be precise information. It is obvious that technical or other aspects of the digital material to be preserved are Ó÷üëéï: kika i boken! indeed important to deal with, but those are just means of preserving information while the digital "technology is a live".

We do not know how long this technology and its tools are going to be a part of our society. Perhaps in just some years from now a new informational paradigm will occur. Another issue concerns the fact it was archival institutions that early experienced the need of digital preservation, it was obvious that the first efforts on preservation started from archival work practices.

Consequently (archival) metadata standards were

developed in order to support digital preservation. The archival inheritance spokes for the principle of provenience as one of the stone corners in long-term digital preservation, because this principle supports authenticity and trustworthiness of any kind of digitally recorded information.

Consequently today's "solutions", based on the Archival and/or the Technocratic Approach, supports preservation only in a (relatively) short-term. To approach a solution concerning the question about how to preserve information through technology changes and surpassing the archival inheritance, the LDP Centre's research activities has taken a new view on long-term digital preservation, which puts information in focus.

This includes the development of a detached *Digital Information Preservation Object* that is independent of technology and deals with the question of provenience in a new way. Such preservation object might be transferred between different technologies.

This is viewed as the main key to a viable solution for long-term digital preservation. Such view demands a higher level perspective of information and its continuing value without neglecting the constant changing technical aspects of digital preservation.

Developing the Information Approach

This paper is a result of two research activities, literature review and interaction in the developing R&D team at the LDP Centre. The literature review was carried out with the purpose of developing a definition of Digital Information Preservation Object and the interaction helped to gather data about the developed structure through seminars, (informal) "interviews" and systems development meetings.

There is a large quantity of literature about the concept of information. But in comparison, the amount of literature in the field of long-term digital preservation is relatively small.

The process of critical selection of relevant literature was based upon parameters such as "well known writers", "established perspectives and/or schools", in order to address the key sources, key theories and definitions of the topic. Since our intention was to provide a broad view on the subject, the initial literature review made it clear that several research projects have shown its own approaches to what we call Digital Information Preservation Object.

The development of the base structure, were a joint task of the entire LDP Centre. Everyone (at some extent) was involved in its development and several research observations were made during these activities.

The resemblance with Action Research as research method is purely unintentional. Nevertheless, adopting Action Research as a research method in this work will underpin the scientific value of the paper. Some words about Action Research are then necessary.

Action Research, as research method, is suitable in order to describe the origins of the gathered data (the structure developed by the LDP Centre). Further, some of the parts of the named structure were and still are being developed in joint seminars between system developers and researchers at the LDP Centre. This implies that a social context is set up.

This team interacts together in order to find improvements to already existing drafts. Together, the team define problems, co-generate relevant knowledge, learn and take actions. This "socio-technical" unit, is relatively small (nine persons) self-managing and "posses the skills and authority to control the operation of their technology" and appropriate to carry out Action Research a low-system level. In our work, we tackle questions like: what are the elements of the Information

Approach? what properties/characteristics constitute a definition of the notion Digital Information Preservation Object? Since the LDP Centre intends to develop a general preservation model in which Digital Information Preservation Object is the mediator for preservation, this paper will have influence for further research as well as for what methods, models and techniques that will be developed and used. Furthermore, our result will influence the development of the information systems intended to serve long-term digital preservation.

About Information

The term information is used with different meanings by different groups and in different contexts and there is no well-defined definition of the terms "data" and "information". A common and short definition is that information is interpreted data. Hence, data is signs used to represent information, or signs which carries with them the possibility to compose and/or decompose the text, photo, music etc. from which it is derived.

Thus, retrieving the source provides access to information and we can start reading/viewing/listening but also interpreting and analysing the information existing in the source.

This results in the creation of knowledge, that is, we learn from information. The central idea is that data become information by a process of interpretation. The infological equation states that I = i (D, S, t) where *I* represent the information we can get through the interpretation process *i*, which is operating on data *D*, together with our pre-knowledge *S*, during a certain time *t*. Langefors [ibid.] states that "One of the central insights from infology is that data or texts do not "contain" information (knowledge) but will only, at best, represent the information to those who have the requisite 'pre-knowledge'" and he also means that the infological equation is a representation of this.

Dealing with information systems require a broad view of information, since using a computer implicitly involves information services of some kind, that is, we get service by being informed by data. According to Langefors it is necessary to define information as knowledge, since "information is knowledge and not physical signs".

He regards information as knowledge structured in such a way that it is communicated. Because of this it can also be stored, which leads to information being stored knowledge. Checkland & Holwell provides the view that information is a service that supports decision making within organizations. Data are facts and a starting point for mental processes.

They introduce the concept of "capta", which is the result

of selection of certain data (we pay attention to, create some new category or get surprised by the data). In other words, data that catches our interest transforms to capta, a consciousness of something.

This signifies that turning data into information is done through a mental process and during that process the data changes shape, and will ultimately lead to knowledge. Once we have selected, paid attention to or created some data, or turned it into capta, we relate it to other things or put it in a context, we attribute meaning to it, and by this we once again convert it, this time to information.

This can be done individually or collectively and this process, selection and conversion of data into meaningful information can lead to larger structures of related information, or what we call knowledge. The interpretation process emphasizes is implicit in this reasoning.

This is line with our claim – that information is not equated with knowledge. Just like data must be interpreted in order to become information, so must information be interpreted and analysed in order to be knowledge. Information is never the knowledge itself, the knowledge is within the knower.

We agree with Langefors with his notion that in order to understand information people must have pre-knowledge. This we see as knowledge that consists of the ability to assimilate the information, but also to have an understanding of the information content, or the subject in focus.

If these abilities are found, new knowledge is created the moment someone (individually or in a group) thinks of an issue. When people's ideas, or knowledge, are being shaped and transferred to a media they are made available for others to share. Hence, the knowledge has now once again become information and exists physically (or digitally), available for people who need it in order to learn and increase their knowledge of something, for example within an organization.

Information Continuum Perspective

Runardotter et al., put information in a long-term digital

preservation context that is a new circular view of the information life cycle. Information lives longer than people, organizations and tools. The authors manifested that information is a living concept and is in progress during constant ongoing process.

The fact is that people, organizations and tools are replaced over time. Further, they observed the phenomenon that information never dies provided that it is preserved and used. The statement is based on that information is constantly shaped and reshaped, evolving through time, picking up further information or losing some parts and in that way information is all the time under reconstruction.

To keep information alive demands a set of ongoing activities, both organizational and technical. The idea of living spiral is also supported by the Records Continuum Model and Information Continuum Model. According these models information and records continues to evolve in space/time and therefore are no end products..

The Records Continuum Model is widely known about and discussed in the archival profession, unlike the Information Continuum Model discussion of which is only just beginning to be opened up. The named models are founded on Giddens' structuration theory.

This theory of time/space distanciation has been translated into a "rhythm" for information processing derived from the processes of creating information, capturing it as recorded information, organising it and bringing it together within the plural domains of competition.

Each item of information once created, may or may not be recorded, stored and managed in ways that can benefit individuals, groups, communities, and can push that information out into the plural domains of the further reaches of space/time.

The continua (the dimesions of the model) in the Information Continuum Model are collectively meant to focus analytical attention on the nature of recorded information as an allocative resource, something to be shared and to be used within our activities.

The continua in the Records Continuum Model collectively are meant to focus analytical attention on the nature of recorded information as an authoritative resource, something to be relied upon not because of its content but because of the way, it has been created and maintained with some continuing contact to the original specificities of its occurrence.

According to Upward, information (and its reconstituted products) outwardly spiral from the original act of creation of a document. This idea is also derived from Giddens' theory of structuration. In the Information Continuum Model, information is derived from a principle source (for example, an information object such as an interview), and becomes transformed through the agency of people and technologies for different purposes.

Information Objects are both embedded in the "context of the action in which they are part, and are recursively involved". Information artefacts, as records and outcomes of action, become disembedded and reused in other contexts, for example, a research interview is "unitised" and its parts are reconstituted via different technologies or processes as evidence for particular research and theoretical constructions in academic production.

The interview, or any data, is therefore moved space/time, and is reconstituted, reused, re-embedded according to particular human or machine agency (human speech is transformed by agency of speech recognition software into text), or human agency makes particular interpretive decisions about how ambiguous sounds should be transcribed in transcription.

The interview data (or its constituent parts) become pluralized with the production of different knowledge artefacts: theory, the application of theory and the development of scholarly and practical publications. Its pluralisation can also lead to it being used in other forms of action, such as social action, lobbying, or policymaking.

The incorporation of the time/space dimension is also important for several reasons. First, it recognises that information object have a changing historical life, and in addition, the reconstruction of time and space through modernity, and particularly through the agency of ICTs, gives information objects new potentiality.

We could use Giddens own "words" and transform these to our vocabulary of Information Continuum. Giddens "structure" equals to rules and resources organized as properties of systems.

Systems equal to reproduced relations between actors or collectivities organized as social practices. Finally structuration equals to the continuity or transformation of structures, and therefore the reproduction of systems.

The dynamic of structuration is crucial in our view. "Social practices evolve over time and space and must replicate even to stay the same" (the essence of long-term digital preservation). The term of continuity (i.e. continuum) promotes the reproduction of systems (i.e. memory traces, organized social practices) by means of digitally recorded information and its continuing value. Information is seen as an (allocative) resource, something to be shared and to be used within our activities.

In the long-term gaining access to digitally recorded information (through longterm digital preservation activities) will tell us what sorts of things were out there in the world. We could summarize our view in simple words as "Digital preservation will ensure, through the continuing value of information, that social systems will be reproduced as memory tracks of human activities".

Predominant Approaches in Long-term Digital Preservation

In our research we could observe that there are two predominant approaches trying to define the object of preservation. The first is closely related to Archival (including Records Management) and the second is a technical (or merely a technocratic) perspective. We could also observe the lack of an approach based on Information (and/or Information Continuum) perspective.

The Object of Preservation in the Archival Approach

A definition of Preservation Object is given by Dollar as "Preservation Objects are those to be archived. These objects are physically compound by set of files in maybe different formats. The objects logically are compound by data – the content for instance birth date of a person, and metadata – that should describe the context when the birth date of a particular person was used".

The Records concept opens another view on the object of preservation. Preservation is a key characteristic for records, which is followed by their creation purpose to be re-used. The preservation also makes the record a vital component in the memory of organizations, individuals and in some cases of society. A record is more than just information, it suppose to be trustworthy i.e. being able to serve as evidence, and support accountability. The time for preservation could vary from days or months up to hundreds of years. The International Standards Organization definition of records is: "Information created, received, and maintained as evidence and information by an organizations or person, in pursuance of legal obligations or in transaction of business."

In the Guide for Managing Electronic Records of the International Council on Archives, from an archival perspective, a similar definition of record is given as "recorded information produced or received in the initiation, conduct or completion of an institutional or individual activity and that comprises content, context and structure sufficient to provide evidence of the activity."

Records can occur in different forms and representations.

They are usually represented as logically delimited information objects, for example, as distinct documents. But increasingly we find records in the form of distributed objects, such as relational databases and compound documents.

According to Thomassen a record has four characteristics, which make the record unique in relation to other types of information:

- Records serve as evidence over actions and transactions

- Records support accountability
- Records are related to processes, i.e. information that is generated by and linked to some work processes
- Records are going to be preserved, some even for eternity.

Cox stated that the evidential value of a record can only exist if the content, structure and context are preserved. The context is the link between different records that belongs together, and also to the process where the record was created. According to Dollar the electronic record is more of a logical entity, where integral parts can be managed at different places within an information system, or even in different information systems.

The question "What is a record" has been one of the fundamental issues in debates and discussions in archiving and digital preservation over the past twenty years. Attempts to arrive at general definition of an *electronic record* were made in the last decade by several research projects and have by now being replaced by more constructive approach to define properties and functionalities of electronic records that need to be preserved in a given context.

An electronic record can be understood as a package or a set of technical properties and possibilities, and of administrative context where some of these technical possibilities were put to use. In contrast, one approach in Digital Libraries that might have a significant difference is proposed by Nichols.

In this approach the concept of "artifact" is central an defined as "a physical object produced at some time in the past, and attesting to a given set of practices, thinking, and ways of viewing the world, but whose importance will be defined by present and foreseeable future needs and use. The value of the artifact is strongly influenced, but not completely determined by, the document/object's features that are unique". An artifact is then an object with a set of values such as Evidential, aesthetic,

Associational, Market and Exhibition value. An artifact is of value to the extent that it testifies to the information being original, faithful, fixed, or stable. Although, this approach do not mention the term record but "artefact", we interpret this approach to be similar to the Archival Approach.

The definitions of records are to some extent usable in our perspective. Nevertheless the usage of terms as "legal obligations" or "accountability" or "evidential" are strongly connected to Records Management and Archiving. Information is important but not central. We perceive the evidentiallity of records as the major focus of Archiving and Records Management and less focus is given to records as informational source. Thomassen gives emphasis in the need of preservation of records in order to be reused as memory traces.

This encompasses our Continuum perspective which is beyond of just records. The "big difference" is that our perspective is turning the precedence of information in relation to Archiving. Another difference is that our perspective deals with any kind of digitally recorded information as evidence of human activities not just with records as legal evidence.

The Object of Preservation in the Technocratic Approach

A definition of Digital Object is given by Blanchi & Petrone as "a unique identified data abstraction that encapsulates content and access policies while providing a high-level, self-describing, type definition. Digital Objects are described trough the use of an abstract typing mechanism that we refer to as content type".

The concept of Information Package of the OAIS Reference Model states that data is interpreted using its Representation Information (described in metadata), which produces information, that an information object consists of not only data content, but also the information necessary to interpret that content. In order to successfully preserve such a generic Information Object, it is critical for an Open

Archival Information System (OAIS) to clearly identify and understand the Data Object and its associated Representation Information, which together forms what, is called an Information Package.

The PREMIS data model describes intellectual entities, objects, rights, agents and events. Objects, according to PREMIS, can be bitstreams, files or representations (digital objects "instantiation or embodying an intellectual entity") Further, in scientific material the notion Preservation Object can be compared to the approach of Persistent Object articulated by the US National Archives (NARA) in cooperation with the San Diego Supercomputing Centre (SDSC).

The persistent object method presumes that all records can be represented as objects with their specific characteristics and behaviour.

The concept of Significant Properties, proposed by the National Library of Australia (NLA), are functions or characteristics of an object that are essential to its meaning. Preservation of digital objects, in this approach, in some cases will necessitate changes in look, feel, functionality or content if the object is to remain usable at all. Although significant properties may be seen as individual and specific to a given object, most digital archives try to create classes of objects based on common properties.

In the Cedars project, Significant Properties were associated with the Underlying Abstract Form (UAF) of an object. Therefore, objects with the same UAF have the same significant properties. Conversely, if significant properties varied, than objects that were otherwise similar could have different UAFs.

The PREMIS working group, following on the work of OAIS, Cedars and NLA, defined Significant Properties as those "characteristics of a particular object subjectively determined to be important to maintain through preservation actions", noting that "Significant properties may be objective technical characteristics subjectively considered to be particularly important, or subjectively determined characteristics".

Further, the FEDORA architecture describes a content container abstraction, the Digital Object, and the nature of Repositories that provide access to these containers.

They conceptualize a Digital Object as having:

- A structural kernel, which encapsulates content as opaque byte stream packages
- An interface, or behaviour, layer that gives contextual meaning to the data in the Digital Object.

One useful metaphor for a Digital Object is that of a cell. A similar approach is given by Saidis et al. as Digital Object Prototypes (DOPs) which provides the Digital Library (DL) designer with the ability to model diverse types of digital objects in a uniform manner while offering digital object type conformance.

They described a Digital Object that has constituent components, that is to say files, metadata, behaviours and relationships. The derived digital object typing information – that is, which components constitute each different type of object and how each object behaves – is not realized in a manner suitable for effective use by higher level Digital Library application logic including DL modules and services.

A DOP is a digital object type definition that provides a detailed specification of its constituent parts and behaviours. Digital objects are conceived as instances of their respective prototypes.

The approach to Digital Libraries proposed by Arms et al. described the "digital object" in a slightly different manner. The main building blocks in this approach are: "digital objects", which are used to manage digital material in a networked environment; "handles", which identify digital objects and other network resources; and "repositories", in which digital objects are stored.

From a computing view, the digital library is built up from simple components, notably digital objects. A digital object is a way of structuring information in digital form, some of which may be metadata, and includes a unique identifier, called a handle. First lets have a look to the terms and concepts used by this approach.

Very common are the terms of "data abstraction", "data", "bitstreams", "files", "instantiation", "characteristics and behaviour", "functions", "functionality", "objective technical characteristics", "structural kernel", "encapsulates opaque byte stream packages", "interface", "metadata", "behaviours and relationships", "manage digital material in a networked environment", "stored". Looking to the ontology of this approach is quite obvious that the terms utilized comes from computer science in general and at some extent from Object Oriented terminology.

This spokes for data management through information systems making data central. The term object is also important being conceptualization of data (such as files, bitstreams, etc.) having some behaviour (its functionality or implemented functions in as information system). No emphasis is made on information neither on its contents as traces of human activities.

Towards a Definition of Digital Information Preservation Object

Every other approach to define a the object of preservation has focused from different perspectives of preservation and from different characteristics of the digital object using its own ontology. Furthermore, we found that a) there is no existing or established definition of Digital Information Preservation Object, b) existing concepts are context dependent and focuses specifically on object to be preserved. After our study we came to conclusions that research carried out so far do not handle

Digital Information Preservation Object from Information Continuum perspective and do not contribute with any definition of the notion Digital Information Preservation Object. However, the studied research results merely focus on the structure and physical nature of the digital object. Their described abstractions are conceptualizations of the underlying physical level. Nevertheless, although these approaches support our activities to some extent, the definitions provided by these approaches are not suitable for our view, hence; we experienced the emergence of an own definition of Digital Information Preservation Object that specifically focuses on information.

However, this study gave us insights to take another perspective. To define the notion of Digital Information

Preservation Object it is needed to take a standpoint. We cannot begin the definition from structure of the object; nonetheless, we will begin definition from a global view. If we start from the structure, we are viewing an object as a delimited entity at structural level, since our focus is on information, not the object itself.

We want to distinguish the conventional view to the object that is a construction, a container or a carrier to hold together the elements (depending on level of conceptualization) from the view that is to see an object from continuum perspective. An object there is a piece or pieces of information that reflects human action in a social context in the continuum.

There is an important remark before we provide our tentative definition of Digital Information Preservation Object (DIPO). We need to state that any for any object is to say that its analysis is made depending on the level of abstraction adopted and due a set of variables at that specific level.

The Structure developed at the LDP Centre and the descriptions in section are (technical) conceptualizations of "digital (physical) objects"; they concentrate their efforts in describing or defining (at a very low level) the object to preserve regardless of its continuing information value. Our intention (or level of abstraction) lay merely in the general level or, so to say, we try to define DIPO at an "ethereal" level; we want to define the "thing" DIPO.

We take stand in the philosophy of Dooyeweerd who stated that Meaning rather than Existence is the primary property in created reality. In our perspective, this view encompasses the Information Continuum

Model perspective in which put the continuing value of information (i.e. its reconstruction of human social actions) as the meaning (*raison d'être*) of the DIPO. The DIPO is a recorded result of human's action in form of information pieces. This information is categorized in an information type from social context. These information pieces can have relationships to other information pieces either within its own physical carrier or toward other objects.

The vital characteristic of the information object from

continuum perspective is that new object can be created through the combination of information pieces that can be a piece of other objects. In that way, the information will be reused in another context and reproducing human social actions. It means that information can be related to processes (that is generated by, and linked to work processes). Furthermore, the information in the object must serve as evidence over actions and transactions as well.

The natural question that arises, should be what is this definition good for? Having a definition of DIPO and a clear perspective of the continuum, long-term digital preservation issues might be easier to tackle. Something we observe is that there is a need of a uniform "aspectual abstraction" of the Digital Information Preservation Object.

This level should be based in deep philosophical foundations that should cover several aspects of the object (i.e. its attributes, characteristics or properties), such as physical aspects: decay of materials, biotic: pests eating it the storage material, lingual: language changes over long term, social: social and cultural connotations and meanings change over long-term, juridical: legal matters of e.g. long-term ownership, for instance after someone has died, pistic: the religious or faith, moral ethical, normative contexts that can change, probably slowly (over centuries), so this might provide a better degree of harmony over the preservation period than earlier aspects.

Chapter 12

Digital Curation and the Management of Digital Library

This article summarises a presentation given on behalf of LOCSCOT to the 'Google or Bust: Challenging the Profession' CILIPS day event in Dundee on 27 September 2006. The presentation explored certain issues faced by regional and local libraries regarding management, collection and preservation of digital cultural heritage resources i.e. websites and e-journals. The full presentation is available from the DCC and UKOLN websites.

The availability and growing use of digital information and services online has occasioned increasing expectations of digital services from cultural heritage institutions. Many local and national libraries have already embraced the initial challenge of providing basic administrative and collection information online.

Yet the provision of digital library *objects* online takes the digital library challenge to another level: objects and content must not only be collected or created, but also properly managed, stored, and preserved in order to maximise the initial investment and ensure the objects remain available for users for as long as is deemed necessary.

'Digital Curation' is the way to achieve this, with complete life cycle management to tackle these many challenges in a carefully planned, consistent, and ongoing process.

THE UK DIGITAL CURATION CENTRE

In the UK, research and development into digital curation

requirements and activities are the core activities of the Digital Curation Centre (DCC). The DCC was founded to support UK institutions which store, manage and preserve digital information, and to help them address the enhancement and continuing availability of digital information for long-term use.

As a centre of expertise in digital curation and associated digital preservation, the DCC provides a national focus for research and development into curation issues and promotes expertise and good practice, both nationally and internationally, for the management of digital outputs.

The DCC is a consortium project with four main partners: the University of Edinburgh; UKOLN at the University of Bath; the Humanities Advanced Technology and Information Institute (HATII) at the University of Glasgow, and; the Council for the Central Laboratory of the Research Councils, the CCLRC in Didcot. The DCC has a strong research and development agenda and maintains numerous services and outreach activities.

These include:

- Organisation of workshops and seminars to explore different aspects of curation such as policies, audit and certification, and legal issues;
- Development of a community-developed digital curation manual to assist data creators, curators and re-users to understand better the challenges they face and the roles they play in creating, managing and preserving their digital information over time;
- Production of briefing papers, technology watch papers, and standards watch papers on issues relevant to digital curation and preservation, as well as the first journal to focus exclusively on digital curation: the *International Journal of Digital Curation*; Organisation of the annual DCC Digital Curation conference with peer reviewed papers and posters from an international stage;
- Participation in development of an audit and certification framework for trustworthy digital repositories;

- Provision of an associates network, online forum, and helpdesk service offering on-demand support for individuals and UK HE/FE institutions doing preservation planning and solving challenging curation problems. The DCC is funded by the Joint Information Systems Committee (JISC) and the e-Science core programme. More information about the DCC is available from the DCC website.

Digital Curation

As the term 'curation' has only recently begun to be applied to digital materials, we will at this point take a moment to define what we mean when talking about 'digital curation'.

Digital curation, broadly interpreted, is about maintaining and adding value to a trusted body of digital information for both current and future use: in other words, it is the active management and appraisal of digital information over its entire life cycle.

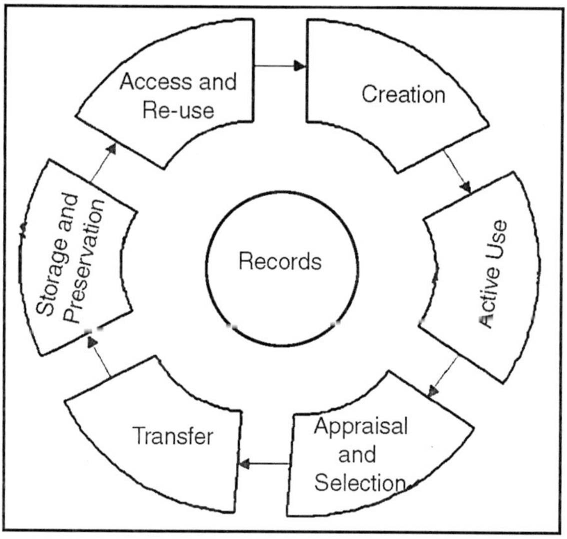

Fig. Sample Life Cycle Model.

The life cycle approach is necessary because:

- Digital materials are fragile and susceptible to

change from technological advances throughout their life cycle, i.e. from creation onwards;

- Activities (or lack of) at each stage in the life cycle directly influence our ability to manage and preserve digital materials in subsequent stages;
- Reliable re-use of digital materials is only possible if materials are curated in such a way that their authenticity and integrity are retained.

Approaching digital information management from a life cycle perspective facilitates continuity of service. This in turn supports verification of the provenance of digital resources despite technological and organisational changes in their context, and helps to maximise the initial investment made in creating or gathering them.

Complete life cycle control is an ideal scenario. However, it is not always possible. Many cultural heritage organisations manage and host resources created by external parties; in such instances it is not always possible to exercise influence over creation and external resource management practices. The active area of life cycle management for such heritage organisations is therefore reduced and can begin only at the point of appraisal or transfer.

This scenario exemplifies how responsibility for curation is shared between different stakeholders, particularly when dealing with transfer of ownership. Communication between these stakeholders and documentation of activities is key to achieving life cycle continuity in such a scenario.

Issues in Developing a Digital Library Collection

The types of digital information held by digital libraries can vary considerably. It may include, for example, relatively straightforward images and textual documents, or more complex audio-visual material and websites. Such items may be digitised from an existing original analogue source, or are 'born-digital'.

Whatever the nature of the collection item, it should always be accompanied by metadata that describes the resource, helps to manage and preserve it, and facilitates its re-use. Both collection items and metadata need to be properly managed across the entire life cycle.

This is not a simple task; nor merely a technical one. Whilst certain aspects are certainly technical, others are cultural and organisational, whilst others are of a legal or financial nature.

For example:

- Organisational and cultural infrastructure may not be geared towards digital longevity: resources are often created for the here and now, but such practices can be incompatible with the sustainability of authentic resources. Addressing this issue requires not just the proper technical storage infrastructure, but also education, training, managerial support, and dedicated funding;
- Curation and preservation is an ongoing commitment, but what of funding? What are the cost benefits in proper management of digital information? Is there a business model, and what are the options for revenue generation?
- The copying and provision of information online must comply with legal requirements, including Intellectual Property legislation and the Data Protection Act. Which legislation affects the creation of digital surrogates, and how? What solutions would support legal compliance whilst still providing access to the materials in digital form?
- What tools are available to ease the processes of harvesting, acquisition, ingest, indexing, and preservation? Which storage mechanism is most suitable, what metadata are needed, and how can the threat of technological obsolescence be addressed?

The active management and appraisal of digital information over its life cycle – in other words, digital curation – requires that these risks are addressed.

Forward planning and an understanding of the life cycle elements is key to achieving this, and a proactive approach is better than a reactive approach although in practice elements of both are usually required. Each stage in the life cycle must be broken down so that the challenges relevant for that stage are identified and tackled.

To complicate matters, challenges cannot necessarily be mapped to a single stage of the life cycle but may persist across different stages: for example, preservation is not simply a storage challenge and may require attention during earlier stages of the life cycle, depending upon time periods and resource availability. Funding and organisational issues such as infrastructure and training can also require attention at several different stages.

Useful Projects and Initiatives

Developing and implementing a curation strategy is not an easy task; yet neither is it one that each organisation must tackle alone. The library, archives, curation and preservation communities have already invested a great deal of time and effort in tacking these solutions.

National institutions are a very useful starting point for organisations starting to address curation, and many national libraries have undertaken initiatives for preservation and accessibility upon which local and regional libraries can draw.

A number of further national and international initiatives can also prove useful, including: The Internet Archive, a non-profit organisation based in the US that crawls the Internet to collect websites and make them available to the public through their Internet site. Harvesting takes place at regular intervals and results in a snapshot of site evolution over time.

The International Internet Preservation Consortium (IIPC), building cooperation between the Internet Archive and national and research libraries. The IIPC is developing an open source web archiving toolkit to support acquisition of websites, collection management, storage & maintenance, and access & finding aids.

The UK Web Archiving Consortium (UKWAC), which collects selective web content relevant to the UK.

The LOCKSS Project (Lots of Copies Keeps Stuff Safe), an open source solution, harvesting and preserving subscription e-journals through duplication of copies within a prescribed network.

Finally, the Digital Curation Centre is the UK's premiere source of information on curation and preservation. In addition to developing guidance and advice of its own, the DCC resource centre also includes one of the largest virtual collections of international curation and preservation resources.

Addressing the Issues

Recommendations for dealing with some of the challenges introduced above are listed below. This is not an exhaustive list, but is intended to provide a starting point for preservation and curation planning:

- Develop a written policy and strategy to support activities and help secure resources ·Take a life cycle approach to support curation and preservation planning
- If creating resources, provide good practice guidance for sustainability (eg when digitising or accepting digitised resources)
- Assess collection/selection criteria – are they still valid? Do they need expanding? Identify possible resources. (Remember that digital resources can complement and enhance physical ones and do not have to act as replacements.)
- Be aware of externally produced digital resources (eg websites); check other heritage collections before gathering!
- Identify legal restraints in collection/management/ access
- Consider whether value can be added to resources during acquisition?
- Store objects in a secure environment
- Plan for preservation activities to maintain access to authentic resources over time and avoid incurring extra costs
- Determine access and user requirements

- Implement an integrated approach to collection accessibility
- Adapt and learn from national and other leading activities

Digital curation is vital if resources created now are to be properly preserved and remain accessible for future generations. This is more than simply a technical challenge and requires commitment at a multitude of levels. This brief article has, I hope, provided some insight into the types of challenges involved and some ways in which they may begin to be addressed. The most useful of these is based on that most fundamental aspects of the human condition: communication.

Digital curation and preservation is an issue for almost any organisation with a responsibility for managing digital information. In the age of the computer, that excludes very few! Whilst these organisations currently have varying degrees of experience, they often have experience in different areas.

Communicating to exchange and share different experiences across a network of curation and preservation organisations can therefore be one of the most fruitful and effective ways to move the practice of digital curation and preservation forwards.

Chapter 13

Impact of Digital Library on Higher Education and Research

The library has, since long, been considered to be the source and power of knowledge and also the knowledge base. In higher education ands research, the library has specific functions to facilitate the extensive use of learning resources by students, teachers, and researchers.

With the growth of literature in large numbers even in the same field, these groups of library users have faced problems in identifying the appropriate literature for their use and consultation in a desired timeframe.

Information and communications technology (ICT), particularly during the last two decades, has significantly contributed to open the door of accessing, hidden, knowledge in a highly efficient manner. Initially, the ICT was used in the library environment for developing databases of in-formation resources mainly aiming at storing and retrieving information on various types of publication resources and also to organize various types of information services.

The ICT has put us in the electronic environment to help identify, assess, acquire, record, store, organize, and disseminate information and information resources according to the need of specific requirements and/or of an organization or an individual requirement.

The use of IT in libraries has enhanced efficiency in all aspects of information acquisition, storage, and transfer. Its magical opportunities have dramatically changed the operations of the library and its information services. With the new facilities, the traditional libraries have been modernized to make these as well-equipped and inter-connected electronic resource centres.

In the library and publication fields, computer-based communications have extensively facilitated the transmission of messages, transfer, and exchange of files and text, such as online submission of papers for publication in books and journals, uploading/downloading, access to databases, conduct of interactions, provision of bulletin boards and newsletters, journals, and publications, online orders, inter-library loans, creation of user profiles, consolidation and repackaging of information for specific needs, dissemination of information, and so on.

Uncountable numbers of monographic materials, journals, learning resources, documents, reports, data, databases, and audiovisual materials generated and published by government and non-governmental organizations and commercial agencies/publishers are now available in electronic formats to access even from the remote corner of a country, thereby increasing the use of these materials and enhancing the efficiency of information dissemination.

PURPOSE, SCOPE, AND LIMITATIONS OF THE PAPER

The concept of developing the digital library system is very new in Bangladesh. In Bangladesh, we have 77 (54 private) universities, about 1,800 university colleges, institutes, and colleges, and about 600 organizations and institutions involved in research and related activities.

These organizations and institutions have libraries, but most are run in a traditional way. About 100 libraries have been using IT to carry out various library-related activities, including creation of databases.

Most publications in various fields coming out from Bangladesh are still in printed formats; as a result, the people remain uninformed of these materials.

There have been no formal survey or studies to know the potentials of digital libraries in Bangladesh where the conditions of libraries and information services are rather deplorable in most cases. In Bangladesh, we are moving at database level but not at digital level, except a few cases. The purpose of the present paper is to highlight the potentials and various aspects of digital library and also to highlight its benefits for and impacts in Bangladesh, particularly in higher education and research.

The paper is not based on any research study, rather it is of educative nature. While writing the paper, we had to depend heavily on various publications, particularly the book titled "Introduction to digital libraries" by G.G. Chowdhury and Sudatta Chowdhury published in 2003.

Change in Library-access and use Patterns

Library is used by various categories of people who need to read literature to keep themselves informed, to enhance their knowledge, to meet specific need(s), to educate themselves, to teach and for learning, practical applications, research, and dissemination.

Their major interest is that their desired information/ materials are made available at a minimum effort in an appropriate format and when they need these. Library patrons need information, use literature and knowledge, and again apply that knowledge to generate new knowledge and information. Information and knowledge can be obtained from print materials, audiovisual materials, databases, and the Internet.

With the change in the information-provision system over the last few years, libraries are becoming information resource-access centres, while maintaining also the traditional library and modern library services. With the advent and applications of ICT, libraries are now gradually becoming dependent on web-based resources available through the Internet (network of networks), which was first developed and launched in the USA in 1969.

Full-text journals, publications, data, and audiovisuals are available through the Internet, thereby facilitating access to free and priced online information and learning resources. But monitoring and tracking the availability of, and searching for, needed papers and publications are major problems in the web-based information system because the system is invisible. Library patrons and library professionals can easily register with publishers of journals and other materials through the Internet to be alerted electronically on a regular basis.

These have warranted that both information users and information professionals are well-oriented with the Internet, with web addresses of those organizations/institutions which put materials in their websites, and with searching mechanisms.

Users are now more independent than before, they are self-learners and self-accessors, and they can access web-based information resources even from their home computers and search databases according to their needs.

The technology has been gradually making the traditional libraries to become universal for all those who need, and seek for, information and information resources either from within or out-side the organization or the country where they are located.

Transitions in Library Development

The history of development of libraries started with the preservation of knowledge on bones, wood surfaces, bark, hides, textiles, stones, clay tablets, papyrus, parchment, vellum, etc. and subsequently on paper with the advent of printing machine. The use of paper in recording knowledge helped spread out the use of knowledge all over the world, even spreading up to rural areas. This also helped preserve knowledge for a longer time.

The mechanism for preservation of knowledge on paper has gradually been transferred to the electronic medium since the advent of the computer system which is used all over the world, including Bangladesh. Now, most publishing houses, national, regional and international organizations are putting their publications and public records in the Internet.

In the early stage of human communication and while transferring knowledge, "man may have even developed an 'oral literature' that was handed down from generation to generation." Initially, library was usually conceived of graphics forms of recorded information, and the library was only one of many means of communication. "The library is a means of communication in the sense that it is a storehouse of recorded information..."

So, the library is the fundamental source of organized recorded or stored information. The process of communication, thus, started first with speech, then writing, then printing, and finally with electronic devices.

Each stage of the development of speech/language, writing, books, earlier libraries, and modern libraries passed though a process of considerable time-span to establish each stage of the conceptualization of each process to development, to organization, to implementation, and to management. "The earliest form of library was what we would consider today an archive, since it was really a collection of government or religious documents."

Based on the growth and change in library systems within the traditional and modern concepts, we have, like computers, several generations in the development of the library system since its inception to up till now.

The generations are:

- *First generation*: Generation of the early archival library system with early writing materials
- *Second generation*: Generation of the traditional library system with collection of printed materials and without the use of modern tools of library organization, such as cataloguing rules and classification schemes
- *Third generation*: Generation of the traditional library system organized with modern tools of library organization
- *Fourth generation*: Generation of the computerized library system with the use of IT/ICT
- *Fifth generation*: Generation of the digital library system without any space, time and language barriers and highly depending on the Internet/web-based resources.

Meaning and Scope of Digital Library

The term 'digital library' has synonymously been used for meaning 'automated library', 'electronic library', 'virtual library', and 'digital library'. The concept of digital library began initially with modernization of libraries with electronic devices.

GG and S Chowdhury reports that "Borgman suggests that the first research-oriented definition of digital libraries appeared in 1992 when the phrase 'electronic libraries' was used for what is now called digital libraries." Another name that we come across is 'hybrid library'.

A hybrid library is a library where both "digital and printed information resources co-exist and are brought together in an integrated information service accessible locally as well as remotely." Whatever may be the name, all mean almost the same, which "support full life cycle of creation, storage, preservation, dissemination, and use of data, information and knowledge." The scope of the functionality of these terminologies is almost same.

Unfortunately, as of now, concerned professionals could not conclude an acceptable definition of digital library. Various researchers and information professionals have proposed various definitions. GG and S Chowdhury say, "Two major categories of definitions are available, one focusing on the access and retrieval of digital content and the other focusing on the collection, organization and service aspects of digital libraries." Borgman presents the scope of a digital library (then defined as electronic library) as a combination of: "

- A service;
- An architecture;
- A set of information resources, databases of text, numbers, graphics, sound, video, etc.
- A set of tools and capabilities to locate, retrieve and utilize the information resources available."

He further says, "Digital libraries encompass two comprehensive ideas, one emphasizing that they extend and enhance existing information storage and retrieval systems, incorporating digital data and metadata in any form; the other emphasizing that the design, policy, and practice should reflect the social context in which they exist."

The 1994 IEEE CAIA Workshop on Intelligent Access to On-line Digital Libraries defined "A digital library is an assemblage of digital computing, storage, and communications machinery together with the content and software needed to reproduce, emulate, and extend the services provided by conventional libraries based on paper and other material means of collecting, cataloging, finding, and disseminating information.

A full service digital library must accomplish all essential services of traditional libraries and also exploit the well-known advantages of digital storage, searching, and communication." The Stanford digital library research team defined a digital library as "coordinated collection of services that are based on collections of materials, some of which may not be directly under the control of the organization providing a service in which they play a role".

Oppenheim and Smithson defined a "digital library as an information service in which all the information resources are available in computer processable form and the functions of acquisition, storage, preservation, retrieval, access and display are carried out through the use of digital technol-ogies."

According to Arms, a digital library is a "managed collection of information, with associated services, where the information is stored in digital formats and accessible over a network."

The Digital Library Federation in the USA defines the digital library as "Digital libraries are organizations that provide the resources, including the specialized staff, to select, structure, offer intellectual access to, interpret, distribute, preserve the integrity of, and ensure the persistence over time of collections of digital works so that they are readily and economically available for use by a defined community or set of communities." Access to the entire collection is globally available directly or indirectly across a network.

Review of the above concepts and definitions suggest that the digital library is "the collection of services and the collection of information objects that support users in dealing with information objects and the organization and presentation of those objects available directly or in-directly via electronic/ digital means."

A digital library may contain materials that are already available in digitized format, such as electronic online journals, electronic information resources, or may contain materials that were originally produced in another form, but subsequently digitized.

Need of Digital Library

Many academic and research organizations and libraries in developed countries are building institutional repositories of the institution's books, papers, theses, and other works. Institutional repositories are often referred to as digital libraries.

Cornell University and the Wisconsin State Historical Society are considered leaders in the field of digital archive creation and management. The ICDDR,B in Bangladesh is also in the process of developing an institutional repository of its publications.

With the gradual change in the library-accessing system and with the increased use of IT in libraries, the libraries in Bangladesh will, in the near future, be in a position to put linkages to international online resources and develop their own digital libraries with collection that are relevant to their library patrons.

This is imminent because of the absence of the needed infra-structural facilities in libraries, urgency of the need for information and information resources, information resource-accessing problems in the local environment, e.g. home, shortage of man-power and budget, scarcity of foreign currencies, and pressure from library users and also from the higher authority.

If we consider the advantages and disadvantages of the digital library system, it also guides us to think of developing and establishing the digital library system without wasting any more time.

Benefits and Impact of Digital Library vis-à-vis Traditional Library

A digital library being in the web is not limited by any space/location and time, resulting in an easy and open access to web-based information resources compared to the traditional library system. Any user may access to information resources round the clock, provided he/she has the access facility.

The major important benefits are that users from various locations within and outside the country can simultaneously access the required document without any serious hindrances and download the needed documents without loosing the quality. They can also search for documents by word, by subject, by phrase, by author, by title, etc. as the providers of the digital library system facilitate user-friendly search interfaces.

The digital library system takes very little space in storing information resources, allowing unlimited networking benefits, link-age of documents in any site at a lower cost, handling of the system with minimum staff and at a lesser cost, and adoption of new developments compared to the traditional library system where budget, space, and skilled manpower are the important constraints.

The traditional library system is demarked and/or highly constrained by space and print collection and by provision of time-needed traditional library services. In this system, information-seekers and library users are generally required to personally visit libraries to meet their needs of information and literature and to get services.

Unfortunately, the services do not reach them in our country. On the other hand, the open access or digital libraries are demarked by electronic collection, electronic preservation system, and online access facilities. Time and access problems are important factors in the traditional library system, whereas time and access are not barriers in the digital library system.

Digital libraries can serve the user population very fast and with easy access to online resources. The digital library system can cope with the problem of handling information explosion and can manage large amounts of digital contents.

Implementation of the digital library system has tremendous benefits and impacts. It brings in-formation and information resources to users, provides a one-stop service, facilitates improved searching, manipulation of information, improved information-sharing, timely access to information, improved use of information, and improved collaboration, and reduces the digital divide.

The digital library system permits offering of digital library services, including personalized information services, reference services, SDI and current awareness services, literature-searching services, bibliographic services, transmission and exchange of literature search results, files, and publications, library-to-library cooperation, removal of barriers of space, time, and language, avoidance of dependence on others, improved communications between receivers and providers, e-alerts of table of contents of journals and publications, and many more.

The digital library helps build own personal collection according to need, lessens the dependence on information professionals or intermediaries, facilitates access to information resources wherever they are located, facilitates the use of same information resources simultaneously by various users, and provides access to information resources not owned by the service-providing organizations.

It brings paradigm shift in the creation, distribution, management, and use of information and facilitates the consumption, creation, and sharing of knowledge. It also facilitates better delivery of information than was possible in the traditional library system.

Limitations, and Constraints in Development, of Digital Library

Digital libraries cannot possibly replace the environment of a physical library as we still like to see and browse reading materials physically and get attracted more to read these. Lack of skills in handling computer viruses and lack of standardization for digitized materials are important limitations. While there are obvious benefits of digitization, the major problem is, however, ensuring the quality of digitized materials.

The other problems are access management, determination of authenticity of materials, and control of unauthorized access and use.

Access being open, through the Internet, many people may be indulged in browsing vulgar resources. Sometimes, it may take a long time to access literature that are immediately needed.

It may happen that computers and other related facilities remain paralyzed in absence of regular maintenance and replacements of necessary equipment.

The development of the digital library system at least involves:

- Digitization (data conversion, data organization, etc.)
- Establishment of linkages to digitized publications. Development of databases only does not mean digital library.

Digitization also involves hardware and software costs, staff cost, outsourcing cost, cost of various related activities before and after digitization, such as movement of physical items, copyright clearance, creation of records, indexes, and so on. The development of a digital library system demands incurring of "large costs for the conversion of print materials into digital format, for the technical skills of staff to maintain them, and for the costs of maintaining online access (i.e. servers, bandwidth costs, etc.)."

Data from the old system to the new system would also need additional costs. The initial cost (cost of hardware, software, groundstations or leasing communication circuit, etc.) is rather high. For fast access and transmit files, the system needs high bandwidth. In the Internet environment, it is difficult to monitor and keep track of information resources used for subsequent use. Users face the problem of 'information overload', receive unwanted information, data, or resources, and provision of services may be disrupted unless access or facilities are ensured.

Index

A

Affiliate Funding 85
Architecture 94, 95, 96, 97, 98, 99, 102, 104, 107, 108, 112, 115, 116, 117, 118, 119, 120, 122, 125, 128, 134, 136, 189, 191, 212, 214, 215, 218, 219, 221, 228, 230, 231, 252, 270
Assumptions 2, 5, 99

B

Benefits 35, 73, 77, 130, 149, 220, 221, 259, 261, 265, 266, 271
British Columbia 155, 194, 198

C

California, 94, 181, 194, 198
Citeseer 20, 23
Clustering 161, 162, 164, 166, 167, 168, 169, 171, 174
Coherence 2, 3, 60, 231
Commercial Funding 85
Communication 57, 69, 70, 89, 90, 116, 142, 143, 144, 151, 156, 157, 158, 178, 180, 258, 262, 266, 267, 269
Conclusions 14, 41, 73, 161, 186, 192, 195, 252, 254

D

DBLP 16, 17, 18
Digital Availability 10
Digital Projects 62, 306, 307
Digitisation 50, 51, 56, 58, 59, 60, 65, 73, 80
Diversification 81
Dlps Archetypes 215

E

Electronic 1, 2, 3, 8, 10, 12, 18, 31, 39, 41, 46, 52, 54, 62, 70, 74, 75, 76, 79, 82, 115, 122, 124, 129, 132, 135, 139, 142, 143, 144, 145, 147, 149, 150, 151, 159, 176, 185, 187, 190, 194, 195, 205, 235, 247, 248, 263, 264, 266
Emphasis 44, 71, 85, 156, 184, 193, 225, 249, 252
European 55, 82, 84, 181
Existing Situation 44, 55, 67

F

Fixity 5, 6
Florida 155, 194
Focusing 16, 68, 80, 133, 189, 194, 197, 207, 268
Formation of Dlps 207

Framework 45, 49, 54, 95, 97, 98, 99, 100, 101, 102, 119, 126, 127, 128, 133, 154, 157, 177, 189, 215, 229, 256
Funding Sources 78, 80, 81, 180

G

Google Scholar 15, 16, 20, 21, 23, 31, 145, 146

H

Harmony 133, 134, 254
Hierarchy 167, 171, 172
Holistic 83, 226
Host Institution 77, 78, 79, 86, 87, 89, 92
Hosting Events 86

I

Identity Crisis 25, 26, 27, 29, 34
IEEE Xplore 17
Illinois 194, 229, 232
Infrastructure 39, 42, 92, 114, 115, 116, 121, 129, 138, 139, 156, 179, 181, 195, 205, 209, 212, 227, 228, 229, 230, 231, 234, 236, 259, 260
ISI Web 19, 31

K

Kent 195, 275

L

LabelSOM 166, 167
Lacking 54, 196
Limitations 54, 58, 65, 111, 186, 231, 264
LIS Programs 187, 188, 189, 190, 192, 193, 198, 199
Los Angeles 194

M

Mekentosj Papers 31, 32
Mendeley 30, 31
Metadata 10, 11, 12, 13, 15, 17, 18, 28, 29, 30, 31, 32, 33, 62, 65, 67, 101, 102, 103, 129, 130, 133, 134, 205, 209, 214, 219, 222, 225, 232, 233, 234, 238, 239, 240, 268
Metaphors 2, 4
Michigan 195
Middleware 94, 97, 103, 105, 106, 107, 108, 109, 221
Mission 56, 66, 80, 98, 202, 204, 209, 210, 221, 222, 224, 225, 226, 236
Models-conclusion 224
MyNCBI 18, 31, 32

N

Nomadic 130, 131, 136
North Texas 196

O

Obstacles 13, 37, 61
OpCit 134, 135
Origins 2, 207, 241
Own Institution 84, 181

P

Peak 207, 213, 214, 221, 223

Persistent URIs 40
Pittsburgh 197, 198
Policy Enforcement 119, 121, 122, 123, 124, 125, 130, 132, 136
Priorities 231
Prism 132, 133
Proposals 29, 44, 52, 53, 55, 59, 60, 62, 71, 77, 79, 80, 81, 83, 84, 87, 91
PubMed Central 18, 19, 23, 28

R

Research Areas 115
Rhode Island 197
Rutgers 178, 181, 197

S

Scalability 111, 218
Scale 53, 127, 213, 215, 226, 227
Scholarly Publishing 128, 129
Scopus 16, 20, 31
Seeking 2, 7, 198, 290
Serendipity 36
Simple URIs 12, 15, 21, 22, 40
Situation 44, 48, 50, 54, 55, 58, 59, 63, 67, 87
Sponsorship 82, 85, 86
Strategic Value 63
Summarisation 160, 166, 169, 170, 174, 175
Synonyms 2, 3, 75

T

Tagging 33, 35, 36, 148, 149, 219
Technologies 2, 5, 6, 47, 48, 49, 51, 53, 57, 67, 75, 134, 137, 141, 142, 143, 151, 179, 193, 207, 221, 222, 224, 228, 235, 236, 240, 245

U

University 8, 22, 23, 30, 33, 75, 85, 148, 149, 151, 154, 155, 156, 158, 178, 181, 182, 194, 195, 204, 205, 206, 207, 208, 209, 210, 213, 215, 216, 217, 219, 270
URIs 12, 13, 15, 16, 17, 18, 19, 20, 21, 22, 24, 27, 28, 31, 32, 33, 34, 40

V

Virtual 4, 7, 75, 130, 142, 143, 144, 150, 151, 152, 155, 156, 157, 158, 159, 176, 182, 187, 261, 268

W

Warmer 13, 30, 37, 39
Web Survey 186